D1029604

Unequal

LAW AND CURRENT EVENTS MASTERS

David Kairys, Series Editor

Also in this series:

Unequal

How America's Courts Undermine Discrimination Law

SANDRA F. SPERINO

AND

SUJA A. THOMAS

OXFORD
UNIVERSITY PRESS

Oxford University Press is a department of the University of Oxford. It furthers
the University's objective of excellence in research, scholarship, and education
by publishing worldwide. Oxford is a registered trade mark of Oxford University
Press in the UK and certain other countries.

Published in the United States of America by Oxford University Press
198 Madison Avenue, New York, NY 10016, United States of America.

Library of Congress Cataloging-in-Publication Data
Names: Sperino, Sandra F., author. | Thomas, Suja A., author.
Title: Unequal : how America's courts undermine discrimination law /
Sandra F. Sperino and Suja A. Thomas.
Description: New York, NY : Oxford University Press, 2017. |
Series: Law and current events masters | Includes bibliographical references and index.
Identifiers: LCCN 2017006323| ISBN 9780190278380 (hardcover : alk. paper) |
ISBN 9780190278403 (epub) | ISBN 9780190682279 (online course content)
Subjects: LCSH: Discrimination—Law and legislation—United States. |
Discrimination in employment—Law and legislation—United States. |
Courts—United States. | Justice, Administration of—United States.
Classification: LCC KF4755 .S965 2017 | DDC 344.7301/133—dc23
LC record available at https://lccn.loc.gov/2017006323

9 8 7 6 5 4 3 2 1

Printed by Sheridan Books, Inc., United States of America

CONTENTS

PREFACE AND ACKNOWLEDGMENTS

This book tells the surprising story of what happens when workers file employment discrimination cases in federal court. Judges dismiss many of these cases before a jury can hear them or even after they hear them.

Judges dismiss cases where supervisors grope women, call them whores and sluts, and repeatedly ask them on dates. Judges dismiss cases where supervisors use racial epithets against black workers. Judges dismiss cases where an employer gives an employee a negative evaluation because of her race. In dismissing these cases, judges declare that these actions do not count as discrimination.

Congress passed discrimination laws that offer broad protections against discrimination. Yet, over the past several decades, courts have created ways to analyze discrimination cases that favor employers and disfavor workers. Judges have slowly built up a set of rules that govern discrimination cases allow them to dismiss cases—instead of properly enforcing the laws.

This book examines each of these judge-made "rules." Many of these "rules" are contrary to both the text and the purposes of the discrimination statutes. They are also factually unsupported. While the individual judge-made "rules" are troubling enough, when all of them are put together, workers have little chance of prevailing. Judges use all of these frameworks and doctrines to dismiss employees' cases. Often, cases do not reach a jury. Even in the rare cases that make it to jury trial, judges often overturn verdicts where the jury found in the worker's favor.

This book focuses on the reasons judges use to dismiss cases. Other than the discrimination cases that reached the United States Supreme Court, we have changed the names of the people and employers involved in the cases used as examples in this text. The focus is on the faulty reasoning of the judges—not the outcomes of individual cases. Many of the examples illustrate legal arguments that judges used in many different cases, and the footnotes provide lists of cases that relied on similar reasoning.

In discussing the cases, we describe the evidence presented by the worker and, where relevant, the contrary evidence provided by the employer. We recognize that some of the comments and conduct described is offensive but describing the comments and conduct is necessary to understanding the cases. We do not choose sides or otherwise try to determine what happened in the case. When there is a dispute about the facts of the case, it is the role of the jury to determine who is telling the truth and who is not. Looking at the evidence shows how judges regularly invade the province of the jury, evaluating cases in ways that favor employers, even when the evidence suggests discrimination.

While this book analyzes decisions made by federal courts, its impact extends to the states. Each state has its own laws prohibiting discrimination, but states often follow the lead of federal courts in interpreting their own laws. If a federal court interprets federal law in a particular way, states will often read their state law in a similar way. All state laws and federal laws are not coterminous, however. Some states provide greater protections and remedies for workers than federal law, some provide the same level, and some provide less.

This book focuses on three types of claims raised by workers: claims of individual disparate treatment, harassment, and retaliation. An individual disparate treatment claim is one in which an individual worker or a small group of workers assert that race, sex, or another protected trait played a role in a negative employment outcome. The focus is on such intentional discrimination claims brought by individuals.

There are additional types of claims that workers can raise. They can bring pattern or practice claims. In those cases, they allege that their employer discriminated against an entire group based on its protected trait. Workers can also allege that an employer's practices have a significant effect on a certain group of people—what the courts call disparate impact claims. Further, scholars are theorizing a rich literature about implicit bias and structural discrimination, developing a way for workers to pursue these claims in court. This book does not discuss claims based on pattern or practice, disparate impact, structural discrimination, or implicit bias.

The book begins by describing the overall trajectory of discrimination law, showing how courts have eroded the law's promise over the last several decades. Chapter 2 walks readers through the court process, explaining how cases work and describing the different procedures that judges use to dismiss or affect employment discrimination claims before or after a jury verdict. Chapters 3, 4, 5, and 6 describe the doctrines that courts have created to limit discrimination law. Each chapter describes actual cases and shows how judges reason their way to dismissal.

The next chapters explore why courts limit discrimination law and propose solutions to bring the court doctrine more in line with the federal discrimination statutes that Congress drafted. Chapter 7 addresses the role of politics. Chapter 8 discusses claims made by judges that the courts are flooded with frivolous discrimination lawsuits. Chapter 9 shows how the doctrine of discrimination law pushes cases toward dismissal, even if a particular judge does not have a pro-employer bias. Chapter 10 proposes ways that Congress, the courts, citizens, and others can positively influence the future of discrimination law.

This book would not be possible without the help and insights of many people. Early drafts of this book benefited from the comments of faculty members of the University of Cincinnati College of Law as part of its summer workshop series and junior faculty workshop, and also from workshops at the Benjamin N. Cardozo School of Law at Yeshiva University and the Colloquium on Scholarship in Labor and Employment Law hosted by the Maurer School of Law Indiana University Bloomington. Professor Sperino is especially thankful to colleagues who read early drafts, including Michael Solimine, Janet Moore, and Felix Chang. We also thank Melissa Carrington and Jennifer Morales for their comments on the book and Stephanie Davidson of the University of Illinois College of Law for her help archiving the Internet sources. All Internet references are archived at Perma.cc (available at https://perma.cc).

Research assistant Elizabeth Newman provided valuable feedback and citechecking on the earliest drafts of the book. We also appreciate librarian Ron Jones and research assistants Caitlin Graham Felvus and Erin Alderson Shick for their invaluable help in tracking down resources and assisting with research projects. And thanks to our editors, David Kairys and David McBride, who supported this project from beginning to end.

Introduction

If I had a world of my own, everything would be nonsense.
Nothing would be what it is, because everything would be what
it isn't. And contrary wise, what is, it wouldn't be. And what it
wouldn't be, it would. You see?

—*Alice in Wonderland*

On July 2, 1964, President Lyndon Johnson sat in the East Room of the
White House. With Martin Luther King Jr. standing behind him, President
Johnson signed the Civil Rights Act of 1964 into law. President Johnson
proclaimed that the Act would "eliminate the last vestiges of injustice in
our beloved country."[1]

This historic law prohibited discrimination in a wide range of American
life, including at the ballot box, in restaurants, and in hotels. Title VII of
that law prohibited discrimination in the American workplace. For the
first time in the United States, it became unlawful for many employers
to discriminate against workers because of their race, sex, religion, color,
and national origin.[2] Congress later passed laws making age and disability
discrimination illegal.

This book shows how federal judges approach discrimination cases
brought by workers who are protected under these laws. Over time,
judges have created dozens of frameworks, rules, and inferences to help
them analyze discrimination cases. But all of these frameworks, rules, and

inferences do not help judges determine whether discrimination actually happened.

Instead, this analysis has created an alternative reality. Here, no discrimination happens when a supervisor gropes a woman's breast, so long as the supervisor only does it one or two times. In this world of federal discrimination law, some judges declare it is legal and not discriminatory for an employer to give a worker a negative evaluation based on the color of her skin. This is not discrimination. In this alternative universe, when a supervisor calls a woman a "cunt," a "whore," and a "bitch," this is not evidence that the supervisor is biased. When a supervisor says, "all blacks are lazy" or uses vile racial epithets, this is not evidence of racism. These are simply stray remarks that the judge can disregard. The book tells the stories of workers and how courts dismissed their claims.

1. RACHEL, TINA, ANTHONY, AND JOHN

To introduce you to this world of discrimination law, we start with three stories based on cases in the U.S. federal courts.

Rachel is black. Her supervisor, Bill, is white. Bill accidentally copies Rachel on an email in which he states he will never give a black employee a positive evaluation. Later, Bill gives Rachel a negative evaluation. Is it possible that Bill's conduct is discrimination? According to one federal appellate court, the answer is no.[3] The negative evaluation does not count as discrimination.

Tina is a cashier. Tina sued her employer for sexual harassment. In her suit, she presented evidence that her supervisor asked her out on dates many times, even offering "financial assistance" if she would agree.[4] He once "removed from his pants a large bottle of wine, offered Plaintiff a drink, and then asked her to join him later at a local hotel where they could have a 'good time.'" She also claimed that on at least two occasions, he touched her breasts and touched her buttocks once. The court dismissed Tina's claim, ruling that what happened to Tina was not sexual harassment.

Anthony and John are African American men. They both sought promotions at a company to become shift managers. Neither received a promotion.[5] Instead, the white plant manager promoted two white men. The plant manager admitted that he had not followed the written qualifications for the shift manager job when he made the decisions about whom to promote.[6] Moreover, Anthony and John provided evidence that the manager referred to them as "boy." They also had evidence, though disputed by the employer, that they were better qualified than the white employees who were selected for the promotions.[7] They also submitted evidence that no black worker had ever been promoted to the shift manager position that they had sought.[8]

Though jury trials are rare, Anthony's and John's cases made it to a jury. The jury found the employer discriminated against Anthony and John based on their race. Despite this verdict, the judge who presided in the case decided there was insufficient evidence of discrimination and dismissed the cases, finding for the employer. The judge noted that using the term "boy" when referring to Anthony and John was not "probative of racial animus."[9]

The appellate court that reviewed the case agreed with the trial court on a number of matters. Calling African American men "boy" was not evidence of racial discrimination, and the jury was wrong when it found discrimination in Anthony's case. However, the appeals court ordered a new trial for John, finding that John had more evidence to support his case.[10]

In these cases, the courts made a decision: what happened to Rachel, Tina, and Anthony was not discrimination. In cases like Rachel's and Tina's, the judges were so sure of the correct outcome that they were willing to dismiss the cases before they ever reached juries. In Anthony's case, the judges felt comfortable ignoring a jury's verdict. According to these judges, there was only one right answer in each case: the employer had not discriminated against the employees. The worker should lose the case and the employer should win. These are not isolated cases. Searches of federal cases reveal case after case with similar results, where judges dismiss cases brought by workers who allege they are subject to racial epithets or when workers have evidence, for example, that that their supervisors thought they were too old to do their jobs.[11] Courts dismiss cases when women allege that their boss or their coworkers repeatedly touched their breasts or buttocks, where supervisors repeatedly asked them out on dates or for sexual favors, or where they were repeatedly the victim of unwanted sexualized comments and gestures.[12]

The results of these cases are surprising, especially when you consider the traditional rules of litigation. Under these norms, judges decide legal issues, and when there is a dispute about facts, the jury decides. Federal judges are not supposed to pick winners and losers in cases where the facts are contested. If a case presents facts suggesting discrimination, a jury should decide the outcome. If a case is a close call, it is supposed to go to a jury.

As you will see, federal judges do not apply the traditional rules of litigation to discrimination cases. Instead, judges have created a new set of rules. These rules are not neutral. They favor employers and disfavor workers.

Judges have constructed a complex system of legal frameworks, doctrines, and evidentiary rules that allow them to dismiss claims before trial. Even when a case makes it to trial, and a jury finds that discrimination has occurred, trial court and appellate judges use these same legal frameworks to overturn the jury's verdict. In fact, discrimination cases are some of the most disfavored cases on the federal docket. Judges dismiss these claims at rates far higher than most other kinds of claims.

This book shows how the methods that courts use to evaluate discrimination cases are flawed. These methods do not reliably allow courts to determine whether discrimination occurred in a particular case. Instead, the procedures courts use allow them to declare that no discrimination happened, even when the worker has evidence that her race, her sex, or other protected trait caused her to lose her job or otherwise negatively affected her position.

We start from a simple premise. When a worker presents evidence that he or she faced a negative consequence because of his or her race, sex, or other protected trait, a jury should hear the case, consider the contested evidence, and decide whether discrimination occurred.[13] At a jury trial, the employee (plaintiff) can put forward evidence to convince the jury that the employer discriminated. The employer (defendant) can challenge the worker's evidence and try to convince the jury that the plaintiff has not presented sufficient evidence of discrimination and has not proven by a preponderance of the evidence that he or she was discriminated against.

The stories in this book show that judges have narrowed the definition of discrimination. When a male supervisor touches a woman's breast and buttocks, the supervisor may have engaged in a form of discrimination more precisely referred to as sexual harassment. When a supervisor calls black men "boy," race discrimination might have occurred. When a supervisor says that he would never give workers of certain religions good evaluations and then gives them bad evaluations, that might be religious discrimination. In each of these cases, a jury could determine that race, sex, or religion negatively affected the worker's job. This book shows why judges should not dismiss these cases before or after a jury trial.

2. THE SUPER-STATUTE

There are three federal laws that serve as the cornerstone protections against employment discrimination—Title VII, the Age Discrimination in Employment Act, and the Americans with Disabilities Act.

Congress passed Title VII in 1964. Title VII prohibits employers from discriminating against workers based on race, sex, color, national origin, and religion. It has had a profound impact in reshaping workplace norms and opportunities. Title VII is so important that scholars William Eskridge and John Ferejohn labeled it a "super-statute."[14] To attain super-statute status, the law must embrace a great principle. For Title VII, that principle is combatting employment discrimination.

When Congress deliberated about Title VII, a question arose about whether age should also be a protected class. Although Congress was not ready to add age as a protected category in 1964, it did so three years later when it passed the Age Discrimination in Employment Act (ADEA).

The ADEA protects workers 40 years old and older from age discrimination. Several years later, in 1990, Congress enacted the Americans with Disabilities Act, which expanded discrimination law to cover people with disabilities. Workers can also file claims for race discrimination under 42 U.S.C. § 1981.

Taken together, these laws are supposed to provide a level playing field for workers in these protected categories, and they have had some positive effect in limiting workplace discrimination. In the past, companies had policies that segregated workers. Black employees could hold only certain jobs—often the jobs that paid less.[15] Some companies also had policies that required women to quit their jobs when they married or became pregnant.[16] State laws prohibited women from working at night.[17] Thanks in part to the passage of these laws, all of these actions are now illegal.

3. THE CONVENTIONAL WISDOM

With the election of President Barack Obama in 2008, there were new discussions about America's progress toward equality including entering a new post-racial era. In this allegedly post-racial era, Americans have transcended the legacy of race discrimination. Similarly, many people believe that other types of discrimination are rare and only happen at the hands of a few bad actors.

The American workplace is far less equal than many people would like to believe.[18] One study by Professor Devah Pager[19] shows the magnitude of the inequality. Professor Pager sent out white and black testers to apply for jobs. During the application process, some of the applicants indicated they had no criminal history while others suggested that they did have a criminal record. Professor Pager's study found that white applicants without criminal records received callback interviews for jobs 34 percent of the time[20] while black applicants without criminal records received callback interviews only 14 percent of the time.[21] White applicants with criminal records received callback interviews 17 percent of the time[22] while black applicants with criminal records received callback interviews only 5 percent of the time.[23] So white men *with* criminal records actually received more callbacks than African American men *without* a criminal record.[24]

Race matters in hiring. Depending on the study, white applicants were "anywhere from 1.5 to 5 times more likely to receive a callback or job offer relative to equally qualified black applicants."[25] Over time, the unemployment rate for African American workers, which may be affected by these racialized hiring practices, has typically been about twice the rate of white Americans.[26]

Women and people of color are underrepresented in many jobs in certain industries and in certain positions of power. In 2015, CNN reported that there were only five black CEOs among America's 500 largest companies.[27] When Microsoft promoted Satya Nadella to CEO in 2014, *Fortune* declared that he was "one minority exec in a sea of white."[28]

Women are also underrepresented. The *New York Times* reported in 2015 that "[f]ewer large companies are run by women than by men named John . . . ."[29] In 2014, the *New York Times* reported that seven out of ten people working at Google were men.[30] At Google, three out of thirty-six of its top-ranking executives were women, and 83 percent of its engineers were men.[31] Similar numbers were reported at other large tech companies.[32] Additionally, women hold fewer than 20 percent of the board member seats at companies listed in the Standard and Poor's 500 Index.[33]

In the legal system, people of color and women are similarly underrepresented. In 2015, only about 2 percent of partners at large firms were Hispanic or Latino, and about the same number were African American.[34] In some states, fewer than 3 percent of state judges are persons of color.[35] Women are also underrepresented. Since the late 1980s, even though women make up anywhere from 40 to 50 percent of American law school graduates, fewer than 20 percent of equity partners at law firms are women.[36] Only 21 percent of leaders in corporate legal departments at Fortune 500 companies are women.[37] Almost 80 percent of the deans of American law schools are men.[38] Only 24 percent of federal judges[39] and 27 percent of state court judges are women.[40]

Race and sex also affect pay. In 2014, women who worked full-time earned about 82 percent of what men earned.[41] These numbers become worse when the worker is a woman of color. For example, Hispanic women's median salaries in 2014 were only 61.2 percent of white men's median salaries.[42]

There is debate about how much of the wage gap is due to factors other than discrimination, such as hours worked and career choice. There is also discussion about the actual size of the sex-based wage differential. No matter how you parse the data, there is an unexplained wage gap between women and men.[43] For example, one study took into account students' "college major, occupation, economic sector, hours worked, months unemployed since graduation, GPA, type of undergraduate institution, institution selectivity, age, geographical region, and marital status."[44] The study found a 7 percent difference in the earnings of male and female college graduates one year after graduation that was not explained by any of these factors.[45] The study further found that ten years after graduation, this unexplained wage gap widens to 12 percent.

It is difficult to determine how much bias contributes to these continuing disparities. Other factors, such as class, access to quality education, and societal expectations related to career choice, likely play roles. Nonetheless, the previously mentioned studies show that these factors do not completely explain why there is still so much inequality in American workplaces.

Despite these studies, there is an emerging story about the role that bias plays in this continuing inequality. Under the new conventional wisdom, "old school" race and sex discrimination is rare. A few bad actors may intentionally discriminate against workers, but companies work hard to ferret out these bad apples. Writing in 2001, Professor Michael Selmi noted: "It seems that the general consensus today is that the role discrimination plays in contemporary America has been sharply diminished."[46] The *New York Times* quoted a tech executive as saying: "This is a pretty genteel environment, and you don't usually see outright manifestations of bias. . . . Occasionally you'll have some idiot do something stupid and hurtful, and I like to fire those people."[47]

According to the popular narrative, courts provide robust protections against discrimination in cases alleging traditional discrimination. Within the small group of traditional cases that still exist, so the story goes, the legal system does a good job of adjudicating these cases. Judges police egregious forms of discrimination[48] and separate the plausible cases from the meritless ones.[49] In these traditional cases, judges are largely correct in deciding which cases should proceed to juries.[50] The cases judges dismiss are cases that a litigant would never win. Under this narrative, federal judges are committed to combating traditional discrimination. This judicial commitment is strong, and courts will not interfere with protecting the core anti-discrimination law.[51]

So, how does bias continue to affect the workplace? In the new narrative, workplace inequity continues to exist because of complex phenomena. Scholars have argued that workplace culture and unconscious bias cause race and sex discrimination.[52] As Professor Tristin Green writes: "Race, sex, and other protected group characteristics will continue to factor into employment decisions, but the decisions are more likely to be driven by unconscious biases and stereotypes operating within a facilitating organizational context than by conscious animus operating in isolation."[53] Legal scholar Amy Wax has noted: "Some commentators have gone so far as to suggest that, as overt bigotry has waned in response to antidiscrimination laws and evolving social mores, unintentional or 'unconscious' discrimination has become the most pervasive and important form of bias operating in society today."[54]

Unconscious biases reinforce inequality: these are the "hidden, reflexive preferences that shape most people's worldviews, and that can profoundly affect how welcoming and open a workplace is to different people and ideas."[55] A supervisor may believe he acts in a neutral way, though he may unconsciously be affected by societal stereotypes about race, sex, or age.[56]

Commentator Nicholas Kristof has discussed the "biased brain," arguing that we can better understand the roots of racial division in America by understanding this unconscious bias.[57] *Fortune* magazine has reported: "Equality is a worthy goal—but it's tough to achieve when unconscious bias so pervades the American workplace."[58] Large companies like Google have responded by embracing diversity training that focuses on identifying unconscious biases.

According to the popular narrative, courts handle traditional discrimination claims well, but they are struggling with more complex ideas like unconscious bias. Courts restrict the law where discrimination is not evident. Courts may not be able to adeptly fix problems such as unconscious bias, and it may not even be a good idea to hold employers liable for unconscious bias.[59] Legal scholar Amy Wax has been skeptical of efforts to use the legal system to this end, arguing that there are "no known methods for effectively controlling unconscious bias in the workplace" and that courts would not be particularly good at determining whether workplace decisions resulted from the "intermittent, subtle, and elusive phenomenon" of unconscious bias.[60]

Under this narrative, there is little or nothing left for courts to enforce because judges either cannot fix the problems of unconscious bias or would be bad at fixing them. If judges are dismissing lawsuits, these cases are likely newer kinds of discrimination about which judges feel less comfortable and for which there is no overt evidence that race, sex, or other protected traits directly played a role in an employment decision.

We contest this narrative. In this book, we will show that the federal judiciary often fails to decide traditional discrimination cases in a fair manner. Judges have created a whole host of frameworks, inferences, and doctrines that they use to dismiss cases and keep them away from juries, including cases that present evidence of discrimination.

Modern workplace inequality may very well be caused, in part, by unconscious bias, but this is not all that is happening. Judges do not protect the core of the discrimination statutes. When workers present evidence of traditional discrimination, judges often dismiss their cases.

4. INTERNAL LIMITS

There is another popular myth about American discrimination law. It is easy to win a discrimination lawsuit and also easy to win a very large verdict against an employer. The reality is much different. Congress placed specific limits in the federal discrimination statutes that are different in kind or degree from almost any other type of claim, outside of claims made by prisoners. The discrimination laws on the books, the ones created by Congress, already contain important limits that balance the interests of workers, employers, and the courts. When the courts add on doctrines and rules to restrict claims, they limit an already narrow cause of action.

Congress limits employment discrimination claims in three important ways. First, a person alleging discrimination may not immediately go to court and file a claim. Instead, the person must present her claim to either the Equal Employment Opportunity Commission (EEOC) or a similar state agency. This requirement—to file first with an administrative agency before going to court—is an additional legal requirement. When a person has almost any other kind of claim, he can simply go to court and present his grievance.

The EEOC is a federal agency charged with enforcing many federal civil rights laws. A person alleging discrimination submits a document to the agency called a Charge of Discrimination. The Charge generally describes the worker's allegations against the employer.

The charge-filing process reduces the number of claims filed in court. After a charge is filed, the EEOC or state agency may investigate an employee's claims, possibly eliminating the need for later litigation in the courts. The EEOC also provides a voluntary mediation system to help the parties try to resolve the underlying claim.

As one court noted: "Exhaustion of administrative remedies is central to Title VII's statutory scheme because it provides the EEOC the first opportunity to investigate discriminatory practices and enables it to perform its roles of obtaining voluntary compliance and promoting conciliatory efforts."[61] But the discrimination statutes do not require that the EEOC fully investigate every claim or that the EEOC make a decision about the merits of each claim. In most of the cases that later go to court, the EEOC makes no decision about whether discrimination happened or not. Rather, the EEOC most often issues a Notice of Right to Sue letter. This notice simply declares that the EEOC process is finished, without making any decision about whether the employer violated the law.

In addition to the requirement that applicants or employees must go to the agency first, Congress limits the scope of discrimination law by requiring discrimination claims to be filed within a short period of time after discrimination happens. A person alleging discrimination must submit her Charge of Discrimination within 180 days or 300 days of the discriminatory act.[62] After the EEOC or state agency issues its Right to Sue letter, an employee has 90 days to file a claim in court.[63] The time limits imposed by the discrimination statutes are short compared to limits for other types of claims. By comparison, many states give plaintiffs two or three years to file negligence claims.[64] And some litigants can wait ten years before filing suit.[65]

Even though the EEOC does not make a determination for most claims of whether discrimination occurred, the requirement that a potential litigant go to the EEOC or a state agency within a particular time frame limits the reach of discrimination law. If the worker misses any of the administrative filing deadlines, she usually cannot raise her claim in court. This is true even if the worker otherwise has a good discrimination case.

Workers also may lose the right to file their claims forever if they tell the EEOC about some of their claims, but not all of them. A worker can only file a claim in court that is "reasonably related" to the facts submitted to the EEOC. For example, a worker may go to the EEOC and claim he was terminated because of his race. The worker may not realize that the facts also support a claim for retaliation. If the worker does not mention retaliation to the EEOC, he may not be able to later pursue that claim in court.[66] This requirement to submit all potential claims to the EEOC applies even if the worker did not realize he was required to do this and even if the worker did not understand the different types of legal claims.

Discrimination statutes are also limited in a third important way. Congress placed limits on the types and amounts of monetary relief that a court can award under the discrimination statutes.

The Age Discrimination in Employment Act (ADEA) has the most restrictive damages. Under the ADEA, a worker can receive the wages and benefits she lost as a result of age discrimination. If she proves the age discrimination was willful, she can obtain an additional award of damages, but the ADEA limits the amount of this additional award to the amount of backpay.[67]

Title VII and the Americans with Disabilities Act (ADA) allow employees to receive wages and benefits lost due to discrimination. They also allow workers to obtain punitive damages, which are only available if the employee proves the employer discriminated with malice or reckless indifference to the law.[68] Additional damages, such as damages for emotional distress, are also available.

Title VII caps the total combined compensatory and punitive damages that a plaintiff may recover based on the number of employees employed by the defendant.[69] The highest cap, which applies to employers with more than 500 employees, is $300,000.[70] An employer with 100 or fewer employees only can be liable for up to $50,000 under the cap. This cap does not apply to lost wages and benefits. The damages cap is fixed. It is not adjusted upward if the employer engaged in especially egregious discrimination. Moreover, the cap has not changed since 1991 when it was enacted, and it is not adjusted for inflation.[71]

Congress also limited discrimination law in other ways. Smaller employers are outside the reach of federal discrimination law. Under Title VII and the ADA, an employer must have at least fifteen employees to be liable, while under the ADEA, an employer must have at least twenty employees to be liable for age discrimination.[72] Additionally, not all people who work are covered under the laws. The person bringing a discrimination claim must be an individual who falls within the statutory protections, such as an employee or former employee.[73] Often, federal discrimination law does not protect volunteers, independent contractors, and other similarly situated people.[74] The laws also provide employers with various defenses that either eliminate or reduce potential discrimination liability.[75]

The book describes how federal courts further limit the reach of discrimination law and why they do it. The judiciary, over time, has created a series of complex frameworks to evaluate discrimination cases. Supporting these frameworks are a host of judge-made procedural and evidentiary rules. Judges apply these frameworks and rules to evaluate discrimination claims. Unfortunately, the analysis does not accurately determine whether discrimination happened. In many instances, they actually distract courts away from the central question in many discrimination cases: was the worker treated differently because of her race, sex, or other trait.

The Ways Judges Dismiss Cases

Imagine that a woman sued her employer for sexual harassment. She presented evidence that after she returned from maternity leave, a supervisor called her into his office. She claimed the supervisor grabbed her breast and said "the baby gave you big juicy tits and a big ass."[1] The supervisor denied taking this action and making this statement. The woman alleged that another supervisor later said to her that because "she gave birth to several babies her vagina was so large that during sexual intercourse a man's penis could not touch the sides." This supervisor did not deny making this comment.[2]

A jury did not hear the woman's case. A judge dismissed the case before a jury heard it. The judge ruled that what happened to the woman was not sexual harassment. A judge declared that the only possible outcome in the case was that the employer should win and the worker should lose. This chapter explains the ways that judges can dismiss cases before trial, at trial, after trial, and even on appeal.

1. HOW FEDERAL CASES WORK

An employment discrimination lawsuit begins in federal court when a worker files a complaint. The complaint describes the employer's allegedly illegal actions and the remedy sought by the employee.

Many cases filed in federal court end in settlement, and employment discrimination cases follow this general trend.[3] With a settlement, the worker agrees to dismiss her case, sometimes after receiving money from the employer. The court-created doctrines that push cases toward dismissal affect settlements. When attorneys value a suit for settlement, they consider whether the case is likely to make it to trial and whether the worker is likely to win at trial. If an employer believes a judge will dismiss a case before trial or even after trial, it may offer the employee a lower settlement.

Cases that do not settle rarely make it to a jury trial.[4] For example, in one recent year, juries heard about 2 percent of the employment discrimination cases filed in federal court.[5]

Most of the rest of the cases are dismissed before they reach a jury. This often occurs when the judge grants one of two requests or motions made by an employer under the Federal Rules of Civil Procedure, the rules that govern litigation in federal court. The employer may file a motion asking the judge to dismiss the case at the beginning of the case in "a motion to dismiss" or in a "motion for summary judgment" after the parties have exchanged information about the case.

Even in circumstances where a jury actually hears a case and the jury finds for the worker, she still may lose. Again, using federal rules, a federal trial court judge may reject the jury's verdict by ordering "judgment as a matter of law" or may even reduce the money damages awarded by the jury by ordering a "remittitur."

Outcomes at the trial-court level do not favor workers. If a worker does not settle her case early, there is a high likelihood that the judge will dismiss her case on summary judgment. Studies have found that judges dismiss a high percentage of discrimination cases in which the employer files such a motion, with the percentage of dismissals varying depending on the period and court studied.[6] As another scholar, Professor Katie Eyer, explained:

Indeed, of every 100 discrimination plaintiffs who litigate their claims to conclusion (i.e., do not settle or voluntarily dismiss their claims), only 4 achieve any form (de minimis or not) of relief....

These odds can properly be characterized as shockingly bad, and extend (with minor differences) to every category of discrimination plaintiff, including race, sex, age, and disability.[7]

If the worker makes it through the trial court process, she still might lose on appeal. As three noted scholars opined: "Employment-discrimination plaintiffs swim against the tide." On appeal, [workers] have a harder time in upholding their successes, as well as in reversing adverse outcomes."[8]

For a worker to win a case, she must surmount four hurdles: (1) pre-trial motions; (2) trial; (3) post-trial motions and (4) appeal. Professor Eyer noted that "the extensive adverse outcomes faced by discrimination litigants are virtually unique in the world of federal litigation, exceeding the negative outcomes faced by other litigants in both scope and degree."[9]

2. PRETRIAL MOTIONS

Early in a case, an employer can ask the court to dismiss all or some of the claims raised in the worker's lawsuit. By filing a motion to dismiss, the defendant argues that the plaintiff "fails to state a claim upon which relief can be granted."[10] Used correctly, this rule can serve an important purpose. If the worker could never win the claim because the law does not provide a remedy in cases like hers, there is no reason to waste the court's or the employer's time and resources.

The rules that govern litigation in federal court require judges to approach this motion with caution. The system prefers that cases be decided on their merits, which means that ideally, the judge or jury will decide who should win based on the law and facts of the case. To advance this desire for a decision on the merits, there are specific rules about what a judge must do when considering a motion to dismiss. The judge is required to assume that all of the facts the worker asserted are true and to draw all reasonable inferences from the alleged facts in favor of the worker.[11]

Over time, the Supreme Court has made it easier for judges to dismiss cases at this early stage.[12] Until recently, a plaintiff could survive a motion to dismiss so long as his complaint gave the defendant a general idea about what she was claiming. Under the old standard that interpreted the federal rule, a claim could not be dismissed "unless it appear[ed] beyond doubt that the plaintiff [could] prove no set of facts in support of his claim which would entitle him to relief."[13] Now, under the new standard, the plaintiff is required to provide more information—facts showing her claim is plausible.[14]

The Supreme Court's new reading of the motion to dismiss standard makes it easier for judges to dismiss claims. Moreover, the Supreme Court has stated that judges are supposed to use their judicial experience and common sense to decide whether a claim is plausible.[15] Judges who do not reflect the demographics of the general population and who may have different views of discrimination than the general population may use their own experience and common sense to find against the worker even though a jury could find in favor of the worker.[16] Some judges are using the new, more onerous standard to dismiss cases when the facts plausibly state a claim for discrimination.[17]

The new standard creates problems for employment discrimination cases. Prior to the change in the law, it was uncommon for employers to file these early motions to dismiss. Now that the law has changed in their favor, employers file and win these motions to dismiss more frequently. Professor Alexander Reinert has shown that dismissals in employment discrimination cases increased after the Supreme Court changed the dismissal standard.[18]

For example, in one case, a female worker reported sexual harassment after a coworker asked her out on dates and sent her a picture of his erect penis.[19] According to the worker's complaint, the male coworker then lied to the human resources department and claimed he had a consensual relationship with her.[20] In her complaint, the worker alleged that her male coworker then doctored sexually explicit text messages and a racy picture to make it appear as if she had sent them to her male coworker.[21] The human resources department chose to believe the male coworker, and in an odd twist, the female worker was fired. The worker alleged that the company fired her for sexually harassing her male coworker. The court dismissed the worker's case, finding that even if it believed all of the female worker's allegations, she could not establish that she was fired for reporting sexual harassment.

Summary judgment

A more pressing problem for plaintiffs in discrimination cases is summary judgment. After the parties have exchanged information about the case and before trial, an employer has another opportunity to ask the judge to dismiss some or all of the worker's claims.

In the federal court system, litigants have a right to a jury trial in certain cases, including intentional discrimination cases. In a case where the plaintiff or the defendant wants a jury trial, the jury is supposed to decide whether the facts presented in the case are true or not. If a worker claims her supervisor told her that he was not going to promote her because she was a new mom who would not be dedicated to her job and the supervisor denies saying this, this is a dispute of fact. It is the jury's job to determine who is telling the truth and who is not. The judge is not supposed to be involved in weighing witness credibility.

As a result, under the federal rule governing summary judgment, a claim may be dismissed only if there is "no genuine dispute as to any material fact" and the employer is entitled to win under the law.[22] In other words, the judge can dismiss the claim only if there is no important factual dispute and if the employee has no claim for discrimination under the undisputed facts. Similar to the motion to dismiss, the judge is supposed to assume that the facts the plaintiff presents are true and to draw all reasonable inferences that can be taken from the facts in favor of the worker.

Most of the time when judges rule on summary judgment motions, they never actually see or hear the parties' witnesses. Instead, judges make their decisions based on the written material provided by each party to support its case. For example, a worker might present sworn statements about what happened to her from her and other witnesses. She might supplement that with testimony from depositions or other documents. Likewise, the employer typically submits evidence to support its defense—that it acted for a legitimate reason and did not discriminate.

The judge then decides whether to grant summary judgment by determining whether a reasonable jury could find for the worker.[23] If a reasonable jury could find for the worker, the jury decides the case. If not, the case is dismissed because it would be inefficient to permit a jury to hear the case in which it could not find discrimination. Although it is possible for workers to request summary judgment, it is rare for them to do so and even rarer still for a judge to grant such a motion.

In employment discrimination cases, who decides factual disputes is especially consequential. For example, discussing sex discrimination cases, federal judge Jack Weinstein has noted:

> The factual issues in this case cannot be effectively settled by a decision of an Article III judge on summary judgment. Whatever the early life of a federal judge, she or he usually lives in a narrow segment of the enormously broad American socio-economic spectrum, generally lacking the current real-life experience required in interpreting subtle sexual dynamics of the workplace based on nuances, subtle perceptions, and implicit communications.... The dangers of robust use of summary judgment to clear trial dockets are particularly acute in current sex discrimination cases.[24]

As described in this book, judges often decide that a reasonable jury could not find for an employee who has alleged that her employer discriminated against her. A federal judge may have a different perspective than a jury on what the evidence shows and, as a result, may come to a different result than a jury would. Federal judges are appointed by the President of the United States and have elite backgrounds and credentials. Almost 75 percent of these judges are men,[25] and approximately 80 percent of them are white.[26] Juries, on the other hand, include more of a mix of the population, with, for example, more income levels, women, and people of different races and religions. Because of these differences, it is possible for a jury to believe that discrimination did occur, while a federal judge may think that discrimination may not have occurred. These differences make it even more important for these disputed cases to be left to juries.

Despite then Judge Weinstein's warning, in case after case, some judges improperly use summary judgment, dismissing worker's claims when the worker has evidence of discrimination. In these cases, judges do not follow the required legal standard: they view the facts in the light most favorable to the employer, or they undervalue or ignore the worker's evidence. Then, the judges simply repeat the mantra that "no reasonable jury could find in favor" of the worker. In many circumstances, it appears that judges are simply deciding based on their own views of the evidence, not what a reasonable jury could find.[27] As discussed in Chapters 3 through 6, some judges also create legal doctrines that make it easy to disregard worker's evidence. Moreover, some judges label questions of fact that juries are to decide as questions of law for judges to decide.

Here are examples of some cases in which the judge granted summary judgment in the employer's favor. In each of these cases, the judge determined that the worker could never win. The only allowable outcome was that the employer did not discriminate.

In one case where summary judgment was granted, the plaintiff had sued for discrimination, retaliation, and harassment. He was black and Muslim. Two of the three judges hearing the case on appeal decided that summary judgment in the employer's favor was appropriate. According to the federal court judge who voted against summary judgment, the worker presented evidence that during his six-month tenure of employment he was subjected to the following comments by coworkers: "Today, your skin doesn't look as white as it normally does"; he was referred to as "Mr. Cocoa"; was told "It's very difficult to work with you people"; was told African Americans are "very difficult to work with" because they are "very emotional" and "take things too personally"; and that "black people are expected to leave their blackness behind."[28] The worker also submitted evidence that a fellow worker told him that hiring him for a permanent position was "like raising little terrorist kids."[29]

Additionally, the plaintiff showed he was treated differently than white workers. Some workers had complained to management that the employee was being discriminated against.[30] They testified that they heard a stream of negative comments about Muslims and immigrants in the workplace.[31] The employer countered with evidence of instances of poor work performance. The trial court judge resolved the case in the employer's favor, dismissing the worker's claims, and an appellate court agreed that the dismissal was proper.

In another case, a licensed professional nurse brought a claim against a hospital for race discrimination. The nurse, an African American male, was asked by the charge nurse to perform janitorial duties. He refused and was asked: "Who do you think you are?" He also provided evidence that was disputed that the charge nurse later told him: "Get out of here, I'm not signing anything, you stupid n*****."[32] A short time after these incidents, the hospital requested that the male nurse be reassigned to another facility. Relying on testimony by the employer that other white nurses also had been asked to perform janitorial functions, the judge dismissed the claim on summary judgment. The judge decided that the hospital had not discriminated against the black nurse.

It is common for judges to dismiss cases where there is evidence of discrimination. In another case, an engineer received exemplary performance evaluations for twenty-seven years and at times received bonus payments for outstanding service. Later, the engineer's supervisor asked him "to prepare a chart indicating the ages of the engineering staff, to corroborate a suspicion [the supervisor] had that the average age of the engineers was well into the 40s and 50s."[33] In a meeting with staff, the supervisor explained that "one of the goals for the upcoming year was to get some younger people on board (to raise the IQ of the staff)."[34] He also stated that the current staff was a bunch of " 'alta [sic] cockers,' " which was translated to mean " 'old fogies.' "[35] After a coworker complained about the supervisor's behavior, the supervisor was required to attend diversity training. However, thereafter, the supervisor reiterated that the company "needed a new cast of characters to win new business, and that '[w]e need new blood—new and younger, fresh skills from out of schools.' " The engineer then complained, and subsequently, the supervisor criticized the engineer during his performance review. Ultimately, the engineer was fired after his position was eliminated. The trial court judge decided that the engineer could not win his age discrimination claim and granted summary judgment to the employer.[36]

In each of these cases, the judges dismissed the worker's case, ruling there was so little evidence that a reasonable jury could not find for the worker. The judges decided the employers should win these cases. In each case, we do not know whether discrimination happened. In some cases, there is conflicting evidence and the people involved denied making discriminatory comments or acting in a discriminatory manner. Just as we do not know whether discrimination occurred, the judges also do not know. Yet judges make powerful judgments, dismissing cases brought by workers and deciding no discrimination occurred.[37]

These are just a few examples of the many cases that never make it to trial because the judge decides that no discrimination occurred. Studies show that judges grant a large percentage of summary judgment motions filed by employers, with the exact percentage varying by the time period studied. One Federal Judicial Center study found that in over 70 percent of discrimination cases in which the employer moved for summary judgment, the motion was granted.[38] A more recent study regarding employment discrimination cases in the Atlanta federal courts found that the courts granted 83 percent of summary judgment motions.[39]

3. CHANGING THE VERDICT

Even if a worker's case survives the pretrial motions and makes it to trial, a jury still may not decide his case. Moreover, where a jury decides in the employee's favor, he may not win. Federal procedure provides for trial and post-trial motions through which an employer may ask the judge to dismiss the case before the jury deliberates or even after the jury reaches a verdict.

After the employee has presented her evidence at trial, the employer can move for judgment as a matter of law. When a judge grants this motion, she has decided that no reasonable jury could find for the employee and the employee's case is dismissed.

The judge can also wait until after the jury reaches a verdict in favor of the worker and then decide that insufficient evidence of discrimination was presented and thus find that the jury incorrectly found discrimination. This is called a renewed judgment as a matter of law. As with summary judgment, the rules that govern this procedure are supposed to limit judges' abilities to choose winners or losers. And just as with summary judgment, the court is supposed to disturb the jury's verdict only if "a reasonable jury would not have a legally sufficient evidentiary basis to find for the party."[40]

Whenever this motion is used, a jury already has found in favor of one party. In deciding the motion, the judge is not supposed to re-weigh the evidence.[41] Instead, the rule requires the judge to view the evidence in the light most favorable to the jury's verdict. If the jury ruled in favor of the worker, the judge must view the evidence in the light most favorable to the worker. If the judge grants the motion, he is essentially declaring that the jury acted unreasonably.

As an alternative to requesting dismissal, an employer who loses a case will also usually ask the judge to grant a new trial. So, if dismissal outright is not granted, a new trial may be. In these circumstances, in theory, a second jury will then decide the dispute. Although there are instances where a second trial happens, many times the parties settle the case before the second trial begins, given the costs and inherent uncertainty of another trial.

When a judge does not completely reject the jury's verdict, the judge may still not accept the amount of damages the jury awards. Two post-trial devices allow judges to reduce the amount of damages. Using "remittitur," a judge can decide that the jury awarded excessive damages and determine the amount that a reasonable jury could find. In many cases when a judge is asked to reduce damages, the judge will look at other cases that the judge believes are similar to determine whether a verdict is reasonable. All of the facts of these cases are not evaluated by the judge who is considering the reduction because the judge does not review the actual testimony from the former cases. As a result, it is difficult for the judge to accurately compare the present case to the past cases. Also, not all verdicts are available to judges. The available databases typically contain published appellate cases and only a small fraction of trial court cases. This narrow sample of cases generally includes only other judges' decisions to reduce damages and thus reflects judges' (and not juries') views about the appropriate level of damages.[42]

After the judge decides the amount of damages a jury could have awarded, the worker has a choice: he can take the lower amount or go through a second trial. It is unlikely the plaintiff will take the second trial because the judge has already declared the maximum amount that a reasonable jury could find. Any subsequent higher verdict would be unreasonable.[43] In addition to a reduction in damages because of insufficient evidence, the judge can also reduce a jury award of punitive damages if the judge believes the damages are constitutionally excessive. Taken together, these motions mean that workers often do not receive the amount of damages awarded to them by the jury because judges determine the worker should receive less. These changes to verdicts supplement the limits that Congress has already imposed on the damages that can be awarded in employment discrimination cases.

The limits placed on a judge's ability to second-guess a jury have a constitutional and a statutory dimension. The Seventh Amendment of the Constitution limits how a judge can change the outcome reached by a jury.[44] Moreover, the federal discrimination statutes explicitly provide workers with a right to jury trial.[45] Likewise, the procedural rules that govern federal judges restrict a judge's ability to replace a jury's verdict with her own opinion of the case.[46] Despite these boundaries, judges often violate these limits.

The case of *Ash v. Tyson Foods, Inc.*, introduced in Chapter 1, illustrates the effect of many of these procedures on employment discrimination cases.[47] In that case, Anthony Ash and John Hithon, who are black, alleged they each were denied promotions to shift manager at a poultry plant because of their race.[48] The company promoted two white workers instead.[49]

At trial, the plaintiffs presented evidence that they were each referred to as "boy" by a white supervisor.[50] The supervisor also did not use the posted job criteria when choosing people to promote.[51] Additionally, the workers submitted evidence that they were more qualified for the promotions than the people who ultimately were promoted.[52] They also had evidence that no African American man had ever been promoted to the jobs they sought.[53] The employer countered with testimony from the supervisor who denied that the word "boy" was used in a racial way and with more general denials that the company discriminated against the two workers.[54] During the trial, the judge denied a motion for judgment as a matter of law, allowing the jury to decide the case. After deliberating, the jury found that the company failed to promote both Mr. Ash and Mr. Hithon because of their race. The jury awarded them compensatory and punitive damages to compensate them and punish the employer.[55] The plaintiffs received punitive damages because the jury found that the employer engaged in intentional discrimination "with malice or with reckless indifference to the federally protected rights of an aggrieved individual."[56]

After the jury rendered its verdict, the employer argued that there was insufficient evidence of discrimination for the jury to find for the plaintiffs. Agreeing, the trial court judge ruled that the jury incorrectly found for Mr. Ash and Mr. Hithon.[57] No employment discrimination had occurred.

On appeal, the reviewing court agreed that the employer did not discriminate against Mr. Ash. It further ruled that calling an African American man "boy" was not evidence of discrimination.[58] While the appellate court found that the trial court wrongly ruled in the employer's favor on the other plaintiff Mr. Hithon's claim,[59] the appellate court also decided that the jury should not have awarded Mr. Hithon any punitive damages and that the award of compensatory damages was too high. Ultimately, it ordered a new trial for Mr. Hithon.[60]

Eventually, Mr. Hithon's case was tried by a second jury, which found in Mr. Hithon's favor. The employer filed a motion to overturn the jury's verdict, and this time, the trial court allowed the jury's determination that the employer had discriminated to stand. However, the trial court judge again rejected the jury's award of punitive damages.[61] Even though two juries had awarded Mr. Hithon punitive damages, the judge found that both juries were mistaken. *Ash v. Tyson* has a long history, and we will return to this case later in the book to fill in more of that history.

4. APPEAL

Even if the trial judge does not find for the employer before, during, or after trial, the employer still has one more opportunity to win before the courts. The employer can appeal the case to a federal appellate court. Appellate judges do not see or hear the witnesses in the case, and the evidence they consider is a paper record submitted by the parties. Nonetheless, the court can choose to disagree with both the jury and the trial court judge and declare that no discrimination occurred.[62]

One study showed that when an employer appealed a jury verdict for the plaintiff, the appellate court reversed those wins 42 percent of the time.[63] Scholars have noted that the worker's "chance of retaining victory . . . cannot meaningfully be distinguished from a coin flip."[64]

Discrimination cases fare worse on appeal than many other kinds of cases. For example, Professors Kevin Clermont and Theodore Eisenberg studied what happened in tort and contract cases that went to a jury trial. They found that appeals courts reject the jury's finding in those types of cases only 31 percent of the time.[65] Even if the worker who alleged employment discrimination retains her victory on appeal, the appellate court can also reduce the damages she received from the jury.

If a federal jury finds for the employer or a federal trial court judge dismisses a case or reduces damages, the employee—like the employer—can appeal to a federal appellate court. However, employees fare much worse than employers on appeal. When the worker appealed the jury's verdict in favor of the employer, the appellate court reversed the defendant's win only 7 percent of the time.[66] In these circumstances, again, employment discrimination cases fare less well on appeal than many other types of cases. For example, in torts and contracts cases, plaintiffs who lose before the jury win 13 percent of their appeals.[67] Professor Clermont and his coauthors found "employment-discrimination cases, along with other civil-rights-type cases, show [an] anti-plaintiff effect in as extreme a form as one sees."[68]

Even in the rare cases where the appellate court reverses an employment discrimination decision, this "win" for the worker is not cost-free. The worker is required to spend years litigating on appeal and have a lawyer who is willing to spend time on the appeal.

For example, in *Reeves v. Sanderson Plumbing Products, Inc.*, Roger Reeves alleged that his employer fired him because of his age.[69] At the time he was fired, Mr. Reeves had worked for his employer for forty years and was 57 years old.[70] To support his claim, Mr. Reeves presented evidence that a supervisor who was involved in the termination told Mr. Reeves several months before his dismissal that he was so old that he "'must have come over on the Mayflower,'" and that he was "'too damn old to do the job.'"[71]

Mr. Reeves' case was tried by a jury, and the jury awarded him $35,000 in compensatory damages. The jury also found that the employer's conduct was willful. The trial court entered a judgment for Mr. Reeves for $70,000, which represented $35,000 in compensatory damages and an additional $35,000 damages to reflect the willfulness of the employer's discrimination.

The employer appealed the case, and the appellate court found in its favor, rejecting the jury's verdict. The court disregarded the age-related comments, noting that "[d]espite the potentially damning nature of [the] age-related comments, it is clear that these comments were not made in the direct context of Reeves's termination."[72]

The United States Supreme Court eventually corrected the appellate court's error, but it took Mr. Reeves an extra two years to finally uphold the jury verdict of $70,000. The Supreme Court only takes a tiny fraction of the cases it is asked to review each year, meaning for most workers, once an appellate court rules on their case, the case is over.

In theory, pretrial motions, trial motions, post-trial motions, and appeals are intended for use by judges in limited circumstances. The motion to dismiss, summary judgment, and judgment as a matter of law are supposed to be used to dismiss cases that the worker could never win.

Post-trial motions and appeals are supposed to correct mistakes made by judges and juries. However, pretrial motions, trial motions, post-trial motions, and appeals do not serve such limited functions in discrimination cases. Each of these steps has provided judges with an opportunity to decide against the worker and for the employer. We now turn to the court-created doctrines and inferences that make these dismissals possible.

How Discrimination Disappears

Ron, who is black, sued his employer for racial harassment, which is prohibited under Title VII. Before trial, the employer filed a motion for summary judgment asking a judge to dismiss the case. Ron responded with evidence that he had been repeatedly subjected to racial symbols and racial slurs at work.[1] He testified that some coworkers displayed the rebel flag on toolboxes and work hats, and that he saw the letters "KKK" on a bathroom wall and one other location in the workplace. Ron testified that supervisors repeatedly referred to him using racial epithets or racially charged language, including calling him the N-word and "boy." He also presented evidence that a supervisor told him two or three times that he was going to kick his "black ass," and that another supervisor told him that if he looked at "that white girl" he would "cut" him.[2]

The court dismissed his claim. The court decided that Ron did not have a claim for racial harassment because what happened to him was not serious enough for the courts to treat it as harassment.[3] In many instances, courts have declared that a wide swath of conduct is not discrimination, even though there is evidence that sex, race, or other protected traits negatively affected a worker's employment.

Tina's case, which we discussed in Chapter 1, provides another example of a case with evidence of discrimination, but which a judge dismissed on summary judgment. Tina sued her employer for sexual harassment and submitted evidence of the following conduct. While working as a cashier, she was subjected to degrading treatment from a manager. He asked her on dates many times, even offering "financial assistance" if she would agree.[4] He once "removed from his pants a large bottle of wine, offered Plaintiff a drink, and then asked her to join him later at a local hotel where they could have a 'good time.'" Tina also alleged that on at least two occasions, he touched her breasts and touched her buttocks once. When Tina filed a claim for sexual harassment, the court dismissed her claim, ruling that what happened to Tina was not sexual harassment because what happened to her was not serious enough.

Cases like Tina's and Ron's are not isolated. Searches of federal cases reveal case after case where federal courts ruled that conduct is not sufficiently serious to be considered discrimination. Cases are dismissed where women allege that their bosses or their coworkers repeatedly touched their breasts or buttocks, supervisors regularly asked employees on dates or for sexual favors, or employees were continually the victim of unwanted sexualized comments and gestures.[5] Federal courts have ruled that this conduct is not serious enough to be called sexual harassment.

In other cases, where there is evidence that a negative evaluation or threatened termination is caused by race, sex, or other protected traits, some judges will hold that this conduct is not an "adverse action" and does not count as discrimination. Finally, many federal courts will not find illegal retaliation in circumstances where an employer gives a negative evaluation or threatens to fire an employee who complained about discrimination. Again, courts often find that this conduct is not sufficiently serious and thus does not rise to the level of actionable retaliation.

This chapter explores the ways courts limit harassment, discrimination, and retaliation claims. We show how the court-created doctrines are not driven by the text of the discrimination statutes. Despite broad statutory language, many judges construe the statutes more narrowly than required. Finally, we discuss how—even when employees wait to file suit until more negative actions happen—these employees still may not obtain relief from the courts.

1. HARASSMENT

Under existing federal law, harassment based on a protected trait, like sex or race, is illegal. The Equal Employment Opportunity Commission (EEOC) describes harassment as a work environment that a reasonable person would find to be "intimidating, hostile, or abusive."[6] On its website, the EEOC gives examples of harassment. Harassment includes "offensive jokes, slurs, epithets or name calling, physical assaults or threats, intimidation, ridicule or mockery, insults or put-downs, offensive objects or pictures, and interference with work performance."[7]

One kind of harassment is sexual harassment. Judges often dismiss harassment cases by discounting the seriousness of the conduct about which the employee complains. One example involves Helen, who is a female police officer in a sheriff's office. According to the court, a male officer in the sheriff's office engaged in the following behavior toward Helen:

> (1) tried to kiss her after the 1999 Sheriff's Department Christmas party and called her a "frigid bitch" when she refused, (2) showed up at places Plaintiff was "staking out" in December 1999 and told her "you must be working out" and "you sure do look fine," (3) appeared several times in her driveway in January 2000, once drunk, when he told Plaintiff's son that he loved Plaintiff, (4) suggested she wear certain jeans and commented "your ass sure does look fine," (5) told her "you can just walk into the room and I'd get an erection," (6) stood on his tiptoes to look down her shirt, (7) rubbed up against her, whispered in her ear, and put his arm across her chest, (8) chased her around the . . . office, (9) once picked her up over his head in the . . . office, (10) asked her over the Sheriff's Department telephones if she was dressed or naked, (11) opened the door to the women's bathroom and turned the lights off and on when Plaintiff was inside . . . .[He also] tried to convince Plaintiff to go to the hotel hot tub with him [at a convention]. He called her a "frigid bitch" when she refused. . . . And Plaintiff explained that, in June 2002, before she was scheduled to work security at a private golf

tournament given by a strip club owner, [the officer] told her and other officers about another golf tournament hosted by this owner where strippers acted as caddies. [He] said that the owner directed the strippers to place golf balls into their vaginas and to squirt them onto the green.[8]

The judge overseeing the case dismissed it before trial, and the appellate court agreed, affirming the dismissal. According to the appellate court, this conduct did not constitute sexual harassment because the evidence showed the man touched her "[o]nly three times . . . when he tried to kiss her, when he lifted her over his head, and when he rubbed up against her and reached across her chest."[9] Even though this conduct was what the court called "reprehensible behavior [that] only can be described as crass and juvenile"[10] and what a later court called "outrageous," it was not serious enough to be called sexual harassment.[11]

When courts consider whether conduct rises to the level of harassment that is serious enough to deserve a remedy, they do so under a court-created doctrine that does not derive directly from the text of the discrimination statutes themselves. This doctrine developed originally from two Supreme Court cases and was then further defined by lower courts.

The courts were not originally sure whether the federal discrimination statutes prohibited harassment. When the Supreme Court recognized harassment as a claim in *Meritor Savings Bank, FSB v. Vinson*,[12] it noted that federal discrimination law "affords employees the right to work in an environment free from discriminatory intimidation, ridicule, and insult."[13] The Court also noted that sexually or racially offensive work environments are arbitrary barriers to workplace equality.[14] To prove harassment, the Court stated a worker must show that the behavior was "sufficiently severe or pervasive to alter the conditions of [the victim's] employment and create an abusive working environment."[15] However, Title VII does not specifically include this text or this requirement. Instead, it more generally provides that discrimination occurs when a worker's terms, conditions, or privileges of employment or her work opportunities are negatively affected by her sex or another protected trait.

In *Meritor*, a bank teller alleged that her supervisor "made repeated demands upon her for sexual favors, . . . both during and after business hours; . . . fondled her in front of other employees, followed her into the women's restroom when she went there alone, exposed himself to her, and even forcibly raped her on several occasions."[16] Although the supervisor denied this conduct, if proven, there was no question that the worker's evidence was serious enough to be called harassment.

In a later case, the Supreme Court provided more details about how to decide whether the conduct was severe or pervasive. Conduct is severe or pervasive when the worker perceives the environment as hostile or abusive and a reasonable person in the same circumstances would have the same perception.[17] To determine this, the fact-finder should look at all of the circumstances, including "the frequency of the discriminatory conduct; its severity; whether it is physically threatening or humiliating, or a mere offensive utterance; and whether it unreasonably interferes with an employee's work performance."[18]

Some conduct is clearly so serious that it always counts as harassment. For example, if a supervisor rapes an employee, this would be serious enough to be harassment. If a supervisor subjects a worker to sexual epithets and taunting every day for a lengthy period, this would also be harassment. Some conduct is never going to meet this standard. For example, if on one occasion, a supervisor asks an employee out on a date and otherwise does not treat her differently after she declines, this one incident will not trigger liability.

In the middle, some judges see an area of uncertainty. Courts often find the harassment is not illegal. This is what happened in Tina's case. The judge found that even if Tina could prove the repeated requests for dates, an assistant manager's request to join him later at a local hotel, and the manager's touching of her breasts and buttocks, these acts were not severe or pervasive enough to count as harassment.

Another example involves Julie. Julie worked at a newspaper as its editor.[19] She presented evidence of the following conduct. A coworker would repeatedly brush up against her breasts and her behind. On one occasion, the same coworker slapped her on the behind with a newspaper. Another time, he tried to kiss her. On more than one occasion, he asked Julie to come in early so that they could be alone together. He also told her that another coworker had a nice behind and body. Another female worker also claimed that the same coworker had harassed her. Julie filed a claim of sexual harassment. The trial court dismissed Julie's case before trial, and the appellate court agreed. The appellate court ruled that the conduct Julie alleged was not serious enough to constitute harassment under federal law.

In addition to prohibiting sexual harassment of people of the opposite sex, the law forbids same-sex harassment. A man cannot subject another man to inappropriate sexual touching and other similar conduct. Nor can a woman do this to another woman. However, courts have also been reticent to find harassment in same-sex harassment cases. In the following case, a district court found there was no harassment when a male supervisor allegedly made two or three sexual remarks a day to a male employee over a ten-day period.[20] This is how the court described the supervisor's conduct toward the worker:

- Asked the plaintiff "do you want to feel my pipe?";
- Asked plaintiff "Did you stretch your ass out for me?" when plaintiff returned from the bathroom;
- Told the plaintiff "you're a young strapping man with a nice ass";
- Touched plaintiff's side and knee in a suggestive manner on more than one occasion;
- Asked plaintiff "can I play with your hole?";
- Told plaintiff "hey, handsome, come here and sit in my lap";
- Made comments to plaintiff about having a "fine ass";
- Made comments to plaintiff about "drinking his cum, raping him, and straddling his face";
- Blew plaintiff kisses;
- Told plaintiff he wanted to lick his rear;
- Told plaintiff when he complained that "there was nothing he could do about it";
- Talked about the plaintiff's genitals;
- Told plaintiff he was making him "horny"; telling plaintiff "I'm sweaty between my legs"; and asking plaintiff "can I drill you with my pipe?"[21]

These stories are not isolated cases. In case after case, judges deem similar conduct as insufficient to constitute harassment. Consider the allegations workers presented in the following cases:

- Coworkers and supervisor engaged in conduct such as making comments about the worker's breasts, requesting to lick whipped cream and wine off of her, inappropriately touching her while hugging her, requesting to go on dates with her, rubbing her shoulder, arms, and rear end, and sending an inappropriate text message.[22]
- Supervisor telling worker the only reason she was there was "because we needed a skirt in the office"; asking her to go to hotel room and spend the night with him; asking her "to blow" him; constantly referring to her as "Babe"; unzipping his pants and moving the zipper up and down in front of her; and referring to women using words like "bitch," "slut," and "tramp."[23]
- Supervisor "repeatedly asked employee about her personal life, told her how beautiful she was, asked her out on dates, called her a 'dumb blond,' put his hands on her shoulders at least six times, placed 'I love you' signs in her work area, and tried to kiss her on three occasions."[24]
- Coworker placed his hand on employee's "stomach and commented on its softness and sexiness." After worker told coworker to stop touching her and forcefully pushed him away, the coworker "forced his hand underneath her sweater and bra to fondle her bare breast." After worker told coworker he had crossed the line, the coworker again tried to fondle her breasts but stopped when another employee arrived at the office.[25]
- Supervisor told worker she had been "voted the 'sleekest ass' in the office" and on another occasion "deliberately touched [her] breasts with some papers that he was holding in his hand."[26]

We could fill pages and pages with cases like these.[27] Courts routinely dismiss cases such as these where there is significant evidence of harassment by declaring that the alleged conduct does not constitute harassment.

Sometimes, workers are successful in overturning trial court decisions. In one case that was reversed on appeal, a trial court judge had dismissed the worker's claim even though she had evidence that a person who regularly visited her office called women "bitches," discussed his sexual encounters with women, showed naked pictures of women, discussed wanting to have sex with a coworker's daughter, called the worker a "black bitch," and repeatedly used racial epithets.[28]

The dismissals of the cases can have a kind of domino effect, leading to the dismissal of later cases. After one judge deems a case with significant evidence of harassment as not severe or pervasive enough to be called harassment under the statutes, other judges believe they must dismiss later cases with similar or less evidence of harassment.

For example, in one case, a worker was fired. She alleged that she had been fired after she complained that a supervisor slapped her on the butt.[29] The judge held that it was not reasonable for an employee to think that a slap on the butt was harassment.[30] To justify this holding, the judge cited other cases with worse facts, which had been dismissed. In one, "the alleged harasser told plaintiff that he was 'getting fired up,' rubbed his hip against the plaintiff's hip while touching her shoulder and smiling, twice made a sniffing sound while looking at the plaintiff's groin area and once made a sniffing sound without looking at her groin, and constantly followed and stared at plaintiff in a 'very obvious fashion.'"[31] The judge also compared the case to another case where a woman alleged multiple butt slappings.[32] Because courts had dismissed these cases, the trial court found that it must dismiss this worker's claim as well.

Once an appellate court makes a ruling that certain behavior is not serious enough, it sets in motion a growing body of cases that reach the same result. At times, trial court judges are required to follow these cases because the ruling appellate court presides over the trial court and the trial court is required to follow the appellate court's decision. At other times, trial court judges rely on an appellate ruling to justify dismissal, even if they are not required to follow the particular case. The body of law providing examples of when cases should be dismissed keeps growing, and many judges do not question whether the original cases were correctly decided in the first place.

Judges may disagree about what constitutes harassment. In one case, a federal trial court judge found a claim that the worker's supervisor twice called her a "porch monkey" was not harassment and dismissed the case.[33] Although the judge did "not question that the term is highly offensive to African Africans," the judge found the isolated comments did not rise to the required level. [34]

The worker appealed the case to the United States Court of Appeals for the Fourth Circuit. While the three-judge panel noted that the use of term "porch monkey" was "racially derogatory and highly offensive," it could not constitute harassment because there were only two instances of the comment being made.[35] The worker then asked the Fourth Circuit to hear her case en banc, which is a review by the full appellate court rather than the normal three-judge panel that typically hears appeals.

The full Fourth Circuit en banc reversed both of the prior decisions. It held that a reasonable jury could find that the worker was subjected to racial harassment. The court noted that "no single act can more quickly alter the conditions of employment and create an abusive working environment than the use of an unambiguously racial epithet."[36]

There are other cases from different circuits involving use of the "porch monkey" epithet. Sometimes judges allow the cases to proceed. Other times they do not.[37]

Other cases involving sexual harassment also show differences in judges' opinions of what constitutes harassment. Although less common, there are some courts that will allow a case to go to a jury when a supervisor or coworker touches a worker's breasts or buttocks.[38]

Some judges also try to make factual distinctions about the conduct in the cases. For example, one court has indicated that the direct touching of a worker's breast is enough to constitute harassment, but repeated brushing up against a worker's breast and behind are not.[39] Whether the contact is a direct touch or mere grazes is the difference between the case going forward and dismissal.

These cases are even more problematic when you consider the judge's appropriate role in these cases. As the examples show, judges often make these decisions when the employer files a motion for summary judgment, asking the court to dismiss the case. At summary judgment, the judge is supposed to let the case go to trial if a reasonable jury could find for the worker, and the judge is also supposed to believe all of the evidence offered by the worker.

In addition to establishing the protection of the severe or pervasive requirement, courts created another doctrine that allows employers to escape liability for harassment in some other circumstances.[40] If a worker experiences harassment but fails to complain about that harassment, or if the employer takes steps to prevent future harassment after a complaint, this doctrine sometimes allows courts to deny any relief to the worker. Given this ancillary, court-created doctrine that protects employers, it is unclear why courts limit the harassment doctrine by narrowly construing the severe or pervasive requirement.

Even when cases make it to trial and a jury finds that conduct was severe or pervasive, trial court judges or appellate judges may disagree and reject the jury's findings.[41] For example, Sally, a secretary, worked for a company for a month when she was assigned to a new boss, Michael, who was a regional manager for the company.[42] Sally sued her employer for harassment and testified Michael did the following. Michael called Sally "pretty girl." When she wore a leather skirt to work, he grunted as she left his office. Michael told Sally that his office was not hot until she stepped foot into it and that "[a]ll pretty girls run around naked." He told Sally that he was lonely in his hotel room because his wife had not yet moved from Chicago. He then looked at his hand, a gesture intended to suggest masturbation. He once told her that his wife had told him he had "better clean up [his] act" and "better think of you as Ms. Anita Hill."[43]

Sally's case was one of the rare discrimination cases that made it to trial. A jury found in her favor, finding that Michael sexually harassed her. After the jury awarded her $25,000, the company appealed the verdict. The appellate court reversed the jury's verdict and declared the company should win the case. The court noted that Michael was a "man whose sense of humor took final shape in adolescence"[44] but said his conduct was not serious enough to constitute sexual harassment.

2. DISCRIMINATION

Courts often distinguish harassment claims from discrimination claims. Discrimination typically involves a discrete event or set of events that involve more formal consequences. Just as courts limit harassment doctrine through the "severe or pervasive" requirement, courts also limit discrimination law through a separate legal doctrine called the "adverse action" doctrine. Courts decide that employees' claims of discrimination are not sufficiently serious. In one case, an appellate court was trying to determine what conduct was sufficiently serious to be discrimination. The appellate court imagined a fact pattern to demonstrate this point. Chapter 1 previously introduced this fact pattern.

Rachel, who is black, has a supervisor, Bill, who is white. Rachel has a memo that states that Bill "will never give a black employee a positive evaluation." Later, Bill gives Rachel a negative evaluation. The court stated a negative evaluation does not count as discrimination.[45] In the case in which the court used the hypothetical fact pattern, a black employee had alleged that because of the employee's race, his boss did not recommend him for a prestigious award that came with a large financial reward.[46] The court decided it must dismiss the case because the worker had not alleged sufficiently serious harm.

In discrimination cases, courts use this court-created "adverse action" doctrine to limit the reach of discrimination law. Even if an employee has evidence that the employer took an action because of his race or because of her sex, courts will not label such conduct discrimination. Although the cases are not completely uniform, courts often hold that the following conduct is not discriminatory:

- giving an employee a negative evaluation or write-up;[47]
- denying a lateral transfer;[48]
- transferring an employee to a less desirable job;[49]
- reprimanding or threatening a worker with disciplinary action;[50]
- excessively scrutinizing a worker's job performance;[51]
- threatening to fire a worker;[52]
- assigning additional work;[53] and
- giving more difficult job assignments.[54]

Even if a worker presents evidence that these actions were taken because of a protected trait, the courts will hold that the employee has not suffered the kind of harm for which legal redress is available.

David's case is a good example of this idea. David is a male nurse. He wanted to transfer to a nursing job in the operating room. When David asked the woman responsible for transfers whether he could transfer to the operating room, she told him, "I hate to discriminate against you because you're a man, but the doctors want more female nurses in the OR."[55] The woman disputed saying she would "hate to discriminate against" David, but admitted that she said she wanted a woman to fill the position because of her concerns about having enough female nurses available. After this conversation, David did not formally apply for the operating room position because he was told he would not be hired for the position. A jury did not hear the case.[56] Both the trial court and the appellate court ruled that David's case did not present enough facts to show he was discriminated against because of his sex because being denied a lateral transfer does not count as discrimination under Title VII.

Even when workers allege multiple negative actions, courts often find the combined actions do not constitute enough harm to merit protection under the law.[57] For example, a court might dismiss a claim where a worker alleged that because of his race he received unfavorable performance reviews, did not receive the same level of training as other employees, and was spoken to and treated in a condescending way.[58]

Despite the judges' rulings, the actual words of the discrimination statutes provide workers with broad protection. When courts ignore the text of the statutes, they may act in their own self-interest and also may promote the interests of employers. Employment discrimination cases occupy less than 5 percent of the civil cases filed in federal courts but occupied a greater percentage of the docket in the late 1990s. Ridding the docket of some of these cases decreases judges' workload. Also, as discussed later, courts often defer to employers because they do not want to become involved in many employment decisions. In their words, they do not want to sit as "super-personnel departments." Moreover, as described later, some judges do not believe the evidence presented by workers. These factors shape judges' interpretations of federal discrimination statutes.

3. WHAT THE LAW PROVIDES

When the courts declare conduct to be not serious enough to count as discrimination, they do not consult the text of the federal discrimination statutes. These statutes provide broad protection against discriminatory conduct in the workplace.

Title VII, the federal statute that prohibits discrimination based on race, sex, national origin, color, and religion, has served as the model for the other federal discrimination statutes. It provides that it is an unlawful employment practice for an employer to do the following:

(1) to fail or refuse to hire or to discharge any individual, or
otherwise to discriminate against any individual with respect to
his compensation, *terms, conditions, or privileges* of employment,
because of such individual's race, color, religion, sex, or national
origin; or

(2) *to limit*, segregate, or classify his employees or applicants
for employment *in any way which would deprive or tend to
deprive any individual of employment opportunities or otherwise
adversely affect his status as an employee*, because of such
individual's race, color, religion, sex, or national origin.[59]

The statute makes it an unlawful employment practice to "fail or refuse to hire" because of a protected trait. Likewise, it is clear that termination or compensation decisions cannot be based on race, sex, or another protected trait. Courts have likewise construed the statutory language to provide relief for discriminatory demotions.[60]

However, outside of these fixed categories, the courts have not rigorously protected employees, even though the statutory language provides broad protection. The statutory language that Congress used forbids employer actions that "deprive or tend to deprive" employees of employment opportunities. It also prohibits employers from discriminating in the "terms, conditions, or privileges" of employment.

The words "terms or conditions of employment" are used in a number of other employment-related contexts. In each of these other contexts, this wording is understood to encompass all sorts of conduct—not just conduct like hiring and firing. For example, under the federal labor law, the National Labor Relations Act, employers and unions must collectively bargain with respect to "wages, hours, and other terms and conditions of employment."[61] In these cases, courts have held that the terms and conditions of employment include all sorts of employer actions including:

- The price of food at vending machines and in the company cafeteria;[62]
- Safety rules and practices;[63]
- Rules concerning employee discipline, smoking, and dress;[64]
- The level of heat in a plant;[65]
- The worker's break schedule, an employer policy governing the scheduling of vacations, and the employer policy governing work schedules;[66] and
- Requirements regarding whether employees must accept temporary assignments outside their job classifications and that would subject them to discipline if they failed to do so.[67]

Outside of labor law, courts also define the words "terms and conditions" broadly. For example, when an employer and employee agree to arbitrate all disputes related to the "terms and conditions" of employment, courts interpret those words to include disputes related to all aspects of the employee's work.[68]

Even though the federal discrimination statutes use the same words employed in the labor law context and the arbitration context, the federal courts have interpreted the words differently, sometimes reaching opposite conclusions. Changing an employee's schedule is not deemed as affecting a term or condition of employment for discrimination law purposes. Discipline, short of termination, often does not count either.[69] However, in labor law and in arbitration, these actions count as part of the terms and conditions of employment. Despite the broad reading of the words "terms or conditions" in other contexts, judges give them a narrow reading in discrimination law. Judges created the "adverse action" doctrine, unnecessarily restricting the reach of the discrimination statutes, even though the statutes themselves do not contain such limiting language.

4. ADVERSE ACTION IN RETALIATION CASES

Courts use the phrase "severe or pervasive" to describe how serious conduct must be to be called harassment. They use another phrase, "adverse action," to describe how serious conduct must be to be deemed discrimination. In retaliation cases, courts also use the phrase "adverse action" to limit retaliation claims. It describes how serious conduct must be, but the definition of "adverse action" in this context differs from how it is used in discrimination cases.

Each of the discrimination statutes prohibits retaliation.[70] To prevail on a retaliation claim, a person must show she engaged in protected activity (like complaining to an administrative agency or a human resources department about discriminatory conduct), she suffered an adverse action, and that there was a causal connection between the protected activity and the consequence.[71]

Employee complaints play a central role in the discrimination statutes. The complaint gives the employer or an administrative agency the opportunity to remedy the discriminatory conduct without the need for a lawsuit. At times, the law actually requires a worker to complain to be successful later in a lawsuit. In some harassment suits, the employee will lose her case if she failed to first complain to her employer.[72] Under most discrimination laws, workers must report discrimination to the EEOC or a state agency before they can file suit.[73] Even when the law does not require a formal complaint, employers often encourage employees to complain about discrimination. Employer handbooks often contain complaint procedures and tell employees to report harassment and discrimination.

So, let's imagine that Mary goes to the human resources office and complains that her supervisor Maurice sexually harassed her. Maurice is disciplined for his inappropriate behavior. A month later, Maurice begins to write false reports about Mary, asserting her work performance is bad. He also threatens to fire her.

If Mary filed a retaliation claim, many judges would dismiss Mary's case. Similar to discrimination cases, courts have a high standard for establishing an adverse action in retaliation cases. Many courts have held that an employee could not establish a retaliation claim when she alleged her employer took the following actions in response to her complaint of discrimination:

- threatened to fire the employee;[74]
- gave the employee negative evaluations or disciplinary write-ups;[75]
- threatened the employee with a suspension or disciplinary action;[76]
- failed to nominate employee for awards;[77]
- placed an employee on disciplinary or administrative leave;[78]
- assigned the worker to a less desirable shift;[79]
- removed an employee from her office;[80] or
- falsely reported poor performance.[81]

As with discrimination cases, in retaliation cases, courts also dismiss workers' allegations that multiple events, when added together, constitute an adverse action.[82] Again, the cases are not completely uniform. Some courts will allow these claims to go to trial.[83] Others will not.

5. THE REASONABLE PERSON IN RETALIATION CASES

In the retaliation context, the Supreme Court has defined what kind of adverse action the employer must take against a worker who complains about discrimination for that action to count as retaliation. Employer actions constitute retaliation if the negative action would dissuade a reasonable person from complaining about discrimination in the first place.[84] The idea is that the law should protect employees from actions by employers that would dissuade employees from complaining.

Using this definition, lower courts routinely dismiss cases where workers allege their employers retaliated against them for complaining about discrimination. The courts assert that a reasonable person would not be dissuaded from filing a discrimination complaint if she faced consequences such as threatened termination or negative evaluations. In doing so, judges make factual assertions about what reasonable people think. They determine that workers will complain about discrimination, even if as a consequence their supervisor may later threaten to fire them or place negative performance evaluations in their personnel file. One of us tested this claim using a survey.[85]

Participants were asked to imagine that they witnessed discrimination in the workplace. They then answered a series of ten questions about whether the following actions would dissuade them from submitting a complaint about the discrimination to an employer:

- A coworker stares rudely every day for a week;
- Being fired;
- A negative evaluation in an employment file;
- A supervisor threatened termination, but did not immediately carry out the threat;

- A paid seven-day suspension;
- An office move to another location;
- A demotion;
- Criticism from a supervisor about work performance during a meeting attended by coworkers;
- Social ostracism by coworkers;
- A change in job responsibilities with the same pay.

For each action, the survey participant could answer yes, no, maybe, or do not know.

The study results show strong consensus about the circumstances under which a reasonable person would be dissuaded from filing a complaint. More than 90 percent of the study participants thought they would or might be dissuaded from filing a complaint if they would be fired. About 80 percent would or might be dissuaded if a negative evaluation was placed in their employment file or if they would be demoted. More than half of the study participants indicated that they would or might be dissuaded from filing a complaint if they were threatened with termination, would receive a paid seven-day suspension, would have an office moved to another location, faced social ostracism by coworkers, or faced a change in job responsibilities with the same pay.

Table 3.1 provides the number and percentage of study participants who indicated that they would or might be dissuaded from filing a complaint if a particular negative consequence would happen. The chart is organized to show the actions the participants viewed as most harmful first and then in descending order of perceived harm.

There were only two potential job consequences that a majority of participants thought would be unlikely to keep them from filing a complaint: a coworker staring rudely every day for a week and criticism from a supervisor about work performance during a meeting attended by coworkers. However, a sizable portion of the study participants still thought these actions would dissuade them from filing a complaint, with about 41 percent indicating that they would not complain if they would receive negative criticism from a supervisor at a meeting and slightly more

Table 3.1 PERCENTAGE OF PARTICIPANTS WHO WOULD NOT OR MIGHT NOT
COMPLAIN IF FACED WITH CONSEQUENCE.

Negative Consequence	Percentage of Participants Who Would or Might Be Dissuaded
Being fired	90.53%
Demotion	83.16%
A negative evaluation in an employment file	80%
Supervisor threatened termination but did not immediately carry out the threat	68.42%
A change in job responsibilities with the same pay	62.11%
Office move to another location	55.79%
Paid seven-day suspension	53.68%
Social ostracism by coworkers	50.53%
Criticism from a supervisor about work performance during a meeting attended by coworkers	41.05%
A coworker stares rudely every day for a week	17.89%

than 17 percent indicating that stares from a coworker would or might dissuade them from complaining.

This data shows that the courts are correct in their holdings that termination or demotion is likely to deter a person from filing a discrimination complaint—more than 90 percent of participants would or might be dissuaded if faced with termination, and more than 83 percent would or might be dissuaded by a demotion.

However, if retaliation law is supposed to prohibit an employer from taking actions that would dissuade a reasonable person from complaining about discrimination, this survey suggests that judges are setting the retaliation threshold too high. Many judges hold that a negative evaluation is not an adverse action that is protected because being punished in this manner would not dissuade the employee from complaining. Yet 80 percent of participants responded they would or might be dissuaded by a negative performance evaluation. Judges also hold that a worker is not protected if she complains and, as a consequence, the employer threatens to terminate her. However, more than 68 percent of study participants ranked a threatened termination as likely to dissuade.

While there are limitations to a survey like this, the study results challenge some courts' assertions that reasonable people would not be dissuaded from complaining about discrimination when faced with negative consequences, such as threatened termination or negative evaluations.[86]

6. THE REASONABLE BELIEF DOCTRINE

In retaliation cases, courts use the adverse action doctrine to dismiss cases. The "reasonable belief" doctrine is another requirement that courts use to dismiss retaliation cases. When a worker complains to her employer about discriminatory conduct, she receives the protection of discrimination law only if she reasonably believed the conduct she complained about is discrimination.

Let's return to Rachel's case. Rachel was the employee in the hypothetical fact pattern who accidentally received the memo saying that her supervisor would not give good evaluations to black employees. Rachel then received a bad evaluation. Imagine that Rachel goes to her company's human resources department and tells company officials about the memo and her bad evaluation. She lets the human resources office know that she thinks the negative evaluation is because of her race. Two days later, Rachel is fired.

After going to the EEOC to file a charge, Rachel files two claims in court. She first claims that the employer discriminated against her by giving her a bad review. As discussed, some courts will dismiss this claim because it is not serious enough to trigger protection. Rachel also files a retaliation claim in which she alleges that the company fired her for reporting the discriminatory conduct.

To win on her retaliation claim, Rachel must show that a reasonable person in her situation would think she had faced discrimination.[87] Some judges will dismiss Rachel's claim and argue that no reasonable person in Rachel's situation would think the negative evaluation was serious enough to be discrimination.

Workers in discrimination and harassment cases face a dilemma when it comes to complaints. Legal scholar Deborah Brake calls this dilemma the "reasonable belief trap."[88] In describing harassment cases, she stated that it results in a catch-22 for workers. They must "promptly report harassment to preserve their right to sue . . . , but are unprotected from retaliation if they complain internally too soon, before the perceived harassment could be reasonably understood as severe or pervasive."[89]

This concept is illustrated by *Butler v. Alabama Department of Transportation*.[90] The appellate court described the facts of the case as follows:

> Alvarene Butler is black and Karen Stacey is white. They both worked for the Alabama Department of Transportation. One work day in January of 2005 they were going to lunch together. Stacey was driving a pickup truck, and Butler was the only passenger.
>
> On the way to lunch, the truck collided with another vehicle, which was driven by a black male. After the collision, Stacey turned to Butler and asked: "Did you see that? Did you see that stupid mother fucking [n*****] hit me?" A few minutes later, when the driver of the other vehicle was attempting to re-route traffic around the accident, Stacey said: "Look at him now. Now that stupid ass [n*****] down there is trying to direct traffic. I hope something come [sic] over that hill and run over his ass and kill him." Butler understandably found Stacey's use of racial epithets offensive. She did not, however, believe that Stacey's words were directed at her.[91]

Ms. Butler claimed that after she complained about these comments, she started facing negative consequences and was treated differently than Ms. Stacey. She filed a lawsuit against her employer claiming that she was "(1) forced to perform manual labor at job sites while Stacey, a white co-worker, was excused from doing the same work; (2) required to report to work at 7:00 a.m. while Stacey was permitted to arrive at 7:30 a.m.; (3) disciplined for violating the 'call-in' rule for unscheduled absences while Stacey, who also violated this rule, was not; (4) [and] 'docked' pay for days she was absent even though she was approved for leave with pay."[92]

The case went to a jury. The jury found that the employer retaliated against Ms. Butler for complaining about discrimination. The employer filed post-trial motions, asking the trial court judge to reject the jury's verdict. The trial court judge refused and allowed the verdict to stand.

The employer appealed the case to the United States Court of Appeals for the Eleventh Circuit, and that court rejected the jury's verdict. Although the court characterized the use of the racial epithets as "uncalled for" and "ugly,"[93] it said that Ms. Butler could not receive any protection under federal law for complaining about these comments. Ms. Butler could not have a reasonable belief that the comments were severe or pervasive enough to constitute racial harassment. Her claim failed as a matter of law even though a jury had already decided that Ms. Butler's complaint was reasonable.

Again, this is an area where some courts find reasonable belief for certain facts and others do not for the same facts. Another appellate court has held that when there is evidence that a supervisor twice calls a black employee a "porch monkey," those statements are enough to trigger protection against retaliation.[94] That court recognized that Title VII encourages employees to complain when they face discrimination "in an effort to avert any further racial harassment."[95]

Here are some examples of cases where the court dismissed a case because the workers' complaints were not reasonable:

- A white worker did not have a reasonable belief that discrimination occurred when he reported another white worker had said, "Nobody runs this team but a bunch of [n******] and I'm going to get rid of them."[96] The white worker was not protected after complaining about this conduct because the comment was not severe enough for the employee to reasonably believe it constituted discrimination.

- A worker was fired after he complained that a male district manager engaged in inappropriate conduct toward a female employee at a company-sponsored happy hour and made a racial slur to an African American employee. The jury found in favor of the employee. The trial court judge rejected the jury's verdict, and the appellate court agreed. The employee did not have a reasonable belief that he was reporting discriminatory conduct.[97]
- A worker who complained about being slapped on the buttocks by a supervisor she had never met before was not protected from retaliation after she complained about this conduct. The court agreed that if the incident occurred, it was "degrading." However, the court noted that "degrading acts and sexual harassment are obviously not synonymous terms under Eleventh Circuit case law."[98] The court dismissed the employee's claim while noting that an assault and battery claim based on the same conduct could go forward.

Professor Brake has noted "the reasonable belief requirement has spawned a now-sizeable body of cases in which internal complaints about harassment are unprotected because the underlying conduct was not severe or pervasive enough to be actionable."[99]

The decisions incorrectly narrow the scope of the retaliation law and stand in stark contrast with employers' policies that encourage employees to report discriminatory conduct. Employers play an important role in teaching their employees about the meaning of discrimination law through their policies, procedures, and employee handbooks. These documents typically instruct and encourage employees to report the use of racial and sexual epithets and inappropriate touching. Many employers thus have policies that encourage employees to complain about actions that may not even be cognizable under the federal discrimination statutes, or that the employee may not be required to first report to the employer under federal law.

The Society for Human Resources Management (SHRM) is, according to its website, "the world's largest HR membership society" and is dedicated to best practices for human resources issues.[100] It issues sample handbooks for employers to use. SHRM advises employers that their harassment policy should say:

> [The company] is committed to a work environment in which all individuals are treated with respect and dignity. Each individual has the right to work in a professional atmosphere that promotes equal employment opportunities and prohibits unlawful discriminatory practices, including harassment. Therefore, [Company Name] expects that all relationships among persons in the office will be business-like and free of bias, prejudice and harassment.[101]

The model policy goes on to describe harassment as "a range of subtle and not-so-subtle behaviors." It then lists more than a dozen different kinds of conduct that might be harassment:

> [U]nwanted sexual advances or requests for sexual favors; sexual jokes and innuendo; verbal abuse of a sexual nature; commentary about an individual's body, sexual prowess or sexual deficiencies; leering, whistling or touching; insulting or obscene comments or gestures; display in the workplace of sexually suggestive objects or pictures; and other physical, verbal or visual conduct of a sexual nature. . . .
>
> [H]arassment is verbal, written or physical conduct that denigrates or shows hostility or aversion toward an individual because of [a protected trait.] Harassing conduct includes epithets, slurs or negative stereotyping; threatening, intimidating or hostile acts; denigrating jokes; and written or graphic material that denigrates or shows hostility or aversion toward an individual or group and that is placed on walls or elsewhere on the employer's premises or circulated in the workplace, on company time or using company equipment via e-mail, phone (including voice messages), text messages, tweets, blogs, social networking sites or other means."[102]

The sample policy encourages workers to report "all perceived incidents of discrimination or harassment."[103] It also promises that the company will not retaliate against employees for complaining.[104]

If an employee followed this policy and reported unwanted slaps on the buttocks or the use of racial epithets, this employee might not be protected from retaliation under federal law. Even though the employee would be following the company's policies, some courts will hold that she is not protected and will dismiss her claim. As one court indicated: "[A] racially derogatory remark by a co-worker, without more, does not constitute an unlawful employment practice under the opposition clause of Title VII, 42 U.S.C. § 2000e-3(a), and opposition to such a remark, consequently, is not statutorily protected conduct."[105]

Professor Brake has studied how employers' internal complaint procedures intersect with discrimination law. She notes that "[r]eliable data is hard to come by, but it is the rare employer today that lacks an internal policy and complaint procedure for addressing allegations of discrimination in the workplace." [106] These policies shape what employees understand to be discrimination and encourage workers to complain about such conduct.

Not only do employers encourage employee complaints, but the federal courts do as well. The courts have enshrined employee complaints as a key feature of the enforcement structure of discrimination claims. The Supreme Court has repeatedly stated: "Title VII depends for its enforcement upon the cooperation of employees who are willing to file complaints and act as witnesses."[107] The federal courts have interpreted federal discrimination law to require workers to complain in some circumstances to try to avoid further harm that might happen if harassment continued without the employer's knowledge.[108] In many instances, if a worker does not complain about harassment and an employer has an antiharassment policy, the worker will lose her case.

Discrimination case law also encourages employers to create discrimination complaint procedures and rewards them for doing so. The Supreme Court has noted that "Title VII is designed to encourage the creation of anti-harassment policies and effective grievance mechanisms."[109]

Employers can use the existence of complaint and investigation procedures to avoid punitive damages.[110] This gives employers a legal incentive to create complaint procedures, to publicize these procedures to employees, and to encourage employee complaints. The EEOC also encourages employers to adopt effective internal complaint procedures.[111]

Under the current system, workers are told that they must complain in certain circumstances to later maintain a harassment claim. In these and other cases, workers are told it is preferable to complain early because this provides the employer the opportunity to fix problems without litigation. Yet if workers complain, federal law may not protect them.[112]

7. WAITING TO SUE

One reason courts give for the adverse action doctrine in discrimination law or the adverse action doctrine in retaliation law is that the alleged harm is speculative. If a worker receives a bad performance evaluation, that evaluation might be used in later employment decisions or it might not. According to these judges, the law should encourage workers to wait until those later employment decisions happen. When the more significant negative consequences happen, the employee can sue and prevail.

However, when workers wait, their case may be dismissed for other reasons. Assume Betty, who is 63 years old, receives a bad performance evaluation at work from her supervisor, Barry. Betty believes he gave her the bad evaluation because of her age. Barry constantly makes age-related remarks. He tells Betty that she is too old to do her job, that she should retire to give other workers a chance, and that she is an "old hag." A year later, Betty does not receive a promotion for which she applied.

She then files a lawsuit alleging the bad performance evaluation negatively affected her promotion. The evidence shows that many factors went into the promotion decision. The people involved in making the decision looked at her bad performance review and other documents to make the decision. They stated that the bad performance review was one of many factors that affected their decision to choose another candidate for the promotion instead of Betty. Even though there is evidence that the evaluation was biased and that the evaluation was used in making the promotion decision, Betty cannot show exactly how it affected the promotion decision. Even though the bad performance evaluation was a factor in the decision, Betty cannot prove it was the decisive factor. Under the discrimination law, Betty may lose her case even though discrimination played a role in the negative employment decision.[113]

Claims also may be dismissed as untimely. The federal discrimination statutes require a worker to file a charge with the EEOC (or a comparable state agency) within a relatively short period after discrimination happens. These deadlines are one way that Congress chose to limit the reach of discrimination law. This time period is always less than a year and is sometimes as short as 180 days. If Betty does not submit her claim that Barry gave her the negative evaluation within this time period, her different claim for discrimination regarding the promotion claim may fail. Even if she otherwise has a good discrimination claim, she may lose it for failing to meet the deadline for filing an administrative charge about the negative evaluation.[114] The judge may say that the negative evaluation was a separate, discrete act of discrimination and that the law required Betty to go to the EEOC within 180 or 300 days of the negative evaluation. Because Betty did not go the EEOC in time, she cannot use the negative evaluation to support her claim.

Under this view, Betty must go to the EEOC and complain about her negative evaluation. She must do this, even though many judges would not consider her negative evaluation to be the basis for a viable claim. The intersection of the adverse action doctrine and the discrete act doctrine puts workers in the position of having to file potentially nonactionable claims.

Even if Betty submitted her negative evaluation claim to the EEOC, it is not clear that she would be able to use the negative evaluation to support her promotion claim. In order to have a chance to prevail, the worker must file a claim in court within 90 days of receiving the Notice of Right to Sue letter from the EEOC. If Betty filed her negative evaluation claim with the EEOC, she might receive her Right to Sue letter and be required to go to court before the promotion decision is even made. Many courts will then dismiss that claim because it is not an adverse action. When Betty later submits her promotion claim to the EEOC and then files it in court, some courts would find that the dismissal of the performance evaluation claim means that the worker cannot raise that issue again in court.

The way some courts interpret the time-filing requirements and the continuing discrete act doctrine puts workers in a difficult position. If they file a negative evaluation claim right after it happens, the case will be dismissed because the harm is not yet serious enough. If they wait until more serious actions occur, some courts will say that the law required the worker to submit the negative evaluation claim earlier. They will then refuse to allow the employee to use evidence of the bad evaluation to support the rest of her case.

Like most of the doctrines discussed in the book, the courts do not apply these ideas uniformly. Some courts will allow Betty to use her negative evaluation as evidence in her promotion claim.[115] Others will not.[116]

8. CONCLUDING THOUGHTS

Courts have limited the scope of discrimination law by refusing to call lots of conduct discrimination. Many courts will not call the following actions discrimination under any circumstances: giving an employee a negative performance evaluation, threatening to fire a worker, giving a worker more work, giving a worker more difficult work, transferring an employee to a less desirable work location, or removing an employee from high-profile projects. Even when there is evidence that these consequences were influenced by a worker's race, sex, or other protected traits, some judges do not deem these events serious enough to trigger discrimination liability.

This is the case even though the texts of the discrimination statutes provide broad protections for employees. Courts developed their own terminology centered on the words "adverse action." The courts have virtually ignored the language of the discrimination laws that prohibit practices that limit or segregate employees in ways that "deprive or tend to deprive" a worker of employment opportunities or "otherwise adversely affect his status as an employee."

Ignoring broad text, the "adverse action" doctrine and the "severe or pervasive" doctrine result from choices made by the courts. The decision to exclude many workplace actions from the reach of discrimination law is a problem in its own right. It is an even more serious problem when considering the other collateral consequences that flow from this decision.

If a worker complains about conduct that she believes is discriminatory, some judges will allow the employer to legally retaliate against the employee for making that complaint, so long as the employer only engages in retaliatory acts like giving her a bad evaluation or threatening to fire her. Other judges will declare no retaliation claim can stem from that complaint if they deem the complained of conduct not serious enough. At the same time, workers are encouraged by their employers to complain.

Down the Rabbit Hole

Samar is an anesthesiologist. He sued his employer for discriminating against him because of his Iranian ancestry. The employer filed a
motion for summary judgment, asking the court to dismiss the case.
Samar responded with evidence that one of the managers of anesthe-
siology operations called physicians of Middle Eastern descent "god-
dam Arabs."[1] He also stated that the same manager referred to Samar
one time saying, "I hate that worthless Arab son of a bitch" and called
another doctor a "Syrian prick."[2] The court characterized the comments
made by these two physicians as "stray remarks," deciding they did not
count as evidence of national origin discrimination against Samar and
dismissed the case.

The stray remarks doctrine is a court-created doctrine that allows
courts to declare that a remark such as "I hate that worthless Arab son
of a bitch" is not relevant to an underlying claim of discrimination. This
doctrine is one of many evidentiary rules and inferences that courts have
created and use to evaluate discrimination claims instead of leaving these
cases to juries. In addition to the stray remarks doctrine, this chapter
explores the same-actor inference, the honest-belief doctrine, the idea
that courts do not sit as "super-personnel departments," and inference
blindness. These doctrines and inferences are unique to discrimination
law, and they reflect stereotypical thinking and are not justifiable because
they prioritize the employer's explanations over the interests of discrimination victims.

1. STRAY REMARKS

Bobby is a teacher who is black. Bobby sued his employer for race discrimination.[3] In response to the employer's motion for summary judgment, Bobby presented evidence that the school superintendent had told
him that they had "a problem . . . with past black coaches, and if there was
another problem, no matter what it was, that he would do his best to get
rid of [Bobby]."[4] Bobby alleged that in the same conversation, the superintendent also stated that "he [the superintendent] had bad luck with
black men working in" the school district.[5] The superintendent later recommended that the school board refuse to renew Bobby's contract based
on several alleged violations of school policy. Although the school board
did not adopt the superintendent's recommendation, the superintendent
proceeded on his own to terminate Bobby.[6] Despite the superintendent's
statements, the trial court granted summary judgment for the school district, finding that Bobby could not prove to a jury that the school district
had discriminated against him.

Bobby appealed his case, and the appellate court agreed with the trial
court. In doing so, the appellate court stated that there was strong evidence
that the school district terminated Bobby for nondiscriminatory reasons.
The court reasoned that even if Bobby had evidence that the ultimate decision maker had made the discriminatory comments that directly related to
Bobby, the other evidence regarding the reasons for Bobby's termination
were so strong that the court could disregard the comments made by the
school superintendent.[7] The court determined the superintendent's comments were stray remarks and held that there was no substantial evidence
of a relationship between the comments and the decision to fire Bobby.

In another race discrimination case, a judge granted the employer's
motion for summary judgment and dismissed the worker's claim even
though the worker presented evidence that his supervisor referred to
African Americans as "lazy," "worthless," and "just here to get paid."[8] In
an age discrimination case, a court similarly rejected a claim where the
worker submitted evidence his supervisor told him "you are too damn old
for this kind of work" two weeks before he was fired.[9] In both cases, the

courts decided that the comments were stray remarks and could not be considered evidence of discrimination.

Cases where judges disregard such "stray" discriminatory remarks are common.[10] Through this doctrine, judges can refuse to consider discriminatory comments or actions in the workplace if the court deems the comments or actions too remote in time from the contested decision, not made in the context of the decision, or too ambiguous to show discriminatory bias.[11] This doctrine has stood in the way of workers showing that an important decision maker, such as a supervisor, made discriminatory statements in the past or that their workplace was permeated with discriminatory comments. In essence, when courts use this doctrine, they deprive workers the chance to explain the reality of their day-to-day work environment and the context in which supervisors make decisions.

The stray remark doctrine is not required by the text of any of the discrimination statutes. Instead, courts have created it. It first appeared in a concurring opinion by Justice Sandra Day O'Connor in the 1989 case of *Price Waterhouse v. Hopkins*.[12]

In *Price Waterhouse*, Ann Hopkins had alleged that she was not promoted to partner at her accounting firm because of her sex. The Supreme Court noted that when some of the partners evaluated Ms. Hopkins, there "were clear signs" that they "reacted negatively to Hopkins' personality because she was a woman."[13] The evidence in that case showed that some of the male partners stated that Ms. Hopkins was "macho" and that she "overcompensated for being a woman," and some told her that she needed to take "a course at charm school." One partner noted that Ms. Hopkins "ha[d] matured from a tough-talking somewhat masculine hard-nosed [manager] to an authoritative, formidable, but much more appealing lady [partner] candidate."[14] Another advised her that she needed to "walk more femininely, talk more femininely, dress more femininely, wear make-up, have her hair styled, and wear jewelry."[15]

In *Price Waterhouse*, the Justices were wrestling with how discrimination could be proven. The Court decided that a worker could win her case under the Title VII law by showing that a protected trait, like her sex, was

a motivating factor in an employment decision. To explain her views on
this question, Justice O'Connor wrote the following paragraph:

> Thus, stray remarks in the workplace, while perhaps probative of sex-
> ual harassment, cannot justify requiring the employer to prove that
> its hiring or promotion decisions were based on legitimate criteria.
> Nor can statements by nondecisionmakers, or statements by deci-
> sionmakers unrelated to the decisional process itself, suffice to satisfy
> the plaintiff's burden in this regard. . . . Race and gender always "play
> a role" in an employment decision in the benign sense that these are
> human characteristics of which decisionmakers are aware and about
> which they may comment in a perfectly neutral and nondiscrimina-
> tory fashion. For example, in the context of this case, a mere reference
> to "a lady candidate" might show that gender "played a role" in the
> decision, but by no means could support a rational factfinder's infer-
> ence that the decision was made "because of" sex. What is required is
> what Ann Hopkins showed here: direct evidence that decisionmak-
> ers placed substantial negative reliance on an illegitimate criterion in
> reaching their decision.[16]

Justice O'Connor discussed stray remarks in a very narrow context
and also did not provide any support from the statute's language, legislative history, or case law for her opinion about stray remarks. While her
remarks were part of a concurring opinion and are not controlling law,
courts have expanded on her idea. As legal scholar Kerri Lynn Stone has
noted, after *Price Waterhouse*, "the so-called stray comments doctrine . . .
had a groundswell of usage, building in popularity year after year."[17]

Courts can use the stray remarks doctrine at several stages in litigation.
In many cases, judges use the stray remarks doctrine to exclude evidence
and grant summary judgment after discovery occurs. If the case goes to
trial, a judge may deem a certain comment to be a "stray remark" and
exclude it from the evidence that the jury hears. The stray remarks doctrine allows courts to declare that discriminatory statements do not count

as evidence of discrimination. If a comment is a stray remark, the judge can treat the comment as if it were never made.

Consider the evidence workers presented in the following cases in which courts used the stray remarks doctrine:

- A supervisor's references to female workers and the plaintiff in particular as "bitch," "cunt," "whore," "slut" and "tart" were stray remarks and not evidence of sex discrimination.[18]
- A plant manager "commented that he wanted to get rid of the older employees and hire 'young blood.'" After the plant manager took over, "most of the new hires were in their twenties and early thirties." When an older employee was fired, two courts found that the worker could not proceed on her age discrimination claim. The appellate court noted: "Assuming that the age-related comment was made, it was a stray remark uttered two years prior to [the employee's] firing.[19]
- A manager telling a 63-year-old employee, "maybe you are too old to be working here" six to eight weeks before the employee was fired is a stray remark and not evidence of discrimination.[20]
- Evidence that a supervisor referred to an employee as an "old and ugly woman" is a stray remark and does not show potential discrimination.[21]
- A comment by a supervisor that "[w]e don't necessarily like grey hair" and a comment by the vice president of personnel that "[w]e don't want unpromotable fifty-year olds around" were stray remarks and could not be used as evidence for a worker's age discrimination claim.[22]
- Coworkers calling an employee "old man," "old fart," "old son of a bitch," and "fat old bastard" near the time the employee was fired is not evidence of age discrimination.[23]
- Calling a black employee a "colored woman" and referring to her as "n*****" and "bitch" were not evidence of racial animus but rather evidence of a personality conflict.[24]

In each of these cases, the employer might have good evidence to support its claim that it did not discriminate, and the jury might ultimately believe that explanation. But in these cases, judges—aided by their own opinions—have not deferred to juries and instead have decided that comments infused with possible discrimination did not affect the adverse employment decision.[25]

Courts have reasoned that "alleged discriminatory remarks that happen in a casual setting outside discussions regarding the dismissal decision do not support an inference of discrimination."[26] This line of reasoning suggests that a supervisor has to make a discriminatory remark in direct relationship to the negative decision before it counts as evidence of discrimination. When supervisors are making the decision to fire someone—particularly someone who belongs to one of the protected categories—they likely realize that their decision will be scrutinized. At these decisional moments, it is unlikely for a supervisor to exclaim: "I am firing you because you are a woman."

Consider this example. A company fired Leela, a woman of Indian descent.[27] On the day she was fired, Leela met with Ruth. While Ruth denies this, Leela claims that as she left the meeting, Ruth muttered, "Indian bitch." There is also evidence that Ruth played a role in the decision to fire Leela. In granting summary judgment for the employer, a judge reasoned that the "Indian bitch" comment does not count as evidence of discrimination because Ruth did not make the comment in connection with Leela's termination and did not make it during the meeting where Leela was fired.[28] The court also described the comment as a "stray remark" because the decision to terminate Leela was made several days before she was actually fired.[29]

Some courts will also state that comments made within a short time after an employee is fired are not evidence that the employer's actions are discriminatory. In one case, a worker alleged that she quit because her employer sexually harassed her and discriminated against her. When she quit, she alleged the supervisor told her "good riddance, bitch."[30] Even though the court recognized the comment was offensive, in granting summary judgment for the employer, it regarded the comment as a stray remark because it was made after her resignation.[31]

Under the current stray remarks doctrine, courts are throwing out too much evidence and often ignoring the summary judgment standard. Some judges have noted this problem. Harvard Law Senior Lecturer and then U.S. District Court Judge Nancy Gertner stated: "Whether a given remark is 'ambiguous'—whether it connotes discriminatory animus or it does not—is precisely what a jury should resolve, considering all of the facts in context. What may be ambiguous to me, the judge, may not be to the plaintiff or to her peers."[32] Judge Gertner also noted the reasons that derogatory terms are potentially powerful evidence of discrimination.

Introduced into evidence, ageist slurs, such as "old bag," "old shoe," or "old pumpkin" may lead a reasonable juror to conclude that the speaker harbors some animus towards a group of people, for example. And they might lead a reasonable juror to further conclude that when that speaker is making a decision concerning the employment of a member of the class about which he holds a bias, he might actually be influenced by that bias. And finally, apart from the speaker's animus, the statements that employers and employees make in the workplace create an environment that may be hostile in itself or an environment in which discriminatory employment decisions are made and tolerated.[33]

Despite this viewpoint, many other judges continue to label discriminatory epithets as "stray remarks." When the judge takes this action, she excludes the "stray remarks" from being considered as evidence of discrimination. The judge can then dismiss the case. In doing so, he takes away from the jury the ability to consider whether the evidence is probative of discrimination or not.

There are other reasons to be concerned about the stray remarks doctrine. When judges use this doctrine, there is usually more evidence than just one comment. Nonetheless, some judges isolate comments from the broader context of the rest of the evidence in the case.[34] As we will discuss in Chapter 9, the stray remarks doctrine is just one doctrine that courts use to "slice and dice" [35] a case. The court looks at each piece of evidence in isolation, dismisses it as inconsequential, and fails to see the evidence as a whole.

Like many of the doctrines we discuss in this book, judges do not uniformly use the stray remarks doctrine. One federal judge stated, "There appears to be no unified test for determining whether certain statements fall within the stray remarks doctrine."[36] These differences are most clearly seen in cases involving racial epithets or other similarly derogatory language. In some cases, using racial epithets to describe black employees or using the word "bitch" to describe female employees is not counted as evidence of discrimination.[37] In other cases, use of such language does count as evidence of discrimination.[38]

2. STRAY REMARKS AND SECOND-GUESSING THE JURY

As already described, a small percentage of cases, including discrimination cases, actually make it to a jury. Fewer still result in a verdict for the worker. Even when a jury finds in favor of the employee, appellate courts sometimes use the stray remarks doctrine to reject the jury's verdict.[39]

In one case, a doctor, who is Puerto Rican, worked at correctional facility.[40] There, she supervised the medical screening and evaluation of inmates. After a reorganization and consolidation, the doctor was assigned to a new supervisor. The supervisor was a man from the Dominican Republic. In the fall of 2013, an office clerk overheard the new supervisor say that "Dominican doctors were better" than "the other physicians who were there, who were Puerto Rican."[41]

In the spring of the next year, the doctor received a letter notifying her that her contract would not be renewed. The executive director of the correctional center, a man who, like her supervisor, was also from the Dominican Republic, signed the letter. When the doctor asked him why her contract was not being renewed, the executive director told her that it was because her position was no longer necessary due to the correctional services' recent consolidation. The doctor filed suit, claiming her employer had discriminated against her because of her sex and her national origin.

At trial, the employer provided multiple reasons why it did not renew the doctor's contract. The jury, however, determined that the employer did not renew the doctor's contract because of her sex and her national origin. After trial, the judge who had presided at the trial denied the employer's motions, letting the jury's verdict stand.[42]

On appeal, the appellate court reversed the jury's findings,[43] holding that the worker had not presented evidence of discrimination. They did not consider the comment overheard by the office clerk about doctors from the Dominican Republic being better than doctors from Puerto Rico as evidence of discrimination. Although the comment was made by the doctor's supervisor in the year prior to the nonrenewal of her contract, this remark did not count as evidence of discrimination. According to the judges, there was no evidence that the comment was related to the doctor or to the decision to not renew her contract.[44]

The use of the stray remarks doctrine after trial is especially problematic because judges second-guess a jury that evaluated the evidence including the possibly relevant discriminatory comments. In a famous stray remarks case, the Supreme Court intervened and reversed the appellate court decision. In that case, first introduced in Chapter 1 of this book, Mr. Ash and Mr. Hithon were superintendents at a poultry plant.[45] Both men, who are African American, sought promotions to fill two open shift manager positions. Two white males were selected instead. Mr. Ash and Mr. Hithon alleged that their employer had discriminated against them on the basis of their race in not selecting them for the shift manager positions. During the trial, they presented evidence that the plant manager, who made the hiring decision, referred to them as "boy." The two men also submitted evidence that the decision maker did not use the written job qualifications to decide whom to promote but instead used his own set of criteria.[46]

The jury found that the employer discriminated against the men and awarded them damages. Upon the employer's request for judgment in its favor, the judge overturned the jury's verdict. The judge noted that even if the supervisor did refer to the workers as "boy," the employees had not shown that the manager's use of that term was racial in nature.[47] The appellate court also found that the use of the word "boy" was not evidence of discrimination. It reasoned: "While the use of 'boy' when modified by a racial classification like 'black' or 'white' is evidence of discriminatory intent, . . . the use of 'boy' alone is not evidence of discrimination."[48]

The Supreme Court reversed the appellate court's decision regarding the use of the word "boy." The Court noted:

> Although it is true the disputed word will not always be evidence of racial animus, it does not follow that the term, standing alone, is always benign. The speaker's meaning may depend on various factors including context, inflection, tone of voice, local custom, and historical usage. Insofar as the Court of Appeals held that modifiers or qualifications are necessary in all instances to render the disputed term probative of bias, the court's decision is erroneous.[49]

The Supreme Court remanded the case back to the Eleventh Circuit for further action. The court reconsidered the use of the word "boy" in light of the Supreme Court's guidance and then found again that "there is nothing in the record about the remaining factors to support an inference of racial animus in the use of the term 'boy.'"[50] As a result, the court completely dismissed Mr. Ash's claim.[51] Believing that Mr. Hithon presented more evidence of potential discrimination than Mr. Ash, the court decided a new trial was necessary. Upon a second trial on Mr. Hithon's claims, the jury again found for Mr. Hithon.

On appeal, the appellate court again rejected the jury's verdict in favor of Mr. Hithon. It found "that the evidence was insufficient to support the jury's verdict that [the company] intentionally discriminated against Hithon based on his race."[52] One judge dissented, noting that two juries had already found in favor of Mr. Hithon.[53] The court later reconsidered its decision and found that at Mr. Hithon's second trial, there was new evidence about the context in which the term "boy" had been used. Finding that the use of the term in this context could be evidence of discrimination, the appellate court changed its decision and permitted the jury verdict to stand.[54]

Mr. Hithon initially filed his claim in 1996, and this last decision by the court of appeals was issued in 2011.[55] The stray remarks doctrine allowed both the trial court and the appellate court to second-guess how juries understood the potential discriminatory use of the word "boy" when referring to African American men.

The Supreme Court also discussed stray remarks in *Reeves v. Sanderson Plumbing Products, Inc.* In that case, Roger Reeves alleged that his employer had fired him because of his age.[56] At the time he was fired, Mr. Reeves had worked for Sanderson Plumbing for forty years and was 57 years old.[57] To support his discrimination claim, at trial, Mr. Reeves presented evidence that a supervisor who was involved in the termination had told him several months before his dismissal that he was so old he "must have come over on the Mayflower," and that he was "too damn old to do the job."[58]

The jury found in Mr. Reeves' favor, also finding that the employer's conduct was willful. Reviewing the jury's decision, the appellate court disregarded the age-related comments as stray remarks and rejected the verdict. It noted: "Despite the potentially damning nature of [the] age-related comments, it is clear that these comments were not made in the direct context of Reeves's termination."[59]

The Supreme Court corrected the court of appeals' mistake and found that the jury's verdict should stand.[60] The Supreme Court reasoned that when a supervisor says that someone is so old he must have come over on the Mayflower, and that a worker is too old to do his job, the jury is entitled to infer that age played a role in the worker's termination.

Even though some judges and law professors have criticized the stray remarks doctrine, some judges continue to use it to disregard evidence and dismiss cases even after juries find discrimination. If a comment is deemed a stray remark, it may not count as evidence of discrimination.

3. THE SAME-ACTOR INFERENCE

Courts also have created a doctrine called the "same-actor inference" that favors employers and disfavors workers. Let's say a supervisor hires a woman for a position. A year later, when the woman applies for a promotion, the same supervisor does not promote the woman and instead promotes a man. Using the same-actor inference, the court will assume that the woman's sex did not affect the promotion decision because the supervisor who originally hired the woman did not give her the promotion. The court will infer that this subsequent decision by this supervisor is not driven by discriminatory bias.

Another example of the same-actor inference is found in *Brown v. CSC Logic, Inc.*[61] There, the CEO of a company hired a 54-year-old worker.[62] Four years later, that same CEO made the decision to terminate the worker. In support of his age discrimination claim, the worker presented evidence that the CEO had made several age-related comments, most of which were made in the time immediately before the CEO fired him.[63] The worker alleged that after the worker remarried, the CEO stated, "you don't need to be remarrying a young woman again; you can't even get it up."[64] On several occasions, the CEO called the worker an "old goat."[65] On another occasion at a meeting, "when [the worker] was unable to remember a number, [the CEO] stated, 'you just can't remember, you're getting too old.'"[66] He also once asked the worker if "senility was setting in."[67] The court dismissed the worker's claim.

The court in *Brown* also used another inference—the "same protected class" doctrine. If a court uses the same protected class doctrine, it will presume that someone who is in the same protected class as the worker would not discriminate against the worker based on that protected trait. The general idea is that women will not discriminate against other women, older workers will not discriminate against other older workers, and so forth. In *Brown*, the court noted that the CEO was 56 years old when he hired the worker and 60 years old when he fired him.[68]

The appellate court affirmed the trial court's dismissal of the worker's claim. It reasoned:

> This "same actor" inference has been accepted by several other circuit courts, and we now express our approval. The rationale behind this inference is [that] claims that employer animus exists in termination

but not in hiring seem irrational. From the standpoint of the putative discriminator, [i]t hardly makes sense to hire workers from a group one dislikes (thereby incurring the psychological costs of associating with them), only to fire them once they are on the job.[69]

In some cases, courts have stretched the same-actor inference even further. In one case, a worker alleged that he was not promoted because of his Iranian descent.[70] In ruling against the worker on his promotion claim, the court noted that the company had hired him five months prior to the adverse promotion decision.[71] The court did not note which person within the company hired the worker. Because the company in general was aware of the worker's Iranian ancestry when it hired him, the court ruled there could be no inference of discrimination when certain people within the company later made a decision not to promote him. The court used this inference even though the worker presented evidence that his work leader and other coworkers "abused him almost daily, calling him names like 'the local terrorist,' a 'camel jockey' and 'the Emir of Waldorf.' "[72]

Like many of the doctrines discussed in this book, courts do not use the same-actor inference uniformly. In an early case involving the same-actor inference, the court applied the doctrine when the time lag between hiring and firing was four months.[73] However, some courts have used the doctrine when the time between the initial positive decision and the later negative decision was as great as seven years.[74] Other courts have criticized the doctrine when there is a long period between the positive decision and the later negative decision.[75]

It is not clear why the inference is logical in many cases. If a supervisor hires a woman for one job and then fails to promote her, bias could have played a role in the promotion decision. The widely known idea of the glass ceiling suggests that some people think women are qualified for some lower-level jobs but not for jobs with higher levels of responsibility. Moreover, where one person or group of people made an initial positive employment decision and then different people are involved in the subsequent negative employment decision, the same-actor inference should not apply. Bias could have affected the adverse decision.

Despite these criticisms, courts in every federal circuit use the same-actor inference.[76] The Supreme Court has yet to decide a case about the use of this inference.

The assumptions underlying the same-actor and stray remarks doctrines actually conflict. When judges use the same-actor inference, they are asserting that once a supervisor decides to hire someone with a protected trait, the same supervisor will not act in a discriminatory manner when making other employment decisions about that person. This idea presumes that the supervisor has a propensity not to discriminate against this person because he previously hired her.

Yet the stray remarks doctrine makes the opposite inference about discrimination. Under this doctrine, a supervisor's past discriminatory comments are not relevant to show alleged present-day discrimination. The stray remarks doctrine presumes that discrimination by the supervisor in the past does not show a propensity of the supervisor to discriminate in the future.[77] The United States Court of Appeals for the Seventh Circuit recognized this tension between the doctrines:

> This case actually highlights an interesting linkage, or perhaps a disconnect, between the cases using the "common actor" inference and cases dealing with "stray remarks." The common actor inference says it is reasonable to assume that if a person was unbiased at Time A (when he decided to hire the plaintiff), he was also unbiased at Time B (when he fired the plaintiff). Again, that is not a conclusive presumption, but we treat it as a reasonable inference. Some "stray remarks" cases, though, seem to conclude that if a person was racist or sexist at Time A (time of the remark), it is *not* reasonable to infer that the person was still racist or sexist at Time B (when he made or influenced the decision to fire the plaintiff).[78]

This lack of analytical consistency regarding bias shows how court doctrines push cases in one direction—toward dismissal.

4. THE HONEST-BELIEF RULE

The "honest-belief" rule is another doctrine that courts use to dismiss cases before or after juries hear them. This doctrine allows the employer to win a case by arguing that it "honestly believed" it had a good reason to take an employment action. It is often used in cases where the employer was actually wrong about whether an employee engaged in misconduct. Courts will say that an employer's mistaken belief that an employee engaged in bad conduct will not support a claim of discrimination so long as the employer "reasonably believed" the employee engaged in that conduct.[79]

Like many of the doctrines we discuss in this book, this doctrine has some initial intuitive appeal. Take the following example. A bank believes that one of its cashiers is embezzling money. The bank fires the employee. All of the evidence at the time of the firing supports the fact that the employee embezzled the money. The cashier files a lawsuit claiming race discrimination, but the only evidence of discrimination is that the cashier did not actually embezzle the money. Absent other evidence, a court will likely find that the cashier has no evidence of race discrimination. The employer's mistaken but honest belief that the cashier embezzled the money is not evidence of race discrimination.

Legal scholars Ralph Richard Banks and Richard Thompson Ford have noted the role that the honest-belief rule plays in the wider employment law scheme: "[T]he honest-belief rule preserves at-will employment: if the defendant honestly but mistakenly believed the nondiscriminatory reason, it has not discriminated on the basis of race and the plaintiff is simply a victim of a termination without good cause, which is unfortunate but not actionable."[80]

Some judges find the rule problematic and refuse to use it.[81] One federal district court judge noted that "the frequency with which district courts have granted, and the Circuit has affirmed, summary judgment based on such an expansive view of the honest belief rule . . . is concerning." [82]

Under the honest-belief doctrine, the key inquiry is this: what did the person who made the decision honestly believe at the time? Let's return to our embezzlement example. The honest-belief doctrine comes into play in this case if the supervisor mistakenly, but honestly, believed that the employee embezzled money. But in some cases, federal judges apply the honest-belief rule where there is evidence showing that, at the time of the contested decision, the employer did not have such honest belief. In these cases, the judge should recognize that the facts are disputed and should allow the case to go to a jury. Instead, judges often dismiss the worker's claim.

In one case in which a worker alleged she had been fired because of her race, the employer stated that it had fired her for intentionally falsifying her time cards.[83] If true, this would be a nondiscriminatory reason for firing an employee. However, in response to the employer's motion for summary judgment, the worker presented evidence that one of the people involved in the investigation into her time cards had stated that the worker did not purposely falsify her time card.[84] This created an issue of fact about whether the employer honestly believed the employee had intentionally falsified her time cards.

The employee also had evidence that both black and white coworkers had complained to human resources that black employees were being unfairly disciplined.[85] Despite this evidence, using the honest-belief rationale, the court dismissed this case on summary judgment, and the appellate court affirmed that dismissal.[86]

Courts also allow employers to claim that they honestly believed they had fired an employee for violating company policy even when they do not regularly enforce the policy or when there is evidence that the policy does not even exist. As an example, an employer might have an official policy that requires employees to do something in a specific way, like filling out timecards in a particular manner. Many employees do not follow the official policy, and they submit their timecards through another process. The employer fires one worker for not following the process. It does not even discipline, let alone fire, any other employee for violations of the timecard policy.[87] In such a case, the court can still dismiss the worker's suit because of the employer's honest belief that it fired the employee for violating the policy.

In one case, a trial court dismissed a case on summary judgment using the honest-belief doctrine when the employer claimed the worker had violated a company procedure.[88] On appeal, the appellate court upheld the dismissal, even though the dissenting judge pointed out that the evidence "strongly suggests that a clear ... procedure ... simply did not exist."[89] In another case, a trial court dismissed a worker's case at the summary judgment stage, although on appeal, a judge described the employer's factual investigation as "so poor and one-sided as to be 'unworthy of credence.'"[90]

Courts have also used the "honest belief" rule to dismiss cases when there was evidence that the supervisor who complained about an employee's performance made racist remarks. In one case, a black worker was fired after he refused to clean up a mess when ordered to do so by a supervisor. The worker maintained that it was another employee's job to clean up the mess. A foreman at the company stated that the supervisor in question repeatedly referred to black employees using odious language, including calling them "n*****s" and "Black mother fuckers."[91] According to the foreman, this supervisor expressed his opinion that black employees "were generally lazy."[92] This same foreman indicated that the supervisor "would always treat the African American employees more harshly than white employees in almost every nuance of the job."[93] The foreman further recounted that the supervisor made explicit racial remarks about the worker and said "I am going to get rid of him;" that he was going to throw the black employee into the pulper and make him into paper; and that he wanted to "string" up the black employee.[94]

Despite this evidence, the court upheld the dismissal of this case under the honest belief-doctrine. It did so even though the court admitted that management employees who fired the employee may have known the supervisor who reported the insubordination had made racist comments about the worker.[95]

In some cases, there is evidence that the employers should have known when they made their decisions that they were basing their decisions on unreliable information. Even in these cases, courts permit employers to use the honest-belief rule.[96]

Judges also will credit a supervisor's reasons for acting, even if the supervisor is not able to explain why he made a decision. In one case involving a reduction in force, a worker presented evidence that his supervisor previously had stated that in a reduction, he would "have to take care of my kids," referring to younger employees in the department.[97] The company later decided to reduce its workforce and asked the supervisor to rate the employees in his department. The supervisor rated an older employee lower than two younger employees.[98] When the supervisor was asked why he rated the older employee lower, the supervisor "could not identify any specific observations or experiences to justify his comparatively low rating."[99] Nonetheless, the court chose to believe that the older employee deserved to be ranked lower, and the court dismissed the case on summary judgment, finding no evidence of age discrimination. As one court noted in criticizing the honest-belief rule, the rule allows employers to "provide an honest reason for firing the employee, even if that reason had no factual support."[100]

Courts have even dismissed cases under the honest-belief rule when employers change the reasons for their actions. For example, the employer might originally state that it fired an employee for one reason but then during litigation, it changed the reason for the firing.[101]

Some judges will hold, however, that this change in reasoning means the judge cannot dismiss the case under the honest-belief doctrine. As one judge noted: "While the Court does not question business decisions, the Court does question a defendant's proffered justification when it shifts over time. When the justification for an adverse employment action changes during litigation, that inconsistency raises an issue whether the proffered reason truly motivated the defendant's decision."[102]

In other cases, courts may determine that there was an honest belief in another reason for the adverse employment decision even though the employer did not offer this reason. Let's say an employer gives one reason for its decision, claiming, for example, that it fired an employee because he had stolen money. However, when all of the evidence is present, there is a dispute of fact about whether the employer believed the employee stole money. In our theft example, the evidence might show that the employer actually knew that no money was missing at the time it fired the worker. This evidence calls into question the employer's "honest belief." However, during the litigation, another legitimate reason for firing the employee emerges.

In cases like this, some courts find that the employer honestly believed this second reason for the termination and then decide that the employer wins.[103] There are many problems with this type of reasoning. Under the at-will employment doctrine, the employer can make an employment decision for any reason that is not contrary to the law or to a contract. It can make decisions for good reasons, no reasons, and even bad reasons. There are thousands of reasons that potentially justify dismissal under at-will employment. In fact, most reasons do. This makes it too easy for an employer to present evidence of a new "honest belief" arising after the litigation starts.

These cases also seem to contradict Supreme Court precedent.[104] The Court has held that discrimination can be shown by demonstrating that the employer's articulated reason for its decision is not true. In other words, evidence that an employer is not providing the real reason for its decision may be evidence of discrimination. The employer may be lying about the reason for its actions to cover up discrimination. Alternatively, the employer may not have discriminated and has given an untrue reason for other purposes. Discrimination may or may not have occurred. The jury is supposed to resolve the underlying factual dispute, not the judge.

When reading honest-belief cases, it is sometimes difficult to tell what happened in the underlying case based on judges' descriptions of the facts in their written decisions. In most appeals, three judges decide the outcome of the case. At times, a judge will dissent from a majority decision to dismiss the case. When an appellate court judge dissents, the facts of the case depicted in the dissent sometimes are quite different from the facts described in the same case by the majority.[105] The way the judges frame the facts is important. The dissenting judge often includes different facts and describes them differently. The dissenting judge also regularly discusses why there is reason to suspect that the employer did not have an honest

belief for taking action against the employee. However, the majority opinion often gives no reason to doubt the employer's assertion.

5. SUPER-PERSONNEL DEPARTMENT

When courts dismiss a worker's case, they often use a particular senti-
ment to describe why the employer should win and the worker's case
should proceed no further. Courts will proclaim that they do not sit as a
"super-personnel department" regarding the employer's practices. This
phrase is an umbrella term that often means that the court will exclude
the worker's evidence of discrimination in a number of different circumstances. Once the evidence is excluded, the court can find that no discrimination occurred. As one academic has noted, although the courts
"fear[] acting as super personnel department, [they end] up acting as a
super jury" by deciding the ultimate question of whether discrimination
occurred.[106]

At times, the courts use the super-personnel department idea to exclude
evidence under the doctrines we have already discussed, such as the stray
remarks doctrine and the honest-belief rule. In addition, this idea under-
lies many other choices federal judges make to exclude or criticize evidence that workers might use to prove their cases.

In every discrimination case, a worker claims that her race, sex, or other
trait led to negative consequences at work. In almost every discrimination
case, the employer denies discriminating and offers a legitimate reason for
its actions. When the courts invoke this super-personnel department idea,
they are usually stating that they will not question, or allow the worker to
question, the employer's reason for its decision.

Using this amorphous super-personnel department idea, courts can
reject or diminish important evidence. Like some of the ideas discussed
in this book, there is some legitimacy to the idea that courts do not sit
as super-personnel departments. The discrimination laws do not make it
illegal to treat employees unfairly. However, the laws do make it illegal for
an employer to treat an employee unfairly because of a trait such as race

or sex. Juries should decide these questions. Instead, when presented with a case, some judges are quick to use the super-personnel department idea to declare the case's facts as simply showing unfair treatment rather than discrimination. Thousands of cases cite the mantra that courts do not sit as "super-personnel departments."[107]

Untrue Reason(s). Judges use the super-personnel department idea to justify believing the employer's reason for acting, even when other evidence suggests the reason may not be true. In 1973, the Supreme Court held that a worker can establish discrimination by showing that the employer lied about its reason for acting.[108] In such cases, the employer might be telling a lie to cover up the real—discriminatory—reason for its action. In these circumstances, a jury determines whether the employer is lying, and if so, why.

Nonetheless, lower courts have consistently used the super-personnel department idea to prevent workers from disproving the employer's asserted reason for its action. This happens in many different ways.

For example, in employment discrimination cases, employers often provide multiple reasons to counter allegations that they took a discriminatory employment action. If the employer lies about one of the reasons, it may be lying about not discriminating. However, if the worker cannot show that all of the reasons offered by the employer are not true, the courts often decide that no discrimination happened.

In one case, a pregnant employee had alleged that her employer refused to hire her after her probationary period because of her pregnancy.[109] The employer gave several reasons for her negative evaluations. One of the reasons was an objective standard that could be verified—the worker's technical proficiency at a particular task. The other reasons were subjective, such as poor attitude. The worker presented evidence that she was as technically proficient as other workers and also that the subjective evaluation of her performance was not correct.[110] After the jury found for the employee, the appellate court rejected the jury's finding of discrimination. In conjunction with reviewing the employer's reasons for its decisions, the court stated that it did not want to sit as a "super-personnel department" and question the employer's reason for acting.[111]

In another case, a 53-year-old employee alleged that he was terminated because of his age during a reduction in force while the company chose to retain a 34-year-old employee.[112] The employer provided six reasons for firing the older worker. Examining these reasons, the court noted that there were important factual questions regarding four of the six reasons.[113] However, the court described that it does "not sit as a super-personnel department." Despite fact questions regarding the reasons the employer gave for its decision, the court dismissed the worker's case, essentially giving additional credence to the employer's reasons.

This is a problem for workers trying to establish discrimination. Often, the worker cannot rebut every reason given by the employer because the reason provided is subjective. In the case of the pregnant employer, her supervisor stated that she had a poor attitude. It is nearly impossible for a worker to rebut this kind of evidence. Most courts will not accept as sufficient evidence the worker's own statement that she was a fabulous employee and did not have a bad attitude.[114] Some courts will even reject testimony from coworkers or other supervisors.[115] Likewise, courts also dismiss cases when the employer accuses the employee of engaging in bad conduct and the employee has evidence to the contrary. When the worker presents evidence, through his own testimony or the testimony of coworkers, that the bad conduct did not occur, judges often assert this evidence is not relevant.[116]

As already stated, these cases contradict Supreme Court case law. The Court has decided that if an employer does not tell the truth about why it acted, this might be evidence of discrimination.[117] Moreover, the Supreme Court has held that workers can try to show they did not engage in the misconduct alleged by the employer.[118] As the Court has noted, "[p]roof that the defendant's explanation is unworthy of credence is simply one form of circumstantial evidence that is probative of intentional discrimination, and it may be quite persuasive."[119]

Not Following Posted Qualifications. Imagine that an employer posts a promotion opportunity. It lists the required qualifications for the job. Sheila, whose qualifications exceed the requirements, applies for the job. Tony also applies for the job, though he does not meet the posted qualifications. Tony is chosen for the job. The supervisor testifies that he did not use the posted qualifications in making the hiring decision but instead applied his own criteria for evaluating the employees. Even if there is other evidence suggesting that Sheila's sex played a role in the decision, many courts will exclude the evidence of changing qualifications as evidence of potential discrimination.

Courts do not uniformly handle an employer's failure to follow its own posted qualifications for a job. Some courts hold there is no inference of discrimination if an employer does not follow its posted job criteria[120] while other courts state this can support an inference of discrimination.[121]

In one case, a judge both permitted and rejected an inference of discrimination based on an employer not following its posted qualifications. In that case, a black employee alleged that her employer had refused to promote her for two different positions because of her race.[122] The court dismissed the employee's claim of race discrimination for the first position but allowed her race discrimination claim for the second position.

For the first position, the employer had posted the essential functions of a job. The worker alleged that she could perform these essential functions but that the person selected for the position could not. In granting summary judgment, the court refused to even consider this evidence because the chosen applicant met the minimum qualifications for the position. Regarding the additional essential requirements, the judge reasoned that although the essential requirements described the job and "a hiring official is expected to use the essential requirements to evaluate candidates for a position," "[t]he Court [was] unaware of any evidence that an applicant must meet these essential requirements of a job."[123]

For the second position, the employer had posted that a college degree was a preferred, but not required, criterion for the position. The person selected for the position did not have a college degree, and the plaintiff in the case did. In denying summary judgment on this claim, the judge held that the fact that the employer hired someone without the preferred criteria could be evidence of discrimination.[124]

Better qualified. Let's say that both Ann and Bobby apply for a position. Based on the employer's job qualifications for the position, which had been posted, Ann has the better credentials. Ann also has evidence that the supervisor in charge of making the promotion decision made sexist comments. Bobby receives the promotion. The employer asserts that Bobby was chosen because he was the most qualified person for the position, but an objective view of the facts shows that Ann was better qualified. In this fact pattern, Ann could try to demonstrate that the employer discriminated by showing that Bobby received the promotion despite the fact Ann was the most qualified person for the job. If Ann is objectively better qualified and Bobby received the position instead, Ann's sex might have played a role in that decision, especially when there is other evidence supporting Ann's case.

In the past, some courts would not allow a worker to use evidence of her qualifications as evidence of discrimination unless the worker presented evidence that "the disparity in qualifications is 'so apparent as virtually to jump off the page and slap you in the face.' "[125] In *Ash v. Tyson Foods, Inc.*, the Supreme Court rejected this standard, finding that "the visual image of words jumping off the page to slap you (presumably a court) in the face is unhelpful and imprecise."[126] The Court noted that a worker can show discrimination by presenting evidence that the employer chose a less qualified candidate.[127] Nonetheless, after *Ash*, some courts still make it very difficult for a worker to prove her case through evidence that she was more qualified for the position than other applicants.[128]

As with the other ideas discussed in this book, some judges do not use the doctrine and allow a worker to show that he was the most qualified person for the position in support of his discrimination claim.[129]

Company Policies. Imagine an employee named Larry. Larry is a 55-year-old white man. His supervisor, Sarah, is 35 years old. Two years ago, she said she was on a mission to make the department younger. Larry violated the company's Internet use policy when he bought a pair of shoes from Zappos during work hours. Sarah fired Larry. The company policy states that when an employee engages in such minor misconduct, the employee should receive a written warning. However, supervisors have discretion not to follow the policy.

As with many of the doctrines discussed in this book, some courts permit the company's failure to follow its own policies to count as evidence of discrimination.[130] However, many courts will find that Sarah's failure to follow company policy is not evidence of discrimination. Courts use the idea that they do not sit as super-personnel departments to decide that an employer's failure to follow its own policies is not evidence of discrimination.[131]

In some sense, the "super-personnel department" idea has an intuitive appeal. Most employees in the United States are at-will employees. Being an at-will employee means that an employer can hire or fire a worker for a good reason, a bad reason, or no reason at all, so long as the employment decision does not violate a contract or other law. The concept of at-will employment gives employers lots of leeway to make bad decisions—and even irrational decisions. The United States Court of Appeals for the Seventh Circuit expressed the idea this way:

> [A] court's role is to prevent unlawful hiring practices, not to act as a super personnel department that second-guesses employers' business judgments. As we have stated, no matter how medieval a firm's practices, no matter how high-handed its decisional process, no matter how mistaken the firm's managers, [antidiscrimination law] does not interfere. Rather, this court must respect the employer's unfettered discretion to choose among qualified candidates.[132]

However, in many cases, the courts disregard important evidence of discrimination. They also disregard procedural rules that do not allow them to make judgment calls about whose evidence to believe.

6. INFERENCE BLINDNESS

As described here, there is a cadre of rules and inferences that allows judges to see the facts in the light most favorable to the employer. Even outside of these doctrines, some judges seem to suffer from what some scholars call inference blindness. They do not recognize when facts favor the worker.

In one case, a worker claimed that his employer terminated him because of his age. He submitted evidence that as he was demoted he was told, "You're sixty years old, aren't you, Don? You don't need the aggravation, stress of management problems, customer problems, taking care of all these salespeople's problems. . . ."[133] Supervisors and others also referred to him as an "old man" and a "grumpy old man."[134]

To both a district court judge and a three-judge panel of appellate judges, these facts did not even suggest discrimination. Rather, the appellate court found that the evidence showed "nothing more than a desire to furnish [the employee] with a graceful exit supported by a dignified official predicate explanation for his status downgrade, namely that, as a man approaching age 60, he no longer possessed the requisite energy or drive demanded of a store manager."[135]

The very reason the court provides for dismissing the case suggests that stereotypes about age played a role in the employer's decision. The dissenting judge pointed out the problem:

These statements made to [the worker] at the time he was being demoted permit the inference that both the president and vice-president . . . adhered to the stereotype that an older manager cannot perform in a high-stress management position where the company would be pushing him to work harder and do more. These are the very stigmatizing beliefs of an underperforming older worker, . . . that the ADEA was intended to target. Nevertheless, instead of drawing inferences favorable to [the worker] from these statements, the lead opinion elects to believe [the employer's] explanation of them, and imposes its own credibility assessment on both parties. The widely differing perspectives on what these statements meant illustrate a classic example of a genuine issue of material fact, i.e., did [the employer] hold stereotypical beliefs about the capabilities of older managers that motivated its decision to demote . . . ?[136]

The Court of Appeals for the Sixth Circuit sitting en banc eventually reversed both of these decisions.

7. CONCLUDING THOUGHTS

This chapter introduced a series of court-created rules and inferences judges use to help them adjudicate discrimination claims. Some legal scholars have criticized these and other concepts that judges have created for analyzing discrimination cases.[137] Noticeably, none of them favor workers. Each of these evidentiary devices makes it more difficult for a worker to win a suit.

These rules and inferences allow judges to make determinations about the facts in a particular case. They often make judgment calls about who is telling the truth and about how to weigh competing evidence. Although the procedural rules that apply to all lawsuits require judges to let factual questions go to juries, the legal rules and inferences discussed in this chapter allow judges to do the opposite.

This example illustrates this problem. Nancy worked as a veterinary assistant. Within a year of being hired, she was promoted to chief veterinary assistant.[138] Her first supervisor was a woman named Elizabeth. Elizabeth supervised Nancy for about two years. Elizabeth testified that Nancy's work was exemplary and that Nancy "had been one of the best Chief Veterinary Assistants she had ever had."[139] Later, Enrique became Nancy's supervisor. He fired Nancy, asserting that she was tardy for work, had several absences, and failed to follow policies for taking and recording samples.[140] Enrique also fired a male worker for violating policies.[141]

Nancy filed a lawsuit, claiming that she was fired because she was a woman and because she had complained about her supervisor's discriminatory treatment. During the lawsuit, she presented evidence that Enrique had said that Elizabeth did not deserve her job because she was a woman.[142] Nancy also tried to present evidence from a coworker that Enrique had stated that he did not have to listen to what Nancy said because she was a woman.[143] Nancy also submitted evidence that Enrique had told her that her absences and tardiness were not serious problems and that he did not follow the employer's policy for reporting her performance problems and notifying her of her work deficiencies.[144]

Both the trial court judge and the appellate court found no evidence of discrimination. In reaching this conclusion that no reasonable jury could find in favor of Nancy, the appellate court made many judgment calls about which party told the truth. The court started its analysis by asserting the super-personnel department idea, noting: "We are not in the business of adjudging whether employment decisions are prudent or fair. Instead, our sole concern is whether unlawful discriminatory animus motivates a challenged employment decision."[145] Although the court recognized that the comment about Elizabeth not deserving her job because she was a woman could be circumstantial evidence of bias against women, the court decided that it was a stray remark.[146] Moreover, the court decided that Elizabeth's and Enrique's differing opinions about Nancy's work were not relevant.[147] The court also disregarded evidence that Enrique did not fol-low the employer's policies about reporting any performance deficiencies and notifying Nancy about them. Additionally, although Nancy had com-plained to her employer that she was being paid less than male employees, the court ignored Nancy's evidence of retaliation.[148]

We do not know whether Nancy's supervisor took discriminatory or retaliatory action against her. More important, neither do the judges who dismissed the case. However, the numerous doctrines that the courts have created allow them to make critical judgments that result in conclusions that no discrimination or retaliation occurred.

Causation

Causation is another legal concept that courts use to dismiss workers' claims. Consider a case where a worker presents the following evidence. A supervisor calls a black employee "Buckwheat," and the employee complains about the comment.[1] The supervisor also refers to him as a "porch monkey."[2] The same supervisor then proceeds to give the employee a bad review and does not promote him. Moreover, the employee was told by another employee that the company "does not hire many people like you . . . you should be happy just to be here."[3]

According to a federal court that dismissed the employee's discrimination claim, the employer did not discriminate against the employee because of his race. In reaching its conclusion, the appellate court questioned the significance of the discriminatory comments and the relationship between the comments and the adverse action of failing to promote the black employee.[4] The court noted that the supervisor called the employee "Buckwheat" only once. Analyzing this comment, it declared that "[t]he mere utterance of a racial epithet is not indicia of discrimination under Title VII," and it decided the remark was a stray one.[5] The court further reasoned that the supervisor's use of the term "porch monkey" and other remarks regarding the company's hiring practices were not causally linked to the supervisor's review of the employee's work and the decision not to promote him.

This outcome was driven by the legal concept of causation. Causation requires some connection between the wrongful conduct and the harm that results. Imagine that a car is driving down a street at 40 miles per hour, exceeding the posted speed limit by 5 miles per hour. A man quickly darts out into the street. The driver is not able to stop fully, and the car hits the man, breaking his leg. Even if the driver had been driving at the correct speed, she would not have been able to stop her car in time. In such a situation, the law would say that the driver's wrongful conduct did not cause the man's injury. Even though the driver's conduct was against the law, the same result would have happened even if the driver had driven carefully and within the speed limit. The idea of causation plays an important role in many kinds of legal claims. Requiring causation ensures that the person or entity being sued is legally responsible for the harm caused.

Similarly, an employer should not face liability under the discrimination statutes if discrimination did not cause the particular negative employment outcome. For example, assume a worker alleges that his employer fired him because of his race. The evidence shows only that the worker punched a coworker and that the employer always fires employees who punch their coworkers. The worker's race did not cause the negative employment outcome and the employer should not be liable for discrimination. In theory, the causation element protects employers' freedom of action, making sure that employers face liability only when race, sex, or other protected traits played an improper role in an employment outcome.

While causation can work as a general principle, courts have developed causation doctrines that unfairly limit discrimination claims. Courts declare that the worker has not shown a causal connection between discriminatory words or conduct and a later employment decision even when a reasonable jury might decide there is evidence of discrimination.

1. STRAY REMARKS AND CAUSATION

The stray remarks doctrine, which was introduced in Chapter 4, is related to causation problems. In those cases, a coworker or supervisor makes discriminatory comments, and the plaintiff later experiences an adverse employment action. The courts may decide the earlier discriminatory comments and the later employment decision are not related. As a result, the courts determine that bias did not cause the negative employment decision.

Consider the following examples. In one case, a worker presented evidence that a supervisor and other workers regularly called him "old fart."[6] The worker was also repeatedly asked when he was going to retire. After the worker declined an early retirement offer, the worker alleged the company changed and increased his responsibilities. The company later fired the worker, alleging that he had a record of poor performance. Despite the worker's allegations of discrimination, the judge ruled that there was no connection between the employer's actions and the age-related comments and granted summary judgment for the employer.[7]

In another case, a worker had evidence that her supervisor repeatedly referred to her as "bitch," "cunt," "whore," "slut," and "tart." However, the judge ruled there was no causal connection between these comments and negative actions against the worker and ordered summary judgment for the employer.[8]

These examples present classic disputes of fact. The worker submitted evidence that sex or age may have played a role in an employment decision, and the employer disagreed, asserting that it took actions against the employee for legitimate, nondiscriminatory reasons. Despite the factual dispute between the employer and the employee, judges dismissed each of these cases, reasoning that the worker did not show a connection between the comments and the later employment decision. If a worker has evidence that biased comments were made, some courts make the employee show exactly how the biased comment affected any later employment decision.[9]

When judges dismiss cases at the summary judgment stage, they are supposed to believe all of the evidence presented by the worker and draw all reasonable inferences in the worker's favor. If a reasonable jury could decide in the worker's favor, the judge is supposed to let the case go to the jury, even if the judge thinks the employer has a stronger case. In each of these cases, the judge decided that under no circumstances could the worker prove discrimination. According to the judges, the workers did not show a strong enough connection between their evidence of bias and the negative employment outcomes.

2. GROUP DECISIONS

Courts also often decide that causation is lacking when several people are involved in an employment decision. Prior to the 1980s, it was common for workplaces to be organized under a strict hierarchal structure in which an employee's supervisor solely determined who was hired and fired. Although some workplaces continue to employ a similar decision-making apparatus for some or all employment decisions, group decision-making is a key feature of the modern workplace.

Since the early 1980s, there have been several innovations in workplace decision-making that have increased the number of people who make or have input into workplace decisions. The human resources department, a common feature of the modern workplace, is one of these changes. Among other functions, the human resources department is often involved in employment decisions, such as whether to fire an employee. It may even possess the sole authority to make these important employment decisions. Other times, the department may advise supervisors on their options, collaborate to make a decision, or simply execute the decision.

There are other workplace innovations that increase the number of people involved in an employment decision. Professor Tristin Green, who has studied recent changes in workplace structure, has noted that companies have been blurring job boundaries, "allocating work on a team rather than an individual basis, and adopting more subjective, skill-based evaluation systems."[10] In team-based work environments, multiple employees may have supervisory responsibilities over different parts of a project. Some employers also use "360-degree" reviews, where several people, including subordinates, peers, and supervisors, evaluate an employee's work performance.

In short, it has become common for workplace decision-making processes to involve more than one person. In this setting, courts must decide how to determine whether race, sex, or other traits caused the employment decision when one of the people involved in the ultimate employment decision was motivated by such traits.

Price Waterhouse, which was introduced in Chapter 4, is a case with multiple decision makers. Ann Hopkins, who worked as a senior manager at Price Waterhouse, alleged that she was not promoted to partnership because of her sex.[11] Hopkins's local office had proposed her for partner, but the firm did not approve her as a partner. Ms. Hopkins sued for sex discrimination under Title VII after the firm refused to reconsider her for partner the following year.

The Supreme Court described the partnership selection process in the following way:

> [A] senior manager becomes a candidate for partnership when the partners in her local office submit her name as a candidate. All of the other partners in the firm are then invited to submit written comments on each candidate—either on a "long" or a "short" form, depending on the partner's degree of exposure to the candidate. Not every partner in the firm submits comments on every candidate. After reviewing the comments and interviewing the partners who submitted them, the firm's Admissions Committee makes a recommendation to the Policy Board. This recommendation will be either that the firm accept the candidate for partnership, put her application on "hold," or deny her the promotion outright. The Policy Board then decides whether to submit the candidate's name to the entire partnership for a vote, to "hold" her candidacy, or to reject her. The recommendation of the Admissions Committee, and the decision of the Policy Board, are not controlled by fixed guidelines: a certain number of positive comments from partners will not guarantee a candidate's admission to the partnership, nor will a specific quantity of negative comments necessarily defeat her application.[12]

At the relevant time, Price Waterhouse had 662 partners, only 7 of whom were women. Hopkins was the only woman proposed for partnership in the year she was considered. In that same year, the firm proposed 87 men for partner. Price Waterhouse selected 47 male candidates for partner and rejected 21 male candidates. The remaining 20 candidates, including Ms. Hopkins, were held for reconsideration the following year. In deciding whether to make Ms. Hopkins a partner, "[13] of the 32 partners who had submitted comments on Hopkins supported her bid for partnership. Three partners recommended that her candidacy be placed on hold, eight stated that they did not have an informed opinion about her, and eight recommended that she be denied partnership."[13]

Some Price Waterhouse partners praised Ms. Hopkins's work. Others, however, criticized her interactions with staff members, finding that she was brusque. The Supreme Court noted that when some of the partners evaluated Ms. Hopkins, there "were clear signs" that they "reacted negatively to Hopkins' personality because she was a woman."[14] The evidence showed that some of the male partners stated that Ms. Hopkins was "macho" and that she "overcompensated for being a woman" and told her that she needed to take "a course at charm school." One partner noted that Ms. Hopkins "ha[d] matured from a tough-talking somewhat masculine hard-nosed [manager] to an authoritative, formidable, but much more appealing lady [partner] candidate."[15] Another advised her that she needed to "walk more femininely, talk more femininely, dress more femininely, wear make-up, have her hair styled, and wear jewelry."[16]

The promotion process at Price Waterhouse involved many different partners who provided input into the partnership decision. Although the vote of the partners and the outcome is known, the motivation for each partner's decision is unclear. In Ms. Hopkins's case, a judge found that some partners evaluated Ms. Hopkins differently because of her sex, but not all of the partners did.[17] Given ordinary group dynamics, it is easy to imagine that some partners were more vocal during the meeting to decide Ms. Hopkins's fate. Also, some members likely exercised more influence over the decision than others. Some partners may have had a strong desire for Ms. Hopkins to be or not to be promoted. Ultimately, the individuals in the group may have had different reasons for reaching the result. While

they decided not to make Ms. Hopkins a partner, there is no single defini-
tive reason for the decision.

Although in *Price Waterhouse* the Supreme Court recognized that sex
discrimination impermissibly affected the partnership decision, many
modern courts struggle with cases involving multiple decision makers. In
some cases, courts will dismiss the worker's claim if she cannot show how
biased comments by one person directly affected the outcome.

For example, in one case, an administrator nearing retirement alleged
that a school discriminated against her based on her age by not giving her
a promotion. The administrator had evidence that the superintendent told
a school board member that she "had been around for a long time, too
long."[18] The superintendent also mentioned the administrator's possible
retirement plans as a reason the administrator should not receive a new
position. In dismissing the administrator's case on summary judgment,
the court noted that the superintendent was not a member of the committee who chose another applicant for the position and that therefore the
administrator could not show a connection between the superintendent
and the decision.[19] However, the evidence showed that the superintendent
had interacted with the board who appointed the interview committee
and that the superintendent had communicated directly with the administrator about why she would not obtain the position.

In another case, workers alleged age discrimination during a reduction in force in which they lost their jobs. The workers had evidence that
during a restructuring meeting, a company official stated "it's going to be
out with the old and in with the new."[20] The employees also showed that
people involved in the individual employment decisions had made age-
related comments.[21] However, the court granted summary judgment for
the employer. While the individuals who made the age-related comments
were part of the committees that made the decisions about which employees to keep, to prevail on an age discrimination claim, the workers were
required to show how the bias of particular committee members impacted
the committee's decision. According to the court, the workers failed to
make this showing.[22]

As with the other ideas discussed in this book, courts do not uniformly apply causation to decisions involving more than one person. Some judges will allow cases to proceed if there is evidence that only one person in a group harbored bias.[23] Others will not.

3. THE CAT'S PAW

There is a special subset of cases involving group decisions. Courts call these cases cat's paw cases.

Sally works for a large bank. Sally's coworker informs her that her supervisor, Bill, repeatedly calls Sally a "cunt," a "whore," and a "bitch."[24] There is evidence that in connection with Sally's eligibility to receive stock options, Bill states: "The bank should not be giving the bitch any stock options." The evidence also shows that Bill regularly talks with his supervisor, Mitch, who decides how much to award for bonuses.[25] Although Sally does receive the stock options, she receives a much lower bonus than some men in her department. While Mitch asserts he made the bonus decision on his own, there is other evidence that Bill talked about Sally to Mitch.

Some judges will decide that there is no evidence of discrimination in this case and the case must be dismissed. A judge might reason that Sally could not show how Bill's comments affected the bonus decision.

The courts have given the name "cat's paw" to a subset of cases like Sally's case. The name is based on a fable in which a monkey wants to recover nuts from a fire.[26] The monkey convinces a cat to retrieve the nuts, but then the monkey steals them from the cat. The monkey obtains the nuts and the cat ends up with a burnt paw. The term "cat's paw" thus refers to one person being used as the tool of another.

A cat's paw case is one in which a biased individual takes an action against another person based on a protected trait, but an unbiased individual ultimately makes the challenged employment decision. For example, a biased supervisor could place a bad evaluation in an employee's file, and a second supervisor (not knowing about the bias of the first supervisor) could then terminate the employee in a reduction in force in part based on the bad evaluation.

Every cat's paw case presents the question of whether the employee's race, sex, or other trait caused the negative employment action. In these cases, the employer alleges that it cannot be held liable for discrimination because a person acting without discriminatory intent actually made the employment decision. In other words, although discriminatory "intent" may be present in these cases, the ultimate decision maker did not possess such intent. The plaintiff typically argues that the decision maker relied on biased information, served as a conduit for the discrimination of others, or merely rubber-stamped a discriminatory decision made by another person.

Some cat's paw cases involve supervisors. For example, an employee might allege that her supervisor did not like women and that the supervisor then lied about the employee's work performance to the human resources department. The human resources department then fired the female employee. A question arises in this case whether the employee can show discrimination since the unbiased human resources department made the ultimate decision.

In a 2011 case, the Supreme Court recognized that workers could get to a jury in a cat's paw case where a supervisor "performs an act motivated by ... animus that is *intended* by the supervisor to cause an adverse employment action, and if that act is a proximate cause of the ultimate employment action, then the employer is liable ...."[27] This standard is not clear. After it, lower courts have dismissed cases in which workers presented evidence that their supervisor was biased and where that bias might have affected a later negative decision.[28]

In one case, a supervisor reported that a worker made a mistake at work and then suspended the worker.[29] As a result of this suspension and a prior incident, the company placed the worker on a last-chance agreement, which stated that the worker might be dismissed if any further problems occurred. The worker complained that he did not make the mistake and that he was being discriminated against because of his race. The company found that the mistake was not the worker's fault. A few months later, the same supervisor again reported a performance problem to another manager. That second manager decided to fire the worker. In this case, the court found that the worker could not establish that the company retaliated against him. The court granted summary judgment for the employer. The court decided that no reasonable jury could connect the worker's complaint to the ultimate decision to fire him.

Courts have noted that the causal chain between a biased supervisor and a later decision is broken if the employer asks the worker to provide his own version of the events related to any reported misconduct. These courts reason that such evidence shows that "the employer has taken care not to rely exclusively on the say-so of the biased" individual.[30] These courts fail to recognize that a reasonable jury could find discrimination in these cases.

Cat's paw cases also arise when companies give nonsupervisors the ability to evaluate the work of other employees but do not give them the ability to make the decision to fire employees. These influential coworkers, who may be biased, can report another worker's negative performance, direct the attention of higher-level supervisors to specific employees, and recommend that supervisors take certain actions. In these circumstances, courts often dismiss the case on causation grounds.

Consider the following case.[31] Pam worked as a sheet metal mechanic for several years, and another coemployee served as a safety inspector. Pam has evidence that on several occasions while they worked together, the safety inspector called Pam a "useless old lady" who needed to retire, a "troubled old lady," and a "damn woman."[32] The safety inspector later reported several problems with Pam's performance to supervisors, who decided to fire Pam. According to the federal courts, no jury could find that Pam's age played a role in her termination. The alleged bias of the influential coworker was not enough because the coworker had "no supervisory or disciplinary authority and [did] not make the final or formal employment decision."[33]

In another case, a female worker complained to the human resources department when a coworker asked her out on dates and sent her a picture of his erect penis.[34] The coworker then lied to the human resources department and said that he was in a consensual relationship with the woman. According to the worker's complaint, the company then fired the woman for sexually harassing her male coworker by sending him sexual messages—even though the harassing coworker had made up those messages.[35] The court dismissed the case, finding that the female worker could not prove that her complaint played a role in her termination.

This, too, is an area where the courts do not uniformly decide cases. Some courts recognize that "explicitly discriminatory remarks ... may implicate the motive of the employer if her conduct set in motion the chain of events that led to ... the adverse employment action."[36] As described in this section, others refuse to see the chain of events that was set in motion.

4. DIFFERENT CAUSATION STANDARDS

In the last decade, courts have interpreted the causation standard to make it more difficult for workers to win age discrimination and retaliation cases. These cases are now more challenging to win than similar cases involving race or sex discrimination.

Imagine Peggy, a female pharmaceutical sales representative. While in her 20s and 30s, Peggy worked on key accounts. Her responsibilities included developing relationships with doctors. She often went to dinner with doctors, took them to baseball games, and joined them for drinks after work. As she entered her mid-40s, her manager stated that she no longer looked young; the manager took away some key accounts and gave her more office responsibilities. A week after she complained to the company's human resources department about this treatment, the company fired Peggy.

In this situation, there is evidence that Peggy was treated differently because of her age. The short time between her complaint and her termination also suggests that the company may have retaliated against her for reporting age discrimination.

If Peggy sues for both age discrimination and retaliation, some courts will find that Peggy cannot establish causation. She must pick a reason for her termination: either age discrimination or retaliation. If she alleges both motives led to her firing, these courts will dismiss both of her claims. The courts reach this outcome because a worker must establish "but for" causation to win an age or retaliation case.

As already described, to prove a discrimination claim, the employee must show causation—that is, the harm or injury must be connected to the worker's race, sex, or other protected trait. For the employer to be liable, how close must the link between the protected trait and the harm be?

The butterfly effect is a causation theory that suggests small actions can lead to larger effects in a complex system. If a butterfly flaps its wings in China, that slightest movement of air might have an impact on the strength of a storm that later strikes South Carolina. If a South Carolina homeowner suffers damage in the storm, it could be argued that the butterfly affected the storm in South Carolina and thus affected the homeowner's damage. But the law, if it could, would not find that the butterfly caused the storm or caused it to be more severe. Other factors like temperature played a role in forming the storm. Other butterflies may have affected the winds. The legal concept of cause requires a tighter link between the harm—here, the homeowner's damages—and the possible wrongdoer—here, the butterfly.

The law can require a lesser or greater connection between conduct and injury. The butterfly represents one end of the spectrum, where there is at best a tenuous connection between action and outcome. On the other end of the spectrum is the idea of sole causation, which would require an injured person to prove that there was one and only one element that caused her injury. Most legal claims require a connection that falls in the middle of the spectrum. In discrimination cases, the key causation question is whether the worker must show her protected trait was a "but for" cause of her injury or whether she must show only that it was a motivating factor.

5. "BUT FOR" CAUSATION

"But for" cause allows a defendant to escape liability in some instances where the defendant engaged in wrongful conduct. Imagine that there is a law that requires all passenger boats to carry life vests.[37] One day, the otherwise careful captain takes tourists out on his boat without the required life vests. A sudden and unpredicted storm rolls in. One of the tourists is swept off the deck of the boat and drowns. Everyone will testify that due to the quickness of the storm, there was no time to throw out a life vest, if one had been available.

Under the concept of "but for" cause, the captain does not face any liability. It is true that the captain did not exercise all required care: he did not have life vests on his boat as the law required. However, the lack of life vests did not cause the injury to the tourist. Even if the life vests had been on board the boat, the tourist still would have drowned. The captain's carelessness in not having life jackets on the boat did not influence the outcome.

The concept of "but for" cause works well in many situations where a single act causes a single harm. However, the law has long realized that this concept has weaknesses in less straightforward situations.

One problem with "but for" cause is that it results in no liability in certain situations where it appears that liability should occur. The two fires hypothetical test explains the shortcomings of this formulation of causation.

Imagine a house in the middle of a forest. On one side of the forest, a teenager who is playing with matches sets trees on fire. The teenager's fire rushes toward a house. At the same time, on the opposite side of the forest, a camper forgets to put out his campfire, and embers from the campfire light the surrounding trees on fire. The camper's fire rushes toward the other side of the house. Both fires converge on the house at the same time, destroying it completely. Either fire on its own could have destroyed the house.

If the homeowner sues the teenager for the loss of his home and if the homeowner is required to prove "but for" cause, the teenager will not be liable for the homeowner's loss. The teenager can argue that even if he had not set his fire, the fire set by the camper still would have destroyed the house. If the homeowner sued the camper, he will still not prevail if he must show "but for" causation. The camper can likewise argue that even if he had put out his campfire, the teenager's fire would have burned the house down.

Here we have two people who acted carelessly—the teenager and the camper. Each independently could have caused the entire injury, yet under the "but for" cause model, both would escape liability. The law has long recognized this problem with the but for causation model. In cases where the but for standard does not work, courts will apply a "substantial factor" or "motivating factor" standard. This motivating factor standard requires a looser connection between harm and injury than does but for cause. Importantly, it still requires that a fairly close connection exists. The homeowner can win in his suit against the teenager if he can show the teenager's misconduct was a substantial factor in bringing about the harm.

Let's return to Peggy's case, where Peggy's supervisor changed her job responsibilities as she became older and when she complained about age discrimination, her employer fired her. It appears that Peggy's age and her complaint about age discrimination led to her being fired. The two fires situation is analogous to this employment discrimination example. In Peggy's case, there are two different reasons for the action: her age and her retaliation for her complaint. Either reason, considered independently, could have been the cause of her wrongfully being fired. It is possible that the evidence will show that the only reason for Peggy's termination was either her age or her complaint. It is more likely, however, that it will be impossible to determine how much her age affected the termination decision and how much her complaint did.

Because of the case law, Peggy cannot win by showing that age or retaliation was a substantial or motivating factor in the decision to fire her. To prevail on an age discrimination claim, Peggy would be required to prove that her age was the but for cause of her employer's decision to fire her,[38] and to prevail on her retaliation claim, she would be required to prove that her complaint was the but for cause.[39] However, Peggy may not be able to establish but for cause if both her age and her complaint caused the employer to fire her, especially when some courts have declared that there can be only one but for cause of an employment outcome.

Causation requirements trap litigants like Peggy, whose claims are consequently dismissed. In one case, a worker alleged multiple unlawful reasons for her demotion, including age discrimination and retaliation. The court dismissed both her age claim and her retaliation claim because she alleged two motives. The court reasoned that "an employee cannot claim that age is a motive for the employer's adverse conduct and simultaneously claim that there was any other proscribed motive involved."[40]

The law has long recognized that but for cause does not work in cases where there are two causes, either of which could have created the full harm and thus that the but for cause standard results in injustice in multiple cause cases. However, the Supreme Court interpreted discrimination law to require a worker to establish but for cause for age discrimination claims and retaliation claims, and so courts continue to require but for cause for these kinds of cases.

In this area, courts also do not uniformly apply the discrimination doctrines. Some courts will allow a worker to proceed if she alleges that both age and retaliation played a role in her termination.[41] However, these courts often note that the worker will not be able to ultimately win her case unless she is able to show that age or retaliation, but not both, was the determining factor in the employment outcome.

6. *PRICE WATERHOUSE* MOTIVATING FACTOR CAUSATION

The Supreme Court first extensively discussed causation in discrimination cases in *Price Waterhouse*. As discussed previously, there, Ann Hopkins claimed that her employer refused to promote her because of her sex,[42] and the decision not to promote her involved many Price Waterhouse partners.

The trial court judge found that there were at least two reasons that Ms. Hopkins did not make partner. The company had been concerned about Ms. Hopkins's interpersonal skills, which the judge deemed a proper criterion for the decision. At the same time, the "partners' remarks about Hopkins stemmed from an impermissibly cabined view of the proper behavior of women."[43] Considering these reasons, the judge decided that Price Waterhouse unlawfully discriminated against Hopkins on the basis of sex by "consciously giving credence and effect to partners' comments that resulted from sex stereotyping."[44]

In *Price Waterhouse*, a case under Title VII, the Supreme Court decided whether discrimination occurred when two motives—one legal and the other illegally discriminatory—contributed to an employment decision. The court decided what causation standard was required to prove a violation of Title VII. Under this statute, it is illegal for an employer to make certain employment decisions "because of" a worker's sex, race, or other protected traits.[45] The words "because of" can arguably describe many different causation standards, such as but for cause or motivating factor cause.

The company Price Waterhouse argued for a but for cause standard, under which a worker wins only if the worker can prove that sex played the decisive role in the employment decision. Thus, it argued that even if sex played a role in the outcome, Ms. Hopkins should win only if she proved Price Waterhouse would have made her partner if the committee members had not considered her sex.

The Supreme Court rejected this argument with six of the Justices explicitly deciding a worker need not establish but for cause to win her sex discrimination claim.[46] Four of those Justices reasoned, "We take [because of] to mean that gender must be irrelevant to employment decisions. To construe the words 'because of' as colloquial shorthand for 'but-for causation,' as does Price Waterhouse, is to misunderstand them."[47] These Justices noted the problem with the stricter causation rules that was discussed earlier in the two fires hypothetical. The Justices reasoned, "It is difficult for us to imagine that, in the simple words 'because of,' Congress meant to obligate a plaintiff to identify the precise causal role played by legitimate and illegitimate motivations in the employment decision she challenges."[48]

At the same time, the Court recognized that the employer is still entitled to make employment decisions based on criteria other than those prohibited by Title VII. To balance the prerogatives of both workers and employers, the Supreme Court created a two-step causation analysis. The worker must come forward with evidence that sex played a motivating role or was a substantial factor in an employment decision. If she does this, the employer has an opportunity to prove that it still would have made the same decision based purely on the legitimate reason. If the employer is able to do this, it will win the case. If the employer fails to show this, then the worker will prevail.[49]

While *Price Waterhouse* sets up a slightly complicated causation framework, it is one that balances the interests of both workers and employers. The Court recognized that it is difficult, if not impossible, for an employee to definitively prove why an employer made a particular employment decision. The best an employee can do is show that her sex played a role.

In her influential concurring opinion, Justice O'Connor reasoned that the worker is required only to show that sex played a role in the outcome. Once the worker does this, "[t]here has been a strong showing that the employer has done exactly what Title VII forbids, but the connection between the employer's illegitimate motivation and any injury to the individual plaintiff is unclear."[50] The worker is not required to make that connection. Rather, as Justice O'Connor noted, the worker has shown that there is smoke. Despite that smoke, it is the employer's responsibility to show there is no fire.[51]

For example, Ms. Hopkins had evidence that some partners considered her sex when evaluating her for partner, but she did not know how sex discrimination affected every person involved in the decision. Some of the partners may have shared the sexist attitude and voted accordingly. Some may not have harbored any animus toward women, but may have allowed sexist, negative comments made by other partners to affect their votes. Others may have rejected the sexist comments but believed that Ms. Hopkins had trouble communicating with staff. And still others may have thought Ms. Hopkins should be partner.

Hopkins did what she was required to do. She showed that sex was a motivating factor. Price Waterhouse was then required to show it would have made the same decision not to promote her based on legitimate, nondiscriminatory reason—not sex. In reaction to this decision, Congress later amended Title VII to make it clear that a worker can establish discrimination by showing that her sex (or other protected trait) was a motivating factor in a negative employment decision.

7. A CHANGE IN CAUSATION LAW

Twenty years after *Price Waterhouse* the Supreme Court changed its opinion about causation. Jack Gross alleged that his employer discriminated
against him on the basis of age in violation of the Age Discrimination in
Employment Act (ADEA).[52] Using the Supreme Court's decision in *Price
Waterhouse*, the trial court judge instructed the jury that Mr. Gross could
prove his case if he could establish that age was a motivating factor in the
company's decision to demote him.[53] The judge also told the jury that age
is a motivating factor "if [it] played a part or a role" in the company's decision to demote Mr. Gross.[54] The judge further instructed the jury that the
company could win the case if it proved that it would have demoted Mr.
Gross regardless of his age.

The jury found that the company discriminated against Mr. Gross
because of his age and awarded him $46,945 in lost compensation.[55] Gross's
employer appealed, and the appellate court, addressing a legal question left
unresolved by *Price Waterhouse*, reversed the jury's verdict, and decided
that a new trial, using different jury instructions, should be held.[56]

On appeal, the Supreme Court did not resolve the legal issue raised
by the parties.[57] Instead, it reconsidered the question of causation. Even
though Title VII and the ADEA use the same "because of" language, the
Court rejected the motivating factor standard it had established in *Price
Waterhouse*. Contrary to its prior holding, a new Court, with a few different Justices, held that workers must meet the higher but for causation
standard to prevail on an age discrimination claim.[58]

To reach its conclusion to require "but for" causation, Justice Clarence
Thomas used a Webster's dictionary and stated the words "because of"
meant "by reason of" or "on account of." He also cited a few cases and a
legal treatise in support of but for causation, as opposed to motivating factor causation. Justice Thomas had also noted that if *Price Waterhouse* had
been decided by the current court, it would likely not have been decided
the same way. A few years later, in *University of Texas Southwestern Medical
Center v. Nassar*, the Court extended *Gross*, holding that the more onerous
"but for" standard also applied to Title VII retaliation cases.[59]

As a result of these cases, workers must prove different causation, depending on the kind of claim they bring. For example, if a woman sues for sex discrimination under Title VII for being fired, she must show that her sex played a motivating factor in the firing. In the same suit, if she alleges her employer retaliated against her by firing her, she will have to meet the more onerous but for standard for the retaliation claim.

After he lost his case, Mr. Gross said the following:

> One of the things I have always counted on was the rule of law. I have always believed it was consistent, it was blind, and it applied to all equally. If the rule of law had been applied to my case, I would have won at the Supreme Court level. Instead, they threw out 20 years of case law precedent and gutted the clear intent of congress and the ADEA. The jury in my case heard the law as written, listened to a week of testimony from both sides, and applied the law to the evidence. They didn't parse each word like the attorneys and judges tend to do, they just measured the law as stated against the evidence. . . .
>
> Age discrimination suits, I've learned, are very hard to win under any rule of law, and only a small percentage of them prevail. And, the process is onerous and not well known to anyone but lawyers who specialize in that area of practice. . . .
>
> I feel like my case has been hijacked by the high court for the sole purpose of rewriting both the letter and the spirit of the ADEA. I am against activist judges, from either party, who use their personal ideology to misinterpret the law as intended."[60]

As already described, using a but for standard makes it much harder for workers to win their cases. *Gross* is a possible example of this difference. After the Supreme Court decided *Gross*, the case was sent back to the lower courts for a new trial.[61] At the new trial, the judge instructed the jury on the new, higher causation standard. The second jury returned a verdict for the company. It appears that the more difficult causation standard resulted in Mr. Gross losing his case.

Senator Patrick Leahy has stated that the *Gross* case shows "that for those employees who are able to pry open the courtroom doors, the Supreme Court has placed additional obstacles on the path to justice."[62] Senator Leahy continued: "I am concerned that the *Gross* decision will allow employers to discriminate on the basis of age with impunity so long as they cloak it with other reasons."[63]

Foster v. University of Maryland East Shore is another example of the difficulties presented by the higher causation standard.[64] In that case, Iris Foster began working as a police officer on a six-month probationary contract. She presented evidence to the court that shortly after she started work, a coworker sexually harassed her on multiple occasions. Among other things, she claimed that a coworker "peeped through a doorknob hole" at her when she was being fitted for her uniform;[65] the coworker told her he had "something on [him] that would stick [her] very hard";[66] and the coworker gyrated in front of her as if he were having sex, pressed his body against hers, and, on another occasion, kissed her on the face.[67]

After Ms. Foster complained about the sexual harassment in May, her employer investigated her claim, found that it had some merit, and reassigned the coworker to work at a different location. Ms. Foster claimed that her supervisor "virtually stopped talking" to her following her complaint and changed her work schedule several times without notice.[68] Ms. Foster notified her employer that she was concerned about retaliation.[69] In August, the employer extended Ms. Foster's employment for another six months, but in October, the employer told her that she would be terminated effective November 29.[70]

Ms. Foster filed suit against her employer prior to the Supreme Court's decision in *Nassar* to increase the causation standard for retaliation claims. Ms. Foster's employer asked the court to dismiss her case on several grounds, including that Ms. Foster could not establish the required causal connection between her sexual harassment complaint and her firing. Rejecting the employer's argument, the court reasoned, "While perhaps Plaintiff does not make the strongest claim of retaliation, and although the jury ultimately may reject her claim, these incidents provide sufficient evidence of 'retaliatory animus' to generate a jury question regarding whether Plaintiff's termination was causally related to her" complaint.[71]

Following the Supreme Court decision that made the causation standard higher, the employer asked the court to reconsider the causation issue in light of the new legal standard. Using the new legal standard, on summary judgment, the court found "that no reasonable juror could determine that Ms. Foster's termination would not have occurred if she had not complained" and the court dismissed Ms. Foster's retaliation claim.[72]

Not all courts dismiss worker's claims when there are contested issues about causation. Several courts have noted that "[t]he determination of whether retaliation was a 'but-for' cause, rather than just a motivating factor, is particularly poorly suited to disposition by summary judgment, because it requires weighing of the disputed facts, rather than a determination that there is no genuine dispute as to any material fact."[73] These courts often emphasize that causation questions should typically be questions for the jury.[74]

As the 1989 Supreme Court noted in the Title VII context, but for cause does not work well in discrimination cases. The concept of but for causation derived from the law of torts. Torts is a term that describes wrongful conduct that results in an injury to the person, property, or reputation of another and that results in liability in the civil legal system. This area of law largely developed to handle physical events.

Car accidents are the quintessential torts in the modern legal system. In a car accident, it is easier to understand how a driver's lack of care created an injury because the careless actions resulted in a collision. For example, a person drives too fast and fails to stop when traffic slows in front of her. Her car rams the back of another car and damages it.

By contrast, traditional discrimination and retaliation cases try to connect an actor's nonphysical, unviewable state of mind, such as intent to take sex or race into account, with a later injury. Because of the nonconcrete character of state of mind, which contrasts with physical torts, but for cause does not work as well in employment discrimination cases.

8. PULLING IT TOGETHER

The new causation standard has created inconsistencies and injustice. Despite the lack of any expressed congressional intent to treat claims differently, workers must prove one causation standard for Title VII discrimination cases and a higher standard for age discrimination cases and retaliation cases.[75] Moreover, courts have used the but for cause standard to justify dismissing cases although there is evidence that workers faced age discrimination or retaliation.

The differences in these legal standards leads to an interesting problem. Courts struggle with what to do when both discrimination and retaliation played a role in an outcome. It is common for workers to allege both discrimination and retaliation because the discrimination statutes and employer policies encourage workers to complain. When an employer then fires the worker, it is often difficult to untangle what caused the firing: the worker's protected trait or her complaint.

Imagine Cecilia, a worker who complains that her supervisor referred to her using racial epithets and then threatened to fire her. The company then fires Cecilia. Cecilia has evidence that she was fired for two reasons: because of her race and because she complained. There are at least four possible ways to describe what happened to Cecilia.

1. The employer became angry when she complained and then fired her because of the complaint.
2. The employer did not consider her complaint. Instead, it fired her for legitimate reasons.
3. Two motives were at play. Cecilia's supervisor wanted her to be fired because of her race and because she complained.
4. Three motives were at play: Cecilia's race, her complaint, and a legitimate reason.

Under the summary judgment standard, the court is supposed to let this factual dispute go to the jury, who will decide what actually happened.

Instead, some judges use the but for standard to dismiss the retaliation claim. To establish race discrimination, Cecilia must show that her race was a motivating factor in her termination. To establish retaliation, she must meet the higher burden of establishing her complaint was the but for cause of her termination.

To decide whether to permit her retaliation claim to proceed, some courts would ask whether the same outcome would have occurred in the absence of her complaint. If the same outcome would have still occurred, then the complaint is not the but for cause of the harm. In Cecilia's case, without her complaint, she alleges she would have been fired because of her race. Therefore, for courts using this reasoning, Cecilia has no retaliation case. Her complaint was not the but for cause of her termination.

Even though her retaliation claim would fail, Cecilia can still win her claim for race discrimination, which is governed by the lower motivating factor standard. Because race discrimination played a significant role in the firing decision, Cecilia can win that claim. Because of the less stringent causation requirement, she can prevail on her race discrimination claim, even if there were other factors at play in the decision, such as the employer's desire to retaliate.

The difference in the causation standard for Title VII discrimination claims and many other claims means that race and sex claims can survive in situations where age and retaliation claims cannot. The following Table 5.1 illustrates how some courts will deal with combined claims, where a worker proves that two illegal reasons caused a negative employment action.

Courts also use the but for standard to dismiss age or retaliation claims when the employer presents evidence that the worker was fired for a legitimate reason. If the court finds that there is at least one legitimate reason for the employer's actions, it reasons that the worker cannot prevail because the illegitimate reason cannot then be the but for cause of the action.[76] In these circumstances, no age discrimination or retaliation can happen to a worker who has violated any workplace rule or policy or who has poor performance.

Table 5.1 How Courts May Treat Combined Claims

Combined Claims	Result
Sex discrimination plus race discrimination	Worker can prevail on both
Sex discrimination plus retaliation	Worker can prevail on sex discrimination, but not retaliation
Sex discrimination plus age discrimination	Worker can prevail on sex discrimination, but not age discrimination
Age discrimination plus retaliation	Worker can prevail on neither claim

Such rulings are incorrect for many reasons. In these cases, judges weigh the employer's evidence against the worker's evidence. The judge improperly decides which evidence should be believed and which evidence should not be believed.

These judges also ignore the factual realities of the modern workplace, where workers are subjected to many rules—some important and some not. Some of the rules are clearly communicated and strictly enforced; others are not. Also, given the numerous workplace rules, it is fairly easy for a supervisor to find infractions. By giving employers so much room to dodge claims, courts are flouting the very intent of antidiscrimination law.

Also recall that under at-will employment, the supervisor's subjective judgments count as valid reasons to make workplace decisions. As discussed in Chapter 4, it can be difficult for workers to challenge the truth of supervisors' subjective evaluations of worker performance. Add but for cause into this mix, and it is even easier to dismiss a worker's claim. All of these doctrines discussed in this book make it too easy to dismiss cases where there is evidence of discrimination or retaliation.

Frameworks

It is difficult to win a discrimination case. To succeed, workers must surmount the procedural hurdles discussed in Chapter 2 and must overcome the doctrines described in Chapters 3, 4, and 5. This chapter discusses another hurdle workers face: the frameworks that courts use to evaluate discrimination cases.

When Congress enacted the federal discrimination statutes, it appeared to formulate a simple way to determine whether discrimination happened. The text of the statutes asks the fact-finder to decide whether a particular employment outcome occurred because of a worker's race, sex, or other protected trait. For example, if a female worker is fired, Title VII asks whether she was fired because of her sex. If she is not promoted, the statute asks whether her sex played a role in that outcome.

Since the 1970s, federal courts have not always used the language of the discrimination statutes to analyze discrimination cases. The Supreme Court has created a set of frameworks to decide whether discrimination occurred. Some of the frameworks have some basis in the words of the statutes, while others have little connection to the texts. Each framework introduces new terms and phrases into the discrimination inquiry, often making it harder for courts to adjudicate discrimination claims. The frameworks also reduce discrimination law to a rote sorting process. Ultimately, in many cases, the frameworks may distract judges and juries from the fundamental question of whether an employer discriminated against an employee.

This book focuses on individual discrimination cases, and so it does not include the additional frameworks the courts have developed for group-based intentional discrimination claims (called pattern or practice claims) or for nonintentional discrimination claims (called disparate impact).

1. MARY'S CASE

Imagine Mary, a 55-year-old woman who has worked for the same company for twenty years and received good performance reviews. A year ago, her employer hired a new supervisor, who is 30 years old. The supervisor starts criticizing Mary's performance. He also calls her "old lady," tells her that she is too old to meet the demands of a busy office, and states he wants some "younger energy" in the office. Additionally, he remarks that men seem to be able to keep it together when they become older, but women do not. He proceeds to give Mary a bad performance review.

Following her company's policy, Mary complains to this supervisor, telling him that his comments and evaluation are discriminatory. Two months later, the supervisor informs the manager of human resources that Mary was insubordinate. The supervisor had asked Mary to clean up a conference room, a task that is not in her job description, and Mary refused. Conducting an independent investigation, the manager determines that Mary refused to clean and fires Mary.

If Mary files a suit against the company alleging discrimination based on her age and sex, the judge in the case will likely first label the type of discrimination she claims happened to her. Over the years, the Supreme Court created names to describe discrimination, such as "harassment" and "individual disparate treatment." Additionally, the statutes label unlawful conduct with words such as "pattern or practice" and "retaliation." A judge will likely label Mary's case with three different names. The supervisor's comments will be regarded as "harassment." The negative evaluation will be referred to as a type of discrimination called "individual disparate treatment." The termination will have two different labels: "individual disparate treatment" and "retaliation."

2. NAME IT, THEN FRAME IT

Most judges approaching a discrimination claim do two things. First, they name or label the type of discrimination. Second, after fitting the case within a kind of discrimination, the judge will use the analytical framework—the rules or sets of rules—that apply to that kind of discrimination. The Supreme Court has formulated these different frameworks that govern the various claims of discrimination described above.

Harassment

As described previously in Chapter 3, harassment may occur where an employee is subjected to taunts, jeers, inappropriate touching, or other similar actions because of a trait that is protected under federal law, such as age, sex, or race. To win her harassment case, Mary must meet several requirements under a framework developed by the Supreme Court in two different cases.[1] The test has four parts, only some of which are required by the words of the discrimination statutes.

First, Mary must show that she is a member of a class protected by the statute. Second, she must show the harassment happened because of that protected trait, such as age or sex. Third, she must show the harassment was unwelcome. Fourth, she must also establish that the harassment affected a term, condition, or privilege of employment.[2] To show the harassment affected a term or condition of Mary's employment, she must also show that she subjectively believed her work environment to be hostile or abusive and that an objective person would view the environment in the same way.[3] In deciding this latter inquiry, the court is to consider all the circumstances of the particular case, including "the frequency of the discriminatory conduct; its severity; whether it is physically threatening or humiliating, or a mere offensive utterance; and whether it unreasonably interferes with an employee's work performance."[4]

Using this framework and the other doctrines that have previously been discussed, a judge is likely to dismiss Mary's harassment claim. Despite many ageist and sexist comments, the judge may reason that the comments are not sufficiently "severe or pervasive" to constitute harassment.

Recall that at times, an employer will not be held liable for harassment that happens in the workplace even when the worker establishes the four elements. The courts have created a separate doctrine that exempts employers from liability in some cases, such as when a worker is harassed by a colleague and fails to report the harassment to the employer.[5]

Individual Disparate Treatment Evaluation Claim

The judge must also evaluate the two claims in which Mary alleges she was treated differently ("disparate treatment") based on her sex and age—the claim that her supervisor gave her a bad evaluation because of her sex and age and the claim that she was fired because of her sex and age.

Direct Evidence. A judge begins by determining whether Mary has what is referred to as "direct" evidence of discrimination. Direct evidence is evidence that links the employment decision directly to a protected trait. For example, it is direct evidence of discrimination when a supervisor informs an employee that he is refusing to promote her because she is a woman. Such evidence unambiguously links an overt bias and the employment decision.

There is a large body of case law that analyzes whether certain remarks or conduct count as "direct evidence." Outside the context of employment policies that are discriminatory on their face, definitions for direct evidence vary because courts have difficulty defining it.[6] Where such evidence exists, the court will ask only the one question that is asked by the words of the discrimination statutes: whether there is evidence that the negative employment outcome occurred because of a protected trait.

With direct evidence, a judge is unlikely to dismiss the case because this evidence strongly suggests that the worker faced discrimination. However, it is rare for workers to have direct evidence of discrimination because employers are unlikely to tell employees that employment actions were taken against them because of their protected trait, such as race.

Additionally, courts are reluctant to label evidence as direct evidence. As a result, very few cases proceed through this simple framework.[7]

However, in many cases, judges still first analyze whether a worker presented direct evidence. As shown throughout this chapter, the frameworks sometimes cause judges to engage in an often lengthy analysis when dismissing cases. Judges often analyze cases through multiple frameworks and at the end of the opinion declare that there was no discrimination. It is likely that a court would find that Mary does not have direct evidence of discrimination.

Circumstantial Evidence. If Mary does not have direct evidence, courts may evaluate her claims under a test the Supreme Court developed for cases involving circumstantial evidence. This test is known as the *McDonnell Douglas* test. The test was developed in a 1973 Supreme Court case, *McDonnell Douglas Corp. v. Green*, in which the Court described the basic contours of the test.[8] This test has three main parts, and the burden for establishing them starts with the plaintiff (often the worker) in step one, moves to the employer in step two, and then moves back to the plaintiff in step three. The *McDonnell Douglas* test is quite complex.

In step one, the court evaluates what is called the prima facie case. The prima facie case has four prongs. Mary must prove (1) that she belongs to a protected class, (2) that she met the objective qualifications for her job, (3) that she suffered an adverse action, and (4) that there were circumstances suggesting discrimination, such as being treated differently than individuals who are not members of her protected class—like men or younger people.[9]

Once Mary establishes her prima facie case, a rebuttable presumption that the employer discriminated against Mary arises. This means that if the employer fails to present any additional evidence, Mary would win her case. Very few cases are decided at this stage as it is rare for the employer to offer no evidence in its defense.

If Mary is able to demonstrate a prima facie case, the employer must then articulate a legitimate, nondiscriminatory reason for giving Mary a negative performance review.[10] This is a low burden. The employer need offer only some evidence that it acted for a nondiscriminatory reason. If it meets this requirement, Mary can still prevail by demonstrating that the defendant's reason for the decision was pretext or a cover-up for discrimination.[11]

Judges are required to modify the prima facie inquiry to apply it in different kinds of discrimination cases.[12] More than forty years after the Supreme Court created the *McDonnell Douglas* test, courts disagree on how to apply it, and the Supreme Court has decided several subsequent cases to explain how the framework operates.[13] Even though the *McDonnell Douglas* decision states that the burden-shifting framework is not the only way for workers to establish discrimination through circumstantial evidence, many courts will only funnel circumstantial evidence cases through that framework.[14]

Causation doctrine further complicates the analysis. The *McDonnell Douglas* test asks a fact-finder to decide whether the employer's or the employee's reason for the negative employment action is true. However, sometimes, employers may take action for more than one possible reason, so the test did not work for these situations. As previously discussed in Chapters 4 and 5, *Price Waterhouse* was one such case. There, evidence was presented that the employer acted for both legitimate and discriminatory reasons. The Supreme Court decided a worker could prevail under Title VII by showing simply that her sex was a "motivating factor" in the employment decision.

Congress later amended Title VII to explicitly include a two-part "motivating factor" proof structure. First, the plaintiff must show that her protected trait was a motivating factor in the challenged employment decision.[15] If she can do this, the plaintiff will win her case, unless the employer can show it would have made the same decision if it had not considered the protected trait.[16] If the employer is able to do this, it will not have to pay certain kinds of monetary damages. For example, the employer would not be required to pay the worker for lost wages or emotional distress.

When the Supreme Court decided the *Price Waterhouse* case, it did not instruct the lower courts on how the motivating factor test should intersect with the *McDonnell Douglas* test. Later, when Congress set forth a motivating factor test in Title VII, it also did not explain how this test related to the *McDonnell Douglas* test. In Title VII cases, some courts have folded the "motivating factor" standard test into the *McDonnell Douglas* test.[17] Most courts separate the inquiries into two tests: the *McDonnell Douglas* test and what courts called the "mixed-motive" test.[18]

As already described, in age and retaliation cases, workers must establish but for causation—not motivating factor causation.[19] The Supreme Court has provided lower courts no guidance on how they should handle claims, like Mary's, where age and sex have combined to create an outcome. As discussed in Chapter 5, courts may not use the motivating factor test for age discrimination cases, but they can use it in race and sex discrimination cases. In cases like Mary's, courts tend to separately analyze the allegations of sex discrimination under Title VII and the allegations of age discrimination under the ADEA, even though these separate analyses might cause the court to diminish the power of the worker's case where two discriminatory motives are at work.

A court presented with Mary's case will first decide whether she has direct evidence of discrimination. If it determines she does not, it will then evaluate her claim using (1) the *McDonnell Douglas* test; (2) the mixed-motive test; or (3) both tests. The court is likely to be presented with many questions, including whether Mary has direct or circumstantial evidence of discrimination and how to perform the mixed-motive analysis in a case that involves a combined claim of age and sex discrimination.

These tests, along with the doctrines discussed in prior chapters, may be used to dismiss Mary's evaluation claim. Some judges might declare that the comments are "stray remarks" and exclude them from evidence altogether. Some judges might say that a bad evaluation is not serious enough to be an adverse action. Courts introduced the concept of "adverse action" into discrimination law as an element of the *McDonnell Douglas* test, even though the phrase "adverse action" does not appear in the statutes themselves. Other judges might say that Mary cannot win her age discrimination claim. These judges would reason that the ADEA requires "but for" cause, which Mary cannot meet because she alleges multiple prohibited reasons—age and sex discrimination—for her bad evaluation.

Individual Disparate Treatment and Retaliation
Termination Claims

A court will separate Mary's termination claim into a disparate treatment discrimination claim and a retaliation claim. That is, it will examine whether Mary was terminated due to her age or sex. It will also determine whether she was terminated to retaliate against her for complaining of discrimination. Her claim that the employer terminated her because of her age will likely be analyzed using the *McDonnell Douglas* framework that was used for the evaluation claim. Her claim that her employer terminated her because of her sex may be analyzed using the *McDonnell Douglas* test and/or the mixed-motive test.

A court will analyze Mary's claim that her employer terminated her for complaining under a separate framework. To establish a retaliation claim, Mary must demonstrate that she engaged in protected activity, that the employer knew she engaged in the protected activity, that an adverse action happened, and that her complaint was the but for cause of her termination.[20]

Mary's claims that her firing was discriminatory and retaliatory may be dismissed under these frameworks and the other previously described doctrines. For example, some courts will dismiss her retaliation claim because the human resources officer could not have retaliated against Mary if she did not know about her complaint. Some courts will apply the cat's paw theory to Mary's case and find that her retaliation claim should survive. The supervisor knew about her complaint, and he played a role in convincing the human resources officer to fire Mary. Some courts will use the cat's paw theory to dismiss the termination claim. The human resource officer's independent investigation of Mary's performance breaks the causal chain between the supervisor and the ultimate decision.

3. COMPLEX FRAMEWORKS

Even though Mary's case seems fairly simple, the frameworks that courts use to evaluate it are not. A court would be required to apply many tests including the supporting doctrines and rules discussed in Chapters 3, 4, and 5. However, it is not clear that these tests help determine whether Mary's sex, her age, or her complaint played a role in her evaluation or termination. These frameworks can distract judges from the main question of whether a person was treated differently because of a trait, such as sex or age.

The history of employment discrimination law could be described as a history of frameworks. In an almost predictable pattern, the Supreme Court has recognized a category of employment discrimination and then, either in the same case or sometime thereafter, created a multipart test for evaluating it. After the establishment of some frameworks, decades of uncertainty follow as lower courts struggle with either the rubric itself or integrating it with other aspects of employment discrimination law. One unfortunate aspect of federal employment discrimination law is how much effort the litigants and courts have wasted figuring out the nuances of the discrimination frameworks. Ironically, when courts dismiss cases as ones in which the employer clearly should prevail, often judges write pages and pages of analysis. The length of the opinions alone suggests that the cases are not so one-sided.

If we look at Supreme Court cases on employment discrimination over the past several decades, many of them are either about creating a framework or explaining a framework. For example, the Supreme Court created the *McDonnell Douglas* test in 1973. Then, the Supreme Court had to decide four subsequent cases to explain how the framework operated.[21] Despite these cases, questions still remain about how the test works.

Discrimination jurisprudence is now filled with a complex and arcane jargon that is far removed from the original words of the statutes. Just looking at a partial list of this jargon in the context of the frameworks illustrates how complicated the doctrine has become: mixed-motive, single-motive, "severe or pervasive," prima facie test, pretext, adverse action, similarly situated employee, direct evidence, and circumstantial evidence.

After a framework is created, courts use it—rather than the statutory language—to decide whether discrimination occurred. Each step in the legal analysis is a place for the judge to determine, perhaps incorrectly, that no discrimination occurred. Because of the complicated nature of the *McDonnell Douglas* test, many judges refuse to instruct juries to use it, believing that it would only confuse them and would not promote a correct decision.[22] Nonetheless, judges still use the formula to analyze whether to dismiss cases.

EEOC v. Abercrombie & Fitch Stores, Inc. is an example of how the tests initially prevented the correct result.[23] The case raised the question of whether an employer could refuse to hire a worker because she wore a headscarf.[24] Under Title VII, an employer cannot discriminate because of religion, and employers must accommodate an employee's religious practice in some cases.[25] An appellate court found that summary judgment should be entered for Abercrombie, disagreeing with the district court. It decided that the worker could not prove she had been discriminated against because she did not explicitly tell her employer that she wore a headscarf because she was Muslim. If the worker did not inform the employer as to why she wore a headscarf and ask for an accommodation, then the employer lacked the requisite knowledge to discriminate on the basis of religion. The court stated:

> Our conclusion naturally rests, first, on our own express articulation
> of the plaintiff's prima facie burden, which is bolstered by a similar
> linguistic formulation of that burden found in rulings of several of
> our sister circuits.[26]

In the end, the court-created tests for proving discrimination distracted this court. The court could not see how refusing to hire a woman because she wore a headscarf could be religious discrimination. The Supreme Court later reversed this decision.[27]

Another relatively simple example is the case of *O'Connor v. Consolidated Coin Caterers Corp.*,[28] a case first discussed in Chapter 4. In that case, a 56-year-old employee alleged that his supervisor stated that the employee was "too damn old," and that the company needed young blood.[29] The company then replaced the 56-year-old employee with a 40-year-old employee.

The trial court judge said that these facts were not enough to go to a jury because the employee did not have enough evidence of potential age discrimination. Using a version of the *McDonnell Douglas* test to evaluate the employee's claim, the judge required the employee to show that the employer treated a similarly situated person outside the worker's protected class better than the older worker. [30] A similarly situated worker is one who holds a similar position to the plaintiff, often with the same supervisor. The Age Discrimination in Employment Act protects only employees aged 40 or older from age discrimination. Because the plaintiff was replaced by a 40-year-old, under the framework, the plaintiff could not prove he had been treated differently than someone outside the protected class, that is, someone younger than 40.

The Supreme Court eventually decided that a worker in an ADEA case is not required to establish that the employer replaced him with someone outside the protected class.[31] The Court held that an inference of discrimination still existed. There was a significant age difference between the two employees, and the comments suggested the action was taken because of age discrimination. The *McDonnell Douglas* framework had directed the lower courts away from the ultimate question of whether the employer had discriminated against the employee because of his age.

In another case, Mr. Harmon, a 57-year-old man, worked for a company for more than twenty years, receiving no negative performance evaluations.[32] Thereafter, he was promoted to district manager, a position he held for several years—again without receiving any negative performance evaluations. The company then hired a 32-year-old to supervise Mr. Harmon.[33] On one occasion, Mr. Harmon claimed that his new supervisor told him: "I bet you think that your older people are your best people. . . . [W]ell, they're not. They're not your best people."[34] Two months later, this new supervisor gave Mr. Harmon a negative evaluation.[35] The new supervisor also hired two younger individuals, ages 25 and 37, into positions similar to plaintiff's position.[36]

Two months later, after the supervisor discovered that two drivers under Mr. Harmon's supervision had vehicle accidents that were not reported to higher management, the supervisor recommended that Mr. Harmon be fired. The supervisor claimed it was company policy to report vehicle accidents, while Mr. Harmon asserted that he did not know about any such company policy.[37] Even though this type of issue would normally result in discipline—not termination under company policy—Mr. Harmon was terminated.[38] An individual who was ten years younger than Mr. Harmon took over Mr. Harmon's duties. Even though there was conflicting evidence about the policy that the company had claimed Mr. Harmon violated, and a company official indicated that the "policy" that had been conveyed to Mr. Harmon was not accurate, the district court granted summary judgment for the employer, which the appellate court affirmed.[39]

The appellate court first considered whether the plaintiff had direct evidence of discrimination. Finding none, it analyzed the facts under the *McDonnell Douglas* test and decided that the employee had not presented a prima facie case of discrimination.[40] His job responsibilities were assigned to a current employee who was ten years younger than Mr. Harmon. Because the plaintiff could not show that he was replaced by a new, younger employee, he did not meet the *McDonnell Douglas* test, and his case was dismissed.[41]

Recall that the primary question under the ADEA is whether the plaintiff was terminated because of his age. Here, the plaintiff had several pieces of evidence including one potentially discriminatory comment, the hiring of a younger manager who immediately began to report problems, the younger manager's hiring of younger workers into similar slots, a twenty-eight-year track record with the company, and two instances where the company possibly did not follow its own policies. This evidence creates an arguable question of fact about whether the termination was because of plaintiff's age. Nonetheless, the *McDonnell Douglas* rubric directed the court away from the more straightforward inquiry of whether the employee's age caused his firing.

The frameworks also make it harder for courts to decide cases with more complicated facts and thus more difficult questions of whether discrimination occurred. In general, courts apply the current frameworks as if they represent a complete lens through which to view discrimination claims.[42] If a set of facts does not fit within a recognized framework, courts will decide there was no actionable discrimination. Many judges would not consider whether the statutory language provides another answer, one that is different from the court-created frameworks. Thus, the frameworks make easy cases harder, but they also are inadequate in helping courts decide more difficult, cutting-edge issues.

Some judges have warned their fellow federal judges about the dangers of the frameworks. For example, some have openly questioned the continued need for *McDonnell Douglas*. Some appellate judges have called attention to the "the snarls and knots" that *McDonnell Douglas* inflicts on courts and litigants.[43] One appellate judge derided the test as "an allemande worthy of the 16th century."[44] She further noted that district courts can decide cases outside the area of discrimination without reliance on a phalanx of complicated tests.[45] Another federal judge has noted that the *McDonnell Douglas* test creates confusion and that it distracts courts away from the ultimate inquiry of whether discrimination occurred.[46]

In some ways, the framework model is very comforting because it gives the appearance that the courts are following an orderly and rational method of making decisions. But as we have seen, adjudicating cases using this model can cause judges to improperly dismiss cases where a worker's protected trait caused a negative employment outcome.

Politics

Chapters 2 through 6 described how the current state of discrimination law favors employers. One possible explanation for this is pure politics. This argument is often framed in a simple dichotomy. Some Republicans want to protect employers' interests, and some Democrats want to protect the interests of workers. Thus, when possible, some federal judges appointed by Republican Presidents might skew discrimination law in favor of employers, and some federal judges appointed by Presidents from the Democratic Party might decide the law to favor workers. This chapter shows how some judges have acted in this partisan way to limit discrimination law. This chapter also shows that the simple dichotomy often fails to explain what is happening in actual cases. Some judges do not discretely fall into categories for or against the discrimination laws. Also some employers do not easily fit these categories.

The chapters that follow this one describe other factors that have contributed to the winnowing away of the employment discrimination law. Chapter 8 describes the willingness of some judges to rely on arguments that are not supported by facts. And Chapter 9 shows how the complex structure of discrimination law can push cases toward dismissal.

1. PURE POLITICS

As described in this chapter, some judges approach discrimination cases in a partisan way. Legal realism refers to the idea that judges are not impartial interpreters of the law. Under this view, judges do not simply look at the words of statutes and objectively report the meaning of those words. Instead, the process of interpretation allows judges to impose their own values and policy judgments—influenced by the politics of the President who chose them—onto the texts of the statutes.

While partisan politics play a role in narrowing the reach of discrimination law, this view is incomplete in a number of important ways. First, it assumes that most or all judges have a well-formed, politically based view of discrimination law. However, there is no evidence that actually supports that all or a majority of federal judges decide discrimination cases based on politics. While politics may play a role, other reasons may be influential. For example, judges might issue decisions that favor employers because much of the current case law pushes the legal analysis to favor employers. Thus, the partisan model overemphasizes the role of political bias when the law favors employers.

Second, the partisan model often overemphasizes the role that the Supreme Court plays in discrimination law. It does not focus sufficiently on the lower federal courts, where most decisions are made. As discussed later, there is no or little Supreme Court precedent for many areas of discrimination law, and most cases never make it to the Supreme Court.

2. SUPREME COURT JUSTICES AS POLITICAL ACTORS

In some circumstances, by narrowly interpreting the statutes, the Supreme Court has pushed discrimination law in the direction of favoring employers and disfavoring workers. In fact, in some of these cases, the Court's reading was so narrow that even Republican Presidents have signed legislation to change the outcome of the Court's decisions to make clear that the discrimination statutes should be construed more liberally.[1] However, in addition to pro-employer or antiworker cases, there are numerous cases in which the Supreme Court has ruled in favor of workers. So the Supreme Court's overall record toward discrimination law is more mixed.

The Supreme Court has split specifically along ideological lines in many important discrimination cases.[2] The new causation analysis that was described in Chapter 5 is one of the clearest examples of politically affiliated members of the Court choosing to favor employer interests over worker interests. As we discussed, causation is the link workers must show between race, sex, or other protected traits and negative employment outcomes. In 1989, the Supreme Court held that a worker could prevail on a discrimination claim by showing that her sex (or other protected trait) played a motivating factor in an employment decision. About two decades later, a Court with a different make-up changed its mind. Members of the Court who had been chosen by Republican Presidents made it more difficult for workers to prove causation in age discrimination cases and retaliation cases.[3]

On a number of occasions, in response to conservative rulings by the Supreme Court that included ideological splits, Congress has stepped in and amended the discrimination statutes.[4] For example, in the late 1980s, the Supreme Court narrowly interpreted many aspects of the federal discrimination statutes with some judges with Republican ties participating in restricting the law. In 1991, Congress responded by passing the Civil Rights Act of 1991, which amended some of the discrimination laws. The Act specifically repudiated the prior Supreme Court decisions and gave greater protection to employees who bring discrimination lawsuits. Despite the protection accorded to employees by this amendment, a Republican President—George H.W. Bush—signed it and it became a law, showing that exact partisan lines are not easy to draw.[5]

During the 1990s, the Supreme Court issued another series of opinions—this time narrowly interpreting the Americans with Disabilities Act (ADA), again with some Justices with Republican ties participating in restricting the law. Congress later again stepped in, amending the ADA. In doing so, Congress explicitly noted that the purpose of the amendments was to reject several Supreme Court decisions, emphasizing that the ADA was intended to broadly cover discrimination on the basis of disability.[6] Here again, the amendments enjoyed bipartisan support, with Republican President George W. Bush signing the amendments into law.

In some areas over the last few decades, the Supreme Court has pushed discrimination law in a pro-employer direction. But when looking at the

Court's record as a whole, the partisan narrative does not completely describe what has happened.

Scholars who study recent Supreme Court cases have found that the decisions are not uniformly conservative. The Court has ruled in favor of workers in more than half of the cases it reviewed. For example, Professor Michael Selmi found that the Supreme Court ruled in favor of the worker in most cases. He reviewed forty-three Supreme Court cases from 1993 until 2010.[7] Workers won in twenty-nine of the forty-three cases, that is, in 67.4 percent of the cases. Employers prevailed in thirteen, or 30.2 percent, of the cases. Professor Selmi found that the remaining case was a functional tie.

Of the forty-three, twenty or 46.5 percent of the cases were unanimous, and eighteen of these unanimous decisions favored plaintiffs. Nearly two-thirds (62.1 percent) of the decisions favoring plaintiffs were unanimous.[8] In other words, in many decisions favoring plaintiffs, Justices appointed by both Republican and Democratic Presidents agreed on outcomes that favored plaintiffs.

Work by Professor Margaret Lemos covering a different time period reached similar results.[9] Professor Lemos conducted a study to compare the views of the Supreme Court with those of the Equal Employment Opportunity Commission (the EEOC),[10] the federal agency tasked with administering many of the federal discrimination statutes. When a contested issue of discrimination law arises, the EEOC often weighs in on the dispute through various means, including guidance documents. Although the EEOC possesses the formal power to interpret the Americans with Disabilities Act, Congress did not give the EEOC the same authority with respect to the substantive meaning of all of the provisions of Title VII. Under Title VII, courts can take the agency's views into account as persuasive authority, but the courts are not required to defer to the EEOC's views on a particular issue.[11]

Professor Lemos reviewed 102 Supreme Court cases, which considered 120 contested issues of law under Title VII. She then identified the EEOC's expressed opinion on 98 of these 120 contested issues.[12] Professor Lemos coded an outcome as liberal if it favored a Title VII claimant and conservative if it favored the employer.[13] She found the "EEOC's position was liberal on eighty-nine, or 91 percent, of the 98 Title VII-related issues that both the Court and the EEOC addressed. The Court, by contrast, took a liberal position on only seventy-three, or 61 percent, of the 120 Title VII-related issues it resolved after oral argument."[14] While this study shows that the EEOC's decisions favored workers more than the Supreme Court did, the Supreme Court favored the worker in most cases.

Care should be taken in drawing inferences from the Supreme Court's overall record. Professor Selmi posits that some of the Supreme Court's proworker decisions show "how conservative some of the lower courts have become," not that the Supreme Court favors workers.[15] For example, in the *Ash v. Tyson Foods, Inc.* case discussed throughout this book, black workers alleged discrimination and presented evidence that a supervisor referred to them as "boy."[16] The Eleventh Circuit Court of Appeals held that this evidence could not demonstrate discrimination, and the Supreme Court reversed.[17] The Court's rebuke of the Eleventh Circuit's flawed reasoning does not show that the Court is liberal, but rather only that the Court was required to rule in the worker's favor because of the extreme position taken by the Court of Appeals.

A more recent case shows this same phenomenon—where an appellate court interpreted discrimination law in a narrow fashion and the Supreme Court intervened to correct the lower court decision that was clearly wrong. In 2015, the Supreme Court decided the case of *EEOC v. Abercrombie & Fitch Stores, Inc.*[18] The EEOC brought the case on behalf of Samantha Elauf who applied to work for Abercrombie & Fitch. Abercrombie had a policy prohibiting employees from wearing caps. Ms. Elauf, a practicing Muslim, wore a headscarf. According to Ms. Elauf, Abercrombie refused to hire her because her headscarf would violate the company's "no cap" policy.[19]

Facially, this seems to be an easy case. If an employer refuses to hire a Muslim woman because she wears a headscarf, this is discrimination based on religion. Federal law requires employers to accommodate religious practices of employees unless doing so would be an undue hardship to their business. The trial court judge granted summary judgment in Ms. Elauf's favor, deciding it was clear that Abercrombie could have hired

Ms. Elauf and allowed her to wear her headscarf without any hardship.[20] The trial court judge then held a trial on damages and awarded Ms. Elauf $20,000 in damages.[21]

Abercrombie appealed the decision, and the United States Court of Appeals for the Tenth Circuit disagreed with the trial court judge. The Tenth Circuit reversed the trial court judge's decision and granted summary judgment instead to Abercrombie. In its opinion, the Tenth Circuit held that Ms. Elauf could not win because Abercrombie did not know that Ms. Elauf wore a headscarf for religious reasons.[22] In a short opinion by Justice Scalia, the Supreme Court reversed the appellate court.[23]

There is also a second way in which the majority proworker outcomes in the Supreme Court cases might be misleading. Professor Selmi noted that the Supreme Court ruled in the employer's favor in the cases that had the broadest impact and thus were most important to discrimination law. These cases tended to be 5–4 decisions, reflecting the ideological split between conservative and liberal justices.[24]

Despite these caveats, in some areas of discrimination law, the Court has generally ruled in favor of workers. For example, over the past decade, the Supreme Court decided a number of retaliation cases, often construing the retaliation provisions to provide workers more protections.[25]

The analysis of Supreme Court case law is currently incomplete in another important way. Studies have analyzed the Supreme Court's docket over the past few decades. However, the Supreme Court laid much of the groundwork for discrimination law in the 1970s and 1980s. In many of the cases, the Supreme Court interpreted the law to favor workers.

However, in some sense, even these past so-called "liberal" Supreme Court cases contribute to the current state of the discrimination law. When the Court divided discrimination law into different kinds of claims, it created a structure that encourages judges to view discrimination claims in a piecemeal fashion. When the Court made frameworks, like the *McDonnell Douglas* test, it also made discrimination law too complex. These frameworks invite judges to devise even more court-created ideas and doctrines. Judges then start to view discrimination law in a technical way. Discrimination law becomes focused on whether litigants can squeeze into the court-created tests. As we discussed in Chapter 6, it is not clear whether these frameworks help judges decide the key inquiry of whether a person's race, sex, or other protected trait played a role in an employment outcome. Thus, even seemingly liberal frameworks have contributed to the current state of discrimination law, and, as a result, the current state of discrimination law cannot be attributed purely to politics.[26]

3. THE SUPREME COURT AND LOWER FEDERAL COURTS

Discussions about judicial bias tend to focus on the Supreme Court. Certainly, the Supreme Court has played a large role. It constructed the overarching frameworks that govern discrimination law. It created the test for harassment law and also devised the doctrines that allow employers to escape liability for harassment in some cases. Additionally, the Court created the *McDonnell-Douglas* burden-shifting framework. It has also played a large role in causation doctrine.

Since creating these employment discrimination standards, however, the Supreme Court has played only a minor role in their development. The Supreme Court issues general instructions through its decisions to the lower federal courts, and then those courts interpret the instructions in the individual cases that come before them. An example helps to show the significant power that the lower federal courts possess in creating the law.

In the late 1980s and early 1990s, the Supreme Court set forth the framework to prove sexual harassment, which required "severe or pervasive" conduct. Since then, it has not defined when conduct is serious enough to be actionable harassment.[27] The lower courts have spent more than two decades defining the severe or pervasive requirement without the Supreme Court intervening. As another example, in 2006, the Supreme Court interpreted the "adverse action" requirement in retaliation cases but has not revisited the question since then.[28] The lower courts have filled in the gaps and largely created the doctrine that exists today.

Moreover, the Supreme Court has played little to no formal role in some areas of discrimination law. Instead, the lower courts created many of the rules and inferences discussed in this book. For example, the Supreme Court has not played a significant role in developing the same-actor inference. Also, even though a concurring opinion by Justice O'Connor set the stray remarks doctrine in motion, the lower courts developed it into the doctrine that it is today.

Practically, the federal trial courts are the only courts with which most litigants will have any contact, and so political bias claims that focus on the Supreme Court are necessarily incomplete. Most litigants do not have the time or the money to appeal cases, especially to the Supreme Court. The Supreme Court also hears only a limited number of cases each year. Additionally, when the Supreme Court takes a case, it tends to focus on one or two specific legal questions, and it does not typically rule on all of the smaller issues that occur in the usual case.

4. PARTISANSHIP IN THE LOWER FEDERAL COURTS?

Although available empirical studies show political bias plays some role in the results reached by lower federal courts, those studies do not conclusively show that ideology drives outcomes.[29] One study did find that judges appointed by Republicans voted for workers in sex discrimination cases 35 percent of the time while Democratic appointees voted in favor of workers 51 percent of the time.[30] However, the study found that the judges voted less on the basis of ideology in cases in which black workers alleged race discrimination.[31] Another study found that appellate judges appointed by Democrats were more likely to vote for workers than judges appointed by Republicans when a black plaintiff alleges disparate impact discrimination.[32] However, the study also noted the possible effect of conservative Supreme Court decisions on case outcomes.[33]

While these studies provide us with some information about the decisions in lower federal courts, the empirical studies are quite limited in reach. For a number of reasons, it is difficult to conduct an empirical study that would provide much useful information about partisanship in the lower courts.

One problem is access to a complete data set. There are two kinds of databases that researchers tend to use for research on federal courts— private databases and the federal courts' public database—both of which have significant limits. The private databases do not contain all of the orders issued by trial court judges. Whenever researchers rely on these private databases, their data set is necessarily skewed because it only contains a small portion of the many orders that trial court judges issue.

The federal courts use PACER (Public Access to Court Electronic Records). This electronic system provides access to judges' orders as well as to pleadings and other documentation related to the courts' dockets. However, PACER is not easy to search. Researchers who use the federal database engage in the time-consuming task of combing through thousands of cases to isolate the relevant ones. To make empirical projects that use PACER more manageable, researchers tend to focus on particular courts. As a result, it is difficult to get an overall picture of what is happening in trial courts across the country.

The lack of a searchable, complete database is not the only limit on empirical studies of decisions by trial court judges. At the trial court level, judges typically rule on dozens of different issues. Although it is possible to determine whether a judge might dismiss a case or not, it is difficult to tell whether all of the judge's rulings align with any particular partisan leanings. There are also conservative federal judges who respect the constitutional division of responsibilities between the judge and the jury. Thus, some judges may be disinclined to rule in favor of workers yet still respect the idea that juries, not judges, are supposed to resolve factual questions.

There are also reasons to doubt the pure politics story in the lower courts. First, scholars look to the political party of the President who nominated the judge as a proxy for the judge's likely political bent, and this is not always a perfect proxy. Finding data about the political affiliation of judges is difficult. Judges do not typically declare their political party. There are a fixed number of available federal judgeships: 9 U.S. Supreme

Court Justices, 179 court of appeals judges, and a little more than 650 district court judges located throughout the United States.[34] Presidents from the Democratic Party appointed some of these judges, and Republican Presidents selected the others.

The judicial process also constrains trial court judges, making it very difficult to determine bias questions. As mentioned earlier, federal trial court judges are required to follow the law established by higher-level federal courts. Accordingly, it is difficult to determine whether lower court judges are acting on their own personal preferences or whether they feel constrained by precedent. For example, a federal trial court judge sitting in Cincinnati, Ohio, must follow the law set forth by the U.S. Supreme Court and also must follow the law provided by the U.S. Court of Appeals for the Sixth Circuit. Even if the judge personally disagrees with the Supreme Court or the Sixth Circuit, the judge must abide by the law created by those courts.

There are similar limits on assessing the political bias of appellate court judges. When appellate judges decide cases, they often sit on three-judge panels, with each judge having a vote on the final decision. With three-judge panels, there may be multiple factors affecting the ultimate outcomes. As Professor Pauline Kim has noted, "scholars have collected considerable evidence suggesting that decision making by a federal court of appeals judge sitting on a three-judge panel differs from what one might expect from that judge sitting alone."[35] Some scholars have noted that judges sitting on three-judge panels might be subject to ideological dampening or ideological amplification.[36] For example, if a federal judge appointed by a Democratic President is on a panel with two Republican judges, the Democratic judge may be less inclined to vote in a partisan way. Likewise, if a Democratic judge is on a panel with two other judges appointed by a Democratic President, we may see more politically aligned outcomes.

Additionally, most empirical studies about appellate courts rely on vote counting. Such studies count whether each judge on the appellate panel voted for an outcome that favored the employer or favored the worker. These studies are limited because they often fail to look at the reasoning underlying the ultimate conclusion. Judges may vote for an outcome that favors an employer but for reasons that do not suggest any particular bias or favor toward employers generally.

Many factors may affect decisions, but the studies focusing on political bias may not fully account for these other factors. For example, some studies have shown that female judges are more likely to vote for workers in discrimination cases than male judges[37] while others have found no effect.[38] One study found that Republican-appointed female judges found in favor of workers in discrimination cases at the same rate as male judges appointed by Democrats.[39] As this study might suggest, sex, class, race, and other characteristics might also affect voting in discrimination cases.

Finally, similar to district court judges, appellate court judges are bound by the prior decisions of the Supreme Court. Professor Kim has noted: "Circuit judges do not vote according to a naïve ideological model, and the large degree of overlap in voting behavior between judges affiliated with opposite parties indicates that factors other than ideology—in all likelihood legal doctrine—influence their decisions."[40] The clarity of the Supreme Court precedent may also affect voting because judges may feel more constrained when the Supreme Court case law is clear than when it is ambiguous and provides room for the appellate court to interpret the law.

Given these limits, it is difficult to determine the role that political bias has played in employment discrimination cases in the lower federal courts. In the end, it may not matter how much of the current state of discrimination law is due to partisanship. If bias based on political party is the primary reason courts sometimes narrowly rule on discrimination claims, the only way to change discrimination law to favor workers is to elect Democratic Presidents and have them appoint Democratic judges.

5. OVERCOMING THE DICHOTOMY

The pure politics narrative rests on assumptions. It assumes that federal judges appointed by Republican Presidents try to serve the interests of employers and likewise those appointed by Democratic Presidents try to appease the interests of employees. Thus, this narrative pits Republicans against Democrats. As already shown, it is not this simple. The history of discrimination law is much more nuanced and calls into question the utility of relying on political bias as the primary driving factor causing the law to favor employers and disfavor workers.

As discussed in this chapter, Republican Presidents and legislators have played important roles in expanding discrimination law. For example, Republican legislators played key roles in creating and passing Title VII of the Civil Rights Act of 1964. Moreover, George H.W. Bush signed the Americans with Disabilities Act (ADA) and the 1991 amendments to Title VII into law. The ADA expanded protections for disabled individuals, and the 1991 amendments greatly expanded the damages available to workers under Title VII and made jury trials available to workers.[41] The 1991 amendments also rejected several Supreme Court decisions that narrowly interpreted Title VII. Later, Republican President George W. Bush signed into law the Americans with Disabilities Amendments Act of 2008, which rejected several Supreme Court decisions that narrowly interpreted the ADA.[42]

Supreme Court Justices appointed by Republican Presidents also authored opinions that broadly interpreted employment discrimination law. Justice Lewis Powell, appointed by Republican President Richard Nixon, authored the Court's 1973 opinion in *McDonnell Douglas Corp. v. Green*.[43] Although the test created by the Supreme Court in that case turned out to be confusing, the initial decision was widely regarded as one that made it easier for workers to prove discrimination cases. Another Nixon appointee, Chief Justice Warren Burger, authored the Court's decision in *Griggs v. Duke Power Co*.[44] In *Griggs*, the Court broadly interpreted Title VII, establishing the method of proving discrimination called disparate impact under which a worker is not required to show bias or intent to prove a claim.[45]

While during the last four decades, the Supreme Court has issued decisions narrowing the reach of discrimination law and many of these decisions were authored and joined by Supreme Court Justices appointed by Republican Presidents,[46] there are a number of cases during this time

period where the Supreme Court interpreted the discrimination statutes broadly, and Republican-appointed Justices authored or joined the
majority decision.[47] Thus, the Republican versus Democrat narrative
is not consistent enough to completely explain the current state of the
discrimination law.

The bias narrative also ignores the fact that many employers support
antidiscrimination efforts. For example, several employers discussed
how they supported diversity efforts in workplaces and schools when
they filed amicus briefs in a case determining whether the University
of Michigan could consider diversity goals in making admissions
decisions. In its friend of the court brief, Exxon Mobil argued that a
"diverse workforce is essential to the success of global companies."[48] BP
noted: "Because BP strongly believes that innovation, one of its core
brand values, can only come from encouraging true diversity of styles
and ideas while leveraging multiple talents, BP has made diversity and
inclusion a strategic focus of its business in the US and around the
world."[49]

However, regardless of these efforts by some companies to diversify
their work forces and provide equal opportunities, when an employer
is sued and they litigate the case, they will argue that they did not
commit any wrongdoing and will attempt to have the law support
their position, which may further narrow the law. Any goals of the
employer for promoting antidiscrimination principles may change
once a worker initiates a discrimination lawsuit and as the company
tries to win that suit.

The ethical rules that govern litigators in these cases—often lawyers
from outside law firms—require them to zealously represent the interests of their clients.[50] Even if an employer is committed to eliminating
discrimination, that goal is often changed in litigation. Once litigation
starts, the lawyers representing the employers have an incentive to either
win the case or to settle it on the best terms possible. For the lawyers
and the employer, the procedural junctures we discussed in Chapter 2
become very important. The employer's attorneys are trying to persuade
the judge to dismiss the case, either through a motion to dismiss or

a motion for summary judgment. If a case makes it past these procedural stages, it will be more difficult to settle and may cost the employer more money. The employer's attorneys will use available arguments to win the case, even if this means diminishing the reach of traditional discrimination law.

Fakers and Floodgates

The structure of discrimination law, with its many pro-employer infer-ences and rules, pushes cases toward dismissal. Over time, courts have significantly restricted the reach of discrimination law, even though those constraints are not justified by the text in the applicable statutes that Congress approved. In this chapter, we explore what we call the "fakers and floodgates" argument, the idea that judges must curtail the reach of discrimination law because the federal court system is flooded with unmeritorious employment discrimination suits.

It is important that concerns about fakers and floodgates be seriously considered. If fake claims were flooding the federal docket, this would be a significant problem. Employers should not be hailed into court to defend against false claims, nor should the court system waste resources litigat-ing them. However, the fakers and floodgates argument is unproven and therefore should not support change to discrimination law. No data shows that the courts are flooded with false claims. If false claims exist, the courts already have an effective way to ameliorate false claims. They can punish litigants who bring false claims.

Nonetheless, the fakers and floodgates argument plays a powerful role in modern discrimination law. A judge who believes the fakers and flood-gates argument could use this argument to justify skewing discrimination law to favor employers. If a judge views each plaintiff as a possible liar, the judge may feel it is her prerogative to sit as what amounts to a "super-juror." The judge may believe that she should protect the judicial system's integrity by helping to eliminate these false claims and that she can appropriately do so by interpreting the statutes narrowly.

1. THE RHETORIC

This assertion that the federal courts are flooded with frivolous discrimination suits has been made both in the media and in court decisions. For example, the *Los Angeles Times* reported that some employers believe discrimination suits are "brought by workers who see dollar signs dancing before their eyes."[1] Federal trial court judges have expressed concern about a deluge of discrimination suits.[2] One judge wrote: "[N]o federal district court can ignore the wave of dubious and potentially extortionate discrimination cases currently flooding the federal docket."[3] Another judge noted: "[J]udicial decisions appear to reflect more concern for 'disgruntled employees' seeking wrongfully to exploit federal resources than for broad social and legal reform."[4] Recently, in *University of Texas Southwestern Medical Center v. Nassar*, the Supreme Court weighed in, stating that to stop the flood of fake lawsuits inundating the courts, it needed to make it harder for workers to win cases.[5]

This belief—that the federal courts are flooded with questionable discrimination cases—may affect how judges interpret the substance of the law. Indeed, federal judges have been taught how to eliminate discrimination cases from their dockets at judicial conferences.[6]

The *Nassar* case shows how concerns about fakers and floodgates have skewed discrimination law. In that case, Dr. Naiel Nassar, who was of Middle Eastern descent, sued his former employer, the University of Texas Southwestern Medical Center, for discrimination and retaliation.[7] Dr. Nassar was both a faculty member at the medical school and a physician at Parkland Memorial Hospital. At trial, he presented evidence that one of his supervisors at the medical school had stated: "Middle Easterners are lazy."[8] This same supervisor noted that the medical school has "hired another one" after it hired another doctor of Middle Eastern descent.[9] Additionally, this supervisor excessively scrutinized Dr. Nassar's work and

billing practices.[10] The medical center responded that it had not discriminated or retaliated against Dr. Nassar.

Because of this treatment by the supervisor, Dr. Nassar no longer
wanted to work at the medical school. He resigned his teaching position
there and arranged to work only as a physician at Parkland Memorial
Hospital. When he resigned from the medical school, he sent a letter to
several people there stating that he was resigning because of harassment
that "stems from . . . religious, racial and cultural bias against Arabs and
Muslims."[11] A doctor from the medical school then contacted the hospital
where Dr. Nassar had worked and where he had arranged to continue to
be employed. The medical school doctor argued that Dr. Nassar's employment at the hospital violated an agreement between the medical school
and the hospital that hospital staff should also be members of the medical
school faculty.[12] The hospital proceeded to rescind its employment offer
to Dr. Nassar.[13] However, contrary to this supposed policy of concurrent
appointments, some members of the hospital staff were not faculty members at the medical school.[14]

Dr. Nassar claimed the medical school discriminated against him
because of religion and race. He also asserted that the medical school
retaliated against him by asking Parkland to rescind his employment offer
after he complained about harassment at the medical school. At trial, after
the jury found that the medical school discriminated against Dr. Nassar
and retaliated against him, it awarded Dr. Nassar more than $400,000 in
back pay for the damages he suffered.[15]

The employer appealed the case, and the appellate court upheld the jury's
finding that the medical school retaliated against Dr. Nassar. The court
noted: "Since credibility determinations, the weighing of the evidence, and
the drawing of legitimate inferences from the facts are jury functions, not
those of a judge, we find no basis to upset the jury's verdict that UTSW retaliated against Nassar because of his complaints of racial discrimination."[16]
Thereafter, the medical school appealed the case to the U.S. Supreme Court.

In its decision, the Supreme Court decided the meaning of Title VII's
retaliation provision. That provision provides: "It shall be an unlawful employment practice for an employer to discriminate against any of

his employees ... because he has opposed any practice made an unlawful employment practice ...."[17] The Court had a choice. It could find that
Dr. Nassar established retaliation if his complaint about discrimination
played a motivating factor in the medical school's decision to ask the hospital to rescind the offer. This reading of the statute would be consistent with
the Supreme Court's prior decision in the *Price Waterhouse* case, which had
held that a worker can prevail in a Title VII discrimination case by establishing a protected trait was a motivating factor in a negative employment decision. Alternatively, the Supreme Court could reject the reasoning in *Price
Waterhouse* and choose to require "but for" causation. As we discussed in
Chapter 5, the but for cause standard makes it more difficult for a worker to
win a case when multiple factors impacted an employer's decision.

The Supreme Court chose to depart from *Price Waterhouse* and decided
that workers are required to meet the higher but for cause standard. The
Court stated that it chose the more employer-friendly causation standard
because to do otherwise would be to "contribute to the filing of frivolous
claims, which would siphon resources from efforts by employers, administrative agencies, and courts to combat workplace harassment."[18] It was
concerned that employees who become aware of a pending negative
employment action may be tempted to raise unfounded discrimination
claims to create a false retaliation claim. The Court provided an example
of the kind of person who could be able to take advantage of a lower causal
standard. Writing for the majority, Justice Kennedy hypothesized:

Consider in this regard the case of an employee who knows that he
or she is about to be fired for poor performance, given a lower pay
grade, or even just transferred to a different assignment or location.
To forestall that lawful action, he or she might be tempted to make an
unfounded charge of racial, sexual, or religious discrimination; then,
when the unrelated employment action comes, the employee could
allege that it is retaliation. If respondent were to prevail in his argument here, that claim could be established by a lessened causation
standard, all in order to prevent the undesired change in employment
circumstances. Even if the employer could escape judgment after trial,

the lessened causation standard would make it far more difficult to dismiss dubious claims at the summary judgment stage. It would be inconsistent with the structure and operation of Title VII to so raise the costs, both financial and reputational, on an employer whose actions were not in fact the result of any discriminatory or retaliatory intent.[19]

Nassar is striking because the Supreme Court used the possibility of false claims to decide to make it harder for all workers to establish retaliation. The fear of too many fraudulent suits outweighed the interests of legitimate claims. After *Nassar*, judges are able to dismiss cases in which employers retaliated against workers, so long as the employer also took another non-discriminatory factor into account when making decisions. As a result, some workers who faced retaliation will find themselves without a claim because of this higher legal standard. In her dissenting opinion, which was joined by three other Justices, Justice Ruth Bader Ginsburg noted the majority's "zeal to reduce the number of retaliation claims filed against employers" apparently drove the Court's holding in favor of the more onerous causation standard.[20] Since *Nassar*, several courts have cited Justice Kennedy's hypothetical in *Nassar* to justify limiting the reach of retaliation claims.[21]

By choosing the but for standard to address fakers and floodgates concerns, the *Nassar* Court chose a blunt instrument to address its underlying concerns and did not balance the concerns of workers who bring legitimate claims. The only interests that mattered were the employers' interests in avoiding litigation and the court system's interest in avoiding a flood of fake cases. While the new reading of the substantive law possibly may limit or deter lawyers from filing frivolous claims, it may also limit and deter them from filing certain legitimate claims.

3. FLOODGATES?

If false discrimination claims flooded the courthouses, there would be good reasons to restrict discrimination law. However, the data does not support the "fakers and floodgates" argument. First, the federal courts are not flooded with discrimination suits.

Instead of a floodgate of employment discrimination litigation, the empirical data shows a decline in the number of civil rights employment cases brought in federal court. While the federal courts witnessed a large increase in the number of these claims filed in federal court between 1990 and 1997,[22] in the last decade, the courts have seen fewer discrimination claims in both raw numbers and as a percentage of their docket.

The Federal Judicial Center, the research agency for the federal courts, maintains data regarding the type and number of cases filed in United States district courts. In the twelve-month period ending March 2003, 20,782 civil rights employment cases were filed.[23] This number steadily declined over time to result in only 12,665 of such cases filed in the twelve-month period ending in December of 2013.[24]

The shrinking number of civil rights employment cases has additional significance when compared to the total civil caseload of federal district courts. While the number of federal cases is growing, the number of employment discrimination cases in federal courts is shrinking. In the twelve-month period ending in March 2003, 256,858 civil cases were filed in federal district court;[25] the number increased to 292,912 cases by the end of 2013.[26]

The number of federal civil rights claims is also not significant when compared to the total number of people in the workforce. In the twelve-month period ending in March 2013, only 12,665 cases were filed[27] in comparison to 143,929,000 people employed in the civilian workforce.[28] In other words, only a tiny fraction of the workforce files a discrimination suit in any given year.[29]

Although the data shows that discrimination claims do not clog the federal courts, the Supreme Court relied on this argument in *Nassar* to support its legal analysis. It appears that the Court did not consider this publicly available information before it made its argument that discrimination claims flood the courts.

4. FAKERS?

In *Nassar*, in addition to the floodgates argument, the Court also stated that retaliation must be made harder to prove to prevent frivolous lawsuits.

This combined fakers and floodgates argument depends on the underlying assumption that a significant number of employees make false allegations. Once again, no data supports this argument.

The majority opinion in *Nassar* cited no empirical or other data regarding the number or likelihood of false cases. It did not provide any information about the costs incurred by the courts, the EEOC, or employers because of these allegedly false claims. The Court also did not provide any examples of cases where workers presented false claims. If the federal courts were flooded with these false claims, it should be easy to provide evidence of them.

The *Nassar* case itself does not appear to present a spurious claim. In *Nassar*, the jury found that the employer retaliated against Dr. Nassar, and the appellate court affirmed that decision.[30] Moreover, some Supreme Court Justices would have affirmed the decision.

In the *Nassar* case, Justice Kennedy and the rest of the majority posited that a worker would be deterred from filing a false claim if the causation standard for retaliation claims was more onerous. To agree with this deterrence argument, you must first believe that a large number of employees want to file fake claims. You must also believe that a substantial number of employees understand discrimination and retaliation law, including that the law protects complaints of discrimination. Because of the required close connection between the employee's complaint and the employer's action, these same employees would also need to complain in the right time period, knowing that their employers soon intended to take some negative employment actions against them.

Additionally, as discussed in Chapter 1, the discrimination statutes require the employee to file a charge of discrimination and/or retaliation with an administrative agency, such as the EEOC. A person who wants to file a fake claim must be motivated enough to go through this administrative process. Moreover, because people who sign charges of discrimination swear that their claims are true, they subject themselves to criminal perjury charges if the claims are false. Employees also must then find an attorney to take their case to court or figure out how to file one on their own. The employee must also pay filing fees to bring a case. If the worker is dishonest in court, he again subjects himself to possible criminal charges.

Available social science evidence does not support any significant faker problem. Instead, it actually shows that employees are reluctant to believe that their employers discriminated against them. In circumstances when they believe discrimination has occurred, they are reluctant to complain to their employer, the EEOC, or a state agency. People can be reticent to make discrimination claims because they may fear retaliation.[31] Employees' hesitancy to believe discrimination has occurred and to make claims is illustrated by Professor Deborah Brake and Joanna Grossman's work. They have shown that only a small percentage of women who experience harassment in the workplace file a formal complaint with their employer.[32]

After *Nassar*, it is more difficult for all workers to prove retaliation. The Supreme Court was willing to make it harder to prove retaliation cases based on the speculative concern that there are fake cases flooding the courts. The Supreme Court never stated how many of these fake claims there were. It did not even balance the interests of the honest claimants against the alleged fakers. Most important, the Supreme Court did not consider whether its new standard would carry out Congress's intent—that is, to protect workers who complain about discrimination.

Unfortunately, after *Nassar*, the fakers and floodgates myth has grown stronger. In court, employers have relied on *Nassar* for the idea that workers are making frivolous claims.[33] Moreover, many lower court judges have quoted *Nassar* in support of this idea.[34] Despite the lack of empirical support for the Supreme Court's fakers and floodgates argument, lower courts have relied on the Supreme Court's assertion about floodgates and fakers as fact.

When judges in discrimination cases use a fakers and floodgates argument to limit substantive law, they fail to recognize that this argument was also used to justify many of the current sanctions and other limits on cases.[35] The rallying cry of frivolous cases has been invoked to justify procedural limits on claims, sanctioning mechanisms, and damages caps. Some of these ways for judges to limit frivolous claims are discussed in the next section.

5. PUNISH ANY FAKERS

There is another reason to be skeptical of the fakers and floodgates argument. Federal judges already possess a wide range of tools to stop fake claims that are brought under any law and to punish those who bring them. And there is no evidence that these devices do not work for discrimination cases.

If a lawyer or unrepresented party files a claim that is, for example, not supported by facts, the defendant's lawyer can ask the plaintiff's lawyer or the unrepresented party to withdraw the offending document. If the plaintiff's lawyer or party does not withdraw the case, the opposing lawyer can file a motion for sanctions, and the judge can require the lawyer, law firm, or party to pay sanctions.[36] The judge also can penalize any lawyer who files false claims. For example, the judge can refer attorneys who file false claims to bar authorities for sanctions, and federal courts may revoke the ability of an attorney to appear before the court. Attorneys also may be sanctioned pursuant to a federal statute for needlessly increasing litigation costs.[37]

When a plaintiff herself engages in misconduct during the suit, the court also has additional ways to sanction that misconduct, such as monetary sanctions, striking the plaintiff's pleadings, or dismissing the case.[38] If a litigant lies or fails to follow a court's order, the judge can hold litigants or their attorneys in contempt of court and send them to jail.

Outside of specific sanctions mechanisms, courts possess inherent authority to manage cases to limit costs.[39] Moreover, the federal discrimination statutes themselves contain a provision to help limit false claims. If a worker brings a meritless claim in court, the court can require the worker to pay all of the employer's attorney's fees.[40]

Additionally, as discussed in Chapter 1, Congress already placed significant limits on discrimination claims that would tend to deter workers who lack legitimate claims. Each of the federal discrimination statutes either contains damages caps or significantly limits the types of damages that a worker can recover.[41] The United States Court of Appeals for the Second Circuit has noted that the purpose of the damages cap in Title VII "is to deter frivolous lawsuits."[42]

Requiring workers to go to an administrative agency before filing a lawsuit can also makes it difficult for frivolous cases to advance. The claim must be filed promptly. Also, while the agency cannot prevent the claim from going to court based on the legitimacy of the claim, it can find that the claim lacks reasonable cause to believe discrimination occurred. In some courts, evidence of the agency's determination would be admissible in later court proceedings. Additionally, workers who submit a charge of discrimination to an administrative agency must sign that document under oath or affirmation and thus are subject to penalties for lying.[43]

The Supreme Court failed to recognize this arsenal of powerful tools to prevent false claims and to punish those who bring them and instead decided the substantive law required change to prevent future spurious claims.

Also relevant to this argument is how the Supreme Court treats potential misconduct by employers. In *St. Mary's Honor Center v. Hicks*, the Court was faced with a case in which the district court judge determined that the employer had provided false reasons for its decisions to demote and dismiss a worker.[44] Instead of changing the law to make it harder for employers to win cases, the Court held that the normal process of litigation could resolve the problem. First, the Court recognized that civil and criminal penalties exist for perjury.[45] Second, the Court noted that fact-finders could determine whether the employer was telling the truth or not.[46] Third, the Court expressed that courts should be cautious about concluding that the employer intentionally provided false evidence.[47] The Court emphasized that discrimination cases often involve complex determinations about actors' state of mind, and the employer must often rely on information provided to it by low-level employees.[48] The Court indicated that it was "absurd" to paint all employers who presented unpersuasive testimony as liars or perjurers.[49]

The Supreme Court believes that courts can handle employer misconduct during litigation without changing substantive law. Judges can use their sanctioning authority, or courts can allow the case to go to trial and let the jury decide who is telling the truth and who is not. As described here, similar mechanisms exist to handle employee false claims.

6. FAKERS, FLOODGATES, AND SUMMARY JUDGMENT

Some might argue that because federal judges dismiss so many cases at summary judgment, these dismissals are evidence that workers are bringing false claims. However, as shown throughout this book, when a judge grants judgment in an employer's favor, there is frequently evidence of discriminatory or retaliatory bias in the workplace. Such cases are often dismissed on summary judgment because of the many court-created doctrines that favor employers and do not necessarily reflect a lack of discriminatory treatment.

The jurisprudence distorts how judges are directed to think about discrimination claims. For example, courts have stated a negative performance review, being denied training opportunities, and a supervisor threatening to fire an employee are not serious enough to be discrimination. One court has noted that negative evaluations are "decisions having no immediate effect upon employment."[50] Some courts find that formal negative actions taken against employees are just a "mere inconvenience."[51] Courts find that actions such as negative employment evaluations are not harmful even though the court recognizes that the negative information in an employment file may hurt the worker in the future.[52]

Judges also make similar claims about harm in the harassment context. In one case, discussed earlier in the book, when a worker returned from maternity leave, she alleged that one of her direct supervisors grabbed her breast and said that "the baby gave you big juicy tits and a big ass."[53] Because the worker alleged that her breast was grabbed only once, the court reasoned that what happened to her was not "extremely serious."[54] The court then cited the general mantra that Title VII does not impose a "general civility code for the American workplace."[55]

As discussed in Chapter 3, according to some judges, a worker suffers no harm when a supervisor repeatedly uses racial epithets, or when there is evidence her supervisor regularly calls her and other women in the workplace "bitch," "cunt," and "whore."

In each of these contexts, discrimination may have occurred. Some judges will dismiss these cases even when the law might provide other limits on the cases. For example, a worker subjected to less egregious conduct would likely obtain more limited damages. These dismissals often reflect the court-created discrimination law rather than evidence that a worker's race, sex, or other protected trait(s) did not play a role in the negative employment decision. Thus, dismissals in these cases do not suggest that a worker brought a false claim.

It may be difficult to understand exactly why judges argue that courts are flooded with fake claims. Chapter 7 explored the possibility of political bias. It also may be that many federal judges' general understanding about work is different than the understanding of other workers. Federal judges are appointed for life and enjoy the kind of job security that most American workers do not. They have more power than the average worker and make more money than those workers. For a federal judge who has been on the bench for some time, likely will never receive an evaluation again, and does not face the prospect of being fired except in extreme circumstances, understanding the impact of a negative evaluation or similar action on employees may be a challenging task.

7. CONCLUDING THOUGHTS

Unfortunately, the fakers and floodgates claim and the doctrines that are embedded in discrimination jurisprudence prevent judges from having more important conversations about discrimination law, including discussions about cost.

It can be expensive for employers to defend against discrimination cases. If a case does not settle quickly, the employer pays its attorneys to file motions and to otherwise defend the case. Presently, there is no readily available public data about how much it costs employers to defend against discrimination cases. Additionally, there is no data about how those costs compare to other suits and what creates any increased costs of discrimination suits.

Actual data is required to have a serious conversation about the costs of discrimination suits. The conversation cannot end there. Costs must be balanced with other values, such as the right to a jury trial and providing an effective antidiscrimination regime. It is difficult to engage in these conversations when courts are willing to accept, without evidence, the fakers and floodgates narrative.

Why Workers Lose

There are multiple reasons why discrimination law favors employers. As discussed in Chapter 7, political bias likely plays a role in some cases, but it does not completely explain what is happening. As examined in Chapter 8, another factor is judges' willingness to dismiss claims because of arguments about fakers and floodgates, even if those arguments are unsupported.

Chapters 2 through 6 discussed how the courts created a complex set of doctrines and frameworks for evaluating discrimination cases that are far removed from the text and the purpose of the discrimination statutes that Congress passed. Each of these doctrines pushes cases toward dismissal. However, a larger problem is what happens when all of these doctrines work together.

The doctrines and frameworks encourage judges to think about discrimination cases out of context by prompting judges to "slice and dice" cases. Using the doctrines and frameworks, many judges will divide the evidence and not look at the evidence as part of a unified whole. The various frameworks, rules, and inferences exclude evidence of discrimination or diminish its importance.

In addition to slicing and dicing, the doctrines and frameworks encourage judges to view discrimination as a series of technical hurdles. As a result, on employers' motions for summary judgment or judgment as a matter of law, many judges use a rote sorting process, asking a predetermined series of questions that lead to an answer. Through this process, many judges appear to decide discrimination cases without much thought on whether discrimination actually occurred.

Indeed, it is not clear whether this body of discrimination law answers the central question in most discrimination cases—that is, was the worker treated differently because of a protected trait? Under this law, judges can become bogged down in questions that do not help us determine whether discrimination occurred, such as what the frameworks require, how the frameworks intersect with each other, or how the various sub-rules and inferences work or fit into the larger body of jurisprudence. Moreover, no judicial opinion has explained how all of these rules, inferences, doctrines, and frameworks work together.

The frameworks and supporting rules and inferences also encourage judges to sit as super-jurors to evaluate the facts of cases. Because many rules require judges to answer threshold questions, such as whether a remark is connected to a decision, before a suit may proceed to trial, the rules give a court permission to make factual judgments that favor the employer.

Finally, the available written case law strongly favors employers. When judges dismiss a case, they often write a lengthy decision explaining why and using the frameworks and doctrines discussed throughout this book. However, when a judge decides to let a case go to trial, those decisions are often shorter or even issued from the bench and not written at all. As a result, judges have an abundance of decisions that favor employers.

1. SLICE AND DICE

All of the discrimination frameworks, inferences, and rules make it easy to "slice and dice" a case.[1] "Slice and dice" means that when a judge is considering whether to dismiss a case, the judge will divide and subdivide the worker's evidence. By breaking down the worker's case, the judge can view the evidence in separate silos. With slicing and dicing, judges use various doctrines to dismiss or diminish the importance of the evidence. The judge sometimes does not consider the totality of the worker's evidence, in which case the lawsuit may be more easily dismissed.

This slicing and dicing is different from how a jury would consider the facts of a case. When a case makes it to the jury, the jury considers evidence that is presented as a whole.[2]

In one case that was sliced and diced, an African American employee alleged that he was fired because of his race and in retaliation for filing a discrimination suit.[3] In the first suit, the worker alleged that he was subject to racial harassment for years, including "being threatened with a hanging noose and being threatened with having a cross burned in his yard."[4] He also claimed that the company learned of the harassment but refused to take action. The litigation ended in a settlement.[5]

After the lawsuit ended, the worker alleged that the general manager of his plant treated him differently than workers who had not filed suit.[6] The worker filed an internal grievance against this manager and also notified the EEOC.[7] The employee later filed another grievance against a supervisor alleging that the supervisor was treating him in a hostile manner because of his complaints.[8]

One day, the supervisor approached the worker and told him to clean up a mess near the employee's work area. According to the worker, he informed the supervisor that it was not in his job function to perform that kind of work.[9] The company then fired him.

The worker was covered by a collective bargaining agreement, and he pursued arbitration to determine whether the company's decision to fire him complied with the terms of the union contract. According to the worker, the arbitrator ordered reinstatement, because the employer did not have an appropriate reason to fire him.[10]

In support of his second court case alleging discrimination and retaliation, the worker presented a sworn statement from a white former employee who had served as a foreman. In his sworn statement, the foreman said the supervisor was "extremely racially offensive" and used "offensive slurs toward black employees, calling them 'n*****s' and 'Black mother f***ers.'"[11] The foreman stated that the supervisor said black employees "were generally lazy and 'Good for nothing.'"[12] Moreover, he stated that the supervisor always treated black employees more harshly than white employees.[13]

According to the court, the foreman's affidavit stated that the supervisor "seemed to single out Plaintiff for his racially based rage."[14] The foreman stated that the supervisor was angry about the worker's prior lawsuit,[15] and he further testified that the supervisor said the worker "is nothing but a f***ing n****r" and "I am going to get rid of him."[16] The foreman noted that the supervisor "wanted to throw Plaintiff in the pulper and string him up."[17] The worker also submitted affidavits from two other workers supporting his claims.

The company moved for summary judgment and submitted evidence suggesting the worker had been fired for refusing to follow the supervisor's order to clean up the mess. The district court judge proceeded to dismiss both of the worker's claims.

The judge first considered whether the worker had direct evidence of discrimination. With very little discussion, the judge ruled there was no direct evidence.[18] The judge also analyzed the facts using the *McDonnell Douglas* framework. Under this framework, once the employee showed a prima facie case, which he did, the employer was required to articulate a legitimate reason for its decision to fire the worker—in this case, the worker's insubordination in refusing to clean up the mess. Once the employer had produced this reason, the judge stated that the law required the worker to "produce sufficient evidence from which the jury may reasonably reject the employer's explanation."[19]

Using the honest belief doctrine, the judge stated that if an employer

honestly, albeit mistakenly, believes in the non-discriminatory reason it relied upon in making its employment decision, then the employer ... lacks the necessary discriminatory intent. [A]rguing about the accuracy of the employer's assessment is a distraction because the question is not whether the employer's reasons for [an adverse employment] decision are *right* but whether the employer's description of its reasons is *honest*.[20]

The judge believed the employer's reason for firing the worker (i.e., the company fired the worker for insubordination) even though the arbitrator had previously found differently (i.e., the company fired the worker without cause).[21]

The judge then implicitly used causation to justify his decision, noting that the general manager, not the supervisor who had allegedly made the racist comments, decided to fire the worker.[22]

The judge proceeded to use the stray remarks doctrine to diminish the importance of the alleged statements to which the white foreman had sworn. The court noted that the statements in the affidavit were "troubling if true," but the statements do not show racial animus by the decision maker at the relevant time.[23] The court likewise downplayed the testimony of the other employees who had supported the worker's claim.[24]

The judge then turned to the retaliation claim. With very little discussion, the court found that the worker did not have any evidence that the company terminated him in retaliation for reporting discriminatory conduct. The worker appealed the case, and the federal appellate court affirmed the dismissal.[25]

The worker had evidence that a supervisor repeatedly referred to black employees using racial epithets and stereotypes, that the same supervisor used that kind of language when referring to him, and that the supervisor was angry about a race discrimination suit that the employee had filed. The worker had evidence that the supervisor said he was going to get rid of the worker, and indeed, the worker was fired for what could be characterized as a minor incident. Additionally, an arbitrator determined that the company did not have cause to fire the employee. Yet by using all of the doctrines and rules that govern discrimination law, a judge was able to say that the case must be dismissed because none of this evidence showed discrimination or retaliation.

2. TECHNICAL HURDLES

Discrimination law also encourages judges to think about discrimination as a series of technical hurdles that a worker must successfully navigate to prevail on a claim. Many workers suffer harm that reasonable people would call discrimination, yet courts have established several doctrines that allow courts to dismiss these claims. The central question in discrimination law is no longer whether a worker suffered discrimination. It is whether the worker can overcome all of the court-created doctrines.

Even the easiest kinds of cases must cross the hurdles. Say a worker's supervisor calls him racist names and then gives him a bad evaluation, claiming the worker engaged in misconduct that the worker denies. This supervisor then recommends to the human resources department that the employee be fired, and the employer proceeds to fire the worker based on the supervisor's recommendation.

The words of the discrimination statutes along with the applicable federal rules require the judge to answer a fairly simple question. Is there enough evidence of discrimination to send this case to the jury? Moreover, if an employer asks a judge to dismiss a case under the rules and the applicable case law, the judge must believe all of the evidence submitted by the worker and must draw all reasonable inferences in the worker's favor.

However, a federal judge is unlikely to view the inquiry as being a simple one. Some of the questions a court might ask to determine whether this case goes to the jury include the following. Did the supervisor call the worker racist names enough times for this to be severe or pervasive harassment? Is the bad evaluation an adverse action? Do the racist comments count as direct evidence of discrimination? Can the worker establish a prima facie case of discrimination under the *McDonnell Douglas* framework? Can the employer articulate a legitimate, nondiscriminatory reason for its conduct? Can the worker establish that the employer's articulated reason is a pretext for discrimination? Are the supervisor's comments stray remarks? Did the employer have an honest belief that the worker engaged in the misconduct? Did the supervisor engage in positive conduct toward the worker such that the same actor inference would apply? Can the court apply a cat's paw theory to this case? Is the worker required to establish that the human resources department personnel had animus as well? Even if the worker can establish harassment, does the agency analysis preclude liability for the employer?

After answering all of these questions, a judge has engaged in a lengthy analysis. The length and the complexity of the judge's analysis suggest that the judge has made a searching inquiry about whether discrimination happened. However, it is not clear that answering these questions helps judges determine whether discrimination occurred.

These frameworks and all of the supporting rules and inferences also tend to bog courts down in technical questions about what the courts meant when they initially created the rules. What is an "adverse action"? When is conduct "severe or pervasive"? How does the "but for" cause standard intersect with the *McDonnell Douglas* test?

The sheer number of frameworks, rules, and inferences means there is often at least one reason a judge may use to justify dismissing a case. Using our example, the judge can declare the racist comments to be stray remarks. Construed this way, the comments no longer count as discrimination. The court can also use the honest belief doctrine to declare that the employer honestly, if mistakenly, believed that the employee engaged in the misconduct. Moreover, the court can find that the worker has not shown a close enough link between the supervisor's comments and the employee's termination to prove discrimination was the reason for the termination. There are so many different ways for a court to dismiss a case. Courts use the adverse action doctrine, the stray remarks doctrine, the reasonable belief doctrine, causation, and a whole host of other doctrines to limit the reach of discrimination law. The only way a worker tries his case before a jury is by overcoming all of these hurdles.

The courts have piled on court-created doctrines that limit claims despite the fact that Congress already substantially limited discrimination claims through express statutory language. The statutes require workers to go to an administrative agency before going to court, and they set forth short time deadlines for filing suit, and both factors curtail workers' ability to move forward with their claims. Some regimes also limit the kinds of damages that a worker can receive. The court-created doctrines thus further limit a discrimination regime where Congress has already determined appropriate ways to balance the interests of workers and employers.

3. SUPER-JURORS

Discrimination law also encourages judges to act as super-jurors. Our constitutional system gives two different groups power in litigation—judges and juries. Judges are supposed to determine the law. In a case where a statute governs, judges are responsible for interpreting what the statutes mean. Juries are supposed to determine the facts.

To maintain the balance of power between judges and juries, procedural rules dictate when judges are allowed to dismiss cases. Judges are not supposed to resolve factual disputes or weigh the credibility of witnesses. If the employer asks the judge to dismiss a case, the judge is supposed to bend over backwards to draw all inferences in favor of the worker. Under the procedural rules that govern litigation, judges are supposed to dismiss cases only when no reasonable jury could rule in the worker's favor.[26] If there are fact disputes, the cases go to a jury. In case after case, however, federal judges assume the role of the jury by determining factual questions, and they defy procedural rules by drawing inferences for employers.

Many of the court-created discrimination rules and doctrines allow or encourage judges to usurp the jury's function. Moreover, most of the discrimination doctrines make choices about which party to favor—the employee or the employer—overwhelmingly telling courts to favor employers.

One of the most egregious examples of this is the same actor inference. If a person makes a positive employment decision about a worker and later that same person makes a negative employment decision about the worker, the same actor inference allows the courts to infer that this person would make decisions in accordance with his past positive actions toward the employee, and thus the negative action was made with no discriminatory intent. The inference automatically favors the employer, regardless of the facts. When an employer moves for summary judgment, although a judge is required to draw inferences in favor of the worker, some judges nonetheless repeatedly invoke the same actor inference to justify dismissing workers' cases at the summary judgment stage and have even used it to overrule jury verdicts.

There are yet more examples of inferences that lead a judge to draw pro-employer conclusions. The honest belief doctrine encourages courts to believe the employer's reasons for acting, even when their reasons are dubious, inconsistent, and mistaken. The stray remarks doctrine tells judges that they have the power to determine whether comments or conduct should count as evidence of discrimination. It encourages judges to parse the facts of a case, declaring that certain facts are not important. When these facts are not counted, it always hurts the employee's case and helps the employer's case.

Judges do not need any of these doctrines to properly perform their gatekeeping function. If the worker presents no evidence of discrimination, then the judge can properly dismiss the case. The problem with each of these doctrines is that they are most often invoked when there is evidence of potential discrimination.

In cases where judges invoke the stray remarks doctrine, the same actor inference, or the honest belief doctrine, the worker has usually presented evidence of comments or conduct that might reasonably be considered to be evidence of discrimination. But judges use the stray remarks doctrine to say the evidence of discrimination does not count as evidence at all, and they use the same actor inference and the honest belief doctrine to find that the employer's version of events trumps the worker's version.

Several of the employment doctrines also encourage judges to transform fact issues into legal questions. Let's take for example a case in which a supervisor regularly refers to a female employee as a "cunt," a "bitch," and a "whore." The supervisor then promotes a man over the female employee. Most reasonable people would concede that there is a question of fact about whether the supervisor discriminated against the female employee because of her sex. Yet the stray remarks doctrine allows a court to transform this factual question into a legal question, thus keeping the matter away from the jury. Courts assess whether they think certain evidence is relevant to the underlying lawsuit. The court can declare that the use of the sexist language is not relevant because it may have occurred a month ago. The court can assert that this is a legal question, and accordingly, it is not usurping the jury's functions when it excludes these facts under the stray remarks doctrine. The jury should never get a chance to consider them. Therefore, there is no question of fact for the jury to resolve.

This same phenomenon happens when courts consider whether harassment is "severe or pervasive" enough to constitute harassment or whether an employer's action is an "adverse action." The text of the statutes provides that actions are sufficiently serious to be discrimination if they negatively affect the terms, conditions, or privileges of employment or if they limit or deprive an employee of opportunities or tend to deprive them of such opportunities.

Courts must determine whether the alleged conduct does not reach the required level. In such cases, it would be appropriate for a court to dismiss a case. Judges have gone far beyond this legitimate role. Instead, many judges will carefully parse the facts of the cases to make fine-grained determinations about whether conduct is serious enough or not. A judge is engaging in such a factual analysis when, for example, he claims that a supervisor brushing against a woman's breast is not serious enough to be harassment, but grabbing her breast is. He is characterizing the manner and in some respects the intent with which the supervisor engaged in the conduct. Brushing up sounds accidental, while grabbing does not. This is the type of factual matter that the jury is supposed to decide.

Using the causation doctrine, courts also transform factual questions into legal ones. When courts claim that a racist supervisor's input into a decision to fire an employee was irrelevant given the human resources department's subsequent investigation of alleged misconduct, the court has determined what happened factually.

By turning fact questions into legal questions, courts can dismiss cases and keep them away from juries. They also are able to use these tools to overturn jury verdicts. By doing this, courts can declare a wide range of racist and sexist comments and conduct does not count as discrimination.

In some cases, judges remind their colleagues about their appropriate limited constitutional role. One appellate court noted that courts should approach summary judgment motions in discrimination cases "with special caution."[27] One district court judge opined that "summary judgment must be granted only with caution in employment discrimination cases, especially those that turn on the employer's intent."[28] Another appellate court stated that "[i]nquiries regarding what actually motivated an employer's decision are very fact intensive, [and] such issues will generally be difficult to determine at the summary judgment stage and thus will typically require sending the case to the jury."[29]

Concerns about the balance of power between judges and juries are especially weighty after a jury trial. As one judge noted, Title VII does not "authorize federal judges to become super-jurors, weighing evidence and drawing independent conclusions regarding the ultimate question of discrimination."[30] The judge continued by noting that "acknowledging that the merits of [a] case are debatable is a far cry from holding that no rational person could agree with the jury's conclusion."[31] Yet, time after time, judges dismiss cases where there is evidence suggesting that discrimination happened. Whether intentionally or not, federal judges have become super-jurors, usurping the jury's function.

4. LOSER'S RULES

The way that judges rule on motions leads to a system that former United States District Court judge Nancy Gertner calls "loser's rules."[32] As discussed in Chapter 2, judges dismiss many employment discrimination cases at the summary judgment stage or at other procedural junctures. When judges dismiss cases, the federal rules require the judge to provide the reasons for dismissing the case. Federal judges often draft a written opinion, detailing all of the reasons why the employer should win the case and the worker should lose.

When a judge allows a case to go to trial, the written decision may be less detailed than the decision to dismiss a case, or there may be no written decision at all. Moreover, when a jury decides a case, there is likely no written record regarding why the jury ruled in a particular party's favor. This dynamic leads to "loser's rules." Most of the written law generated at the district court level is pro-employer because the orders dismissing cases receive more written attention than the orders allowing cases to go to jury trial.

There is another aspect of loser's rules. When federal judges dismiss cases, they are effectively declaring who wins the case and who does not. When they allow a case to go to trial, they are not declaring winners or losers; instead, the jury will find in favor of the worker or the employer. Given this dynamic, written orders that allow cases to go to the jury do not declare that discrimination happened. They simply state that there is possible evidence of discrimination, allowing the case to go to trial.

When judges grant summary judgment, they often declare that no discrimination occurred, given the facts. There is a large body of written law that declares what is not discrimination. There is a smaller body of law that describes what discrimination is, and this body of law is more tentative. Judges who allow cases to go to trial only need to find that discrimination "might" have happened.

When cases are appealed, the appellate judges are often asked to determine whether the trial court judge correctly dismissed the case. When appellate courts affirm these dismissals, they too must declare that no discrimination occurred. They declare that under a given set of facts, there is no way a reasonable juror could have found discrimination. While some appellate decisions reverse the decision ordering summary judgment or judgment as a matter of law and thus may have language favorable for employees, these decisions are not common. There is more written law that favors employers.

Employment discrimination law is crushed under the weight of all the judicial frameworks, doctrines, and inferences that push the law in a pro-employer direction. Although the doctrines are individually objectionable, when put together, they significantly diminish the chances that workers' claims will ever make it to a jury.

The Future of Discrimination Law

The words of the federal discrimination laws explicitly prohibit discrimination. Over time, however, federal judges have created a system of frameworks, rules, and inferences that distract them away from the central question of discrimination law and push cases toward dismissal.

This chapter discusses ways to ensure that the courts robustly enforce the federal antidiscrimination mandates. In this chapter, we set forth measures legislatures, the EEOC, the judiciary, litigants, companies, and citizens can take to introduce more neutrality into discrimination law.

1. CHANGE IS NEEDED

We need to change federal discrimination law now because federal judges have created a body of discrimination law that does not determine whether an employer discriminated against a worker. Judges dismiss cases where there is evidence that supervisors referred to workers using racial or sexist epithets. Judges dismiss cases where supervisors repeatedly touch workers in sexual ways. Judges dismiss cases where employers acted against the employee on the basis of the workers' protected trait by giving them bad evaluations, transferring them, or threatening to fire them.

The reasoning in the cases also shows how courts are making judgment calls that belong with juries. In one case, for example, an African-American cocktail waitress alleged that her supervisor called her a "porch monkey." The trial court judge found that the worker's case must be dismissed as a matter of law because two racial epithets were not enough to create a hostile work environment.[1]

Upon the worker's appeal, a three-judge panel upheld the trial court's decision, finding the worker had no claim.[2] Thereafter, the full appeals court heard the case and disagreed with the other appellate court and the lower court. It held that the worker could proceed with her claim.[3] The court thought that the use of the term "porch monkey" twice, if proven, could lead to liability for harassment under federal law. One court noted that "[p]erhaps no single act can more quickly alter the conditions of employment and create an abusive working environment than the use of an unambiguously racial epithet . . . by a supervisor."[4] Whether a worker's case survives depends on the trial court and the appellate court judges who hear the case. Many of these judges are willing to make factual determinations that racial epithets are not serious enough to constitute discrimination. As shown throughout this book, judges inappropriately make these judgment calls in many discrimination cases and in many different contexts.

More important, change is more generally necessary because the law that is applied in the courtroom is more and more out of step with what the text of the federal discrimination statutes protects.

2. CONGRESS

Thus far, Congress has played an important role in enforcing discrimination law through congressional override. Congress has responded to numerous Supreme Court decisions that narrowed the reach of discrimination law by amending the discrimination statutes to clarify their broad, remedial purposes. There are four ways in which Congress can and should amend the discrimination statutes to clarify the law and further enforce discrimination law.

   (1) Congress should make it clear that workers are not required
       to establish "but for" cause to prevail on any discrimination or
       retaliation claim.

(2) Congress should significantly restrict the "honest-belief" rule and should abolish the stray remarks doctrine and the same-actor inference.

(3) Congress should amend Title VII, the ADEA, and Section 1981 to direct courts to interpret them liberally.

(4) Congress should clarify what it means to discriminate against a person in the terms, conditions, or privileges of employment.

1. Address Causation. One way to correct discrimination law is to fix the doctrines that create the most problems in the enforcement of the law. Because causation plays such a central role in discrimination analysis, it is important to remedy the issues related to it. To address the Supreme Court's retrenchment of the mixed-motive analysis, Congress should amend the ADEA (Age Discrimination in Employment Act), the ADA (Americans with Disabilities Act), and all retaliation provisions to permit a worker to prevail by showing that a protected trait was a motivating factor in an employment decision. As we discussed earlier in the book, courts limit age discrimination and retaliation claims by requiring workers to establish "but for" cause. There is no reason for the courts to require workers alleging age discrimination or retaliation to meet a higher causal burden than those alleging sex or race discrimination. More important, the but for cause standard improperly allows judges to dismiss cases where age or retaliatory motive played a role in a negative employment decision. There has already been some congressional support for expanding the mixed-motive analysis to age and retaliation cases. In prior years, Congress considered, but did not pass, the Protecting Older Workers Against Discrimination Act (POWADA).[5] POWADA would make the causation standard for age discrimination, disability, and retaliation claims the same as it is for race and sex discrimination claims.

2. Abolish or Modify Rules and Inferences. Congress should change or abolish many of the court-created doctrines discussed in Chapter 4. Each of these doctrines contradicts the rules that govern litigation. When an employer asks a court to dismiss a case, the litigation rules require the court to look at the evidence in the light most favorable to the worker. On the other hand, each of the doctrines discussed in this book allows a court to look at the facts in a way that favors the employer.

Congress should abolish the stray remarks doctrine under which courts decide that certain remarks are not relevant to the claim of discrimination because the remarks were remote in time or otherwise exceptional. That doctrine allows judges to declare potential evidence of discrimination is not evidence of discrimination. Employment discrimination law does not need a separate, special evidentiary doctrine. If a piece of evidence possibly shows discrimination, the entity tasked with finding facts should determine whether it does or does not evince discrimination. If a comment is completely irrelevant to the underlying claim, the judge can disregard that comment and does not need a special doctrine to do so. However, where a comment is arguably relevant when, for example, a decision maker has made the comment, the jury should determine whether the evidence supports a finding of discrimination.

Congress also should eliminate the same-actor inference. This doctrine allows a judge to infer that a supervisor who made a positive employment decision about a worker did not discriminate if that same supervisor later takes a negative action against the worker. For a variety of reasons, the same actor may later discriminate against a person whom he hired. For example, the employee may not fit the stereotypical role that the supervisor envisioned for the employee, or the supervisor might think that women or people of color are good entry-level employees but are not good managers. The fact-finder should be able to consider all facts—including that the same actor made the decision—when deciding whether discrimination occurred.

Finally, Congress should significantly restrict the "honest-belief" rule. Under this rule, employers who convince the court that they had an honest belief that they made a decision for a nondiscriminatory reason cannot be liable for discrimination, even where there is evidence that discrimination played a role in the decision. Unfortunately, courts have applied this doctrine even when the employer's decision is baseless or when the employer conducted a shoddy investigation into the underlying conduct.

In most cases, the fact-finder should be permitted to assess all of the evidence to determine whether discrimination occurred.

3. Liberal Construction. Congress could change the federal discrimination statutes in a more wholesale way by instructing courts how to approach their interpretive task. To prevent courts from guessing about legislative intent in conjunction with their decisions, Congress should affirmatively tell courts that it intends to broadly protect workers under the ADEA and Title VII.

Congress already has a road map for this kind of statutory amendment. After the Supreme Court issued a series of opinions in the late 1980s and the 1990s narrowly construing the Americans with Disabilities Act (ADA), Congress amended the statute to reject the way the Supreme Court interpreted particular areas of the statute. Congress also reiterated the underlying purposes of the statute and explicitly provided that the ADA is designed to provide broad protection. Congress indicated that the ADA is supposed to "provide a clear and comprehensive national mandate for the elimination of discrimination against individuals with disabilities" and that the ADA is supposed to provide "broad coverage."[6] Congress then chastised the courts for failing to interpret the ADA in a way that was consistent with the purposes of the Act.[7] It also reminded the courts that the purpose of the ADA is to provide protections for disabled individuals, and it cautioned the courts about creating frameworks that unnecessarily limit disability discrimination claims.[8] Congress should make similar amendments to the ADEA and Title VII.

4. Scope of Coverage. Congress should clarify which actions the discrimination statutes prohibit. Congress should reject the courts' narrow definitions of what constitutes discrimination through the "severe or pervasive" requirement and the "adverse action" concept. In the retaliation context, Congress should make it clear that the underlying conduct does not need to be "severe or pervasive" or an "adverse action" before it is reasonable for a worker to complain. Congress also should amend the retaliation provisions in each of the statutes to make actions taken by the employer that have a negative effect on the employee count as retaliation. For example, the retaliation provisions should provide that employers cannot threaten to fire workers or give them negative evaluations because they complained about discrimination.

Congressional override is the clearest way to solve many of the problems plaguing discrimination law. However, practically, depending on the political climate, it may be difficult, if not impossible, for Congress to act.

Moreover, some of the problems identified in this book are not likely to attract the attention of Congress. To fix a problem, Congress first has to recognize the problem and then see that it is a problem worth fixing. As we have discussed throughout this book, employment discrimination law is complex. It is made up of many different court-created doctrines, inferences, and rules. These rules are often difficult to understand individually. These difficulties increase when trying to understand how they all work together and how they limit discrimination claims. Further, many of the problems stem from the fact that the courts have not been told how all of the doctrines should work together. Because Congress has historically corrected issues related to the Supreme Court's employment discrimination decisions, the fact that many of these doctrines never make it to the Supreme Court also limits the likelihood of congressional override.

In any event, congressional overrides may not fix discrimination law in the long term. While congressional overrides have worked for the particular problem Congress aimed to fix, the federal courts do not otherwise seem chastened by congressional overrides.

One good example of this is in the area of causation. In the 1989 *Price Waterhouse* decision, the Supreme Court broadly interpreted Title VII's causation requirement.[9] However, employers were given an affirmative defense to liability.[10] If an employer proved this affirmative defense, it would not be liable at all under Title VII. In response, Congress amended Title VII, making it clear that the Supreme Court was correct that Title VII allowed a worker to prevail under a motivating factor standard. However, Congress did not agree with the affirmative defense to liability adopted by the Supreme Court. Congress made employers liable once any discrimination was shown. Further, it permitted the employee to recover attorneys' fees and costs, among other things, even when an employer showed it would have made the same decision if it did not take a protected trait into account.[11] Despite this congressional override, the Supreme Court subsequently narrowed the causation requirement in ADEA cases, even though Title VII and the ADEA contain nearly identical language, and courts had previously stated that this broader standard was available in ADEA cases.[12] The court also later narrowed causation in retaliation cases, also not permitting the use of the motivating standard in those cases.

3. THE EEOC

The Equal Employment Opportunity Commission plays an important role in discrimination law. In the past, the EEOC often pushed for the expansion of discrimination law. The agency also has given employers guidance on how to avoid violating the federal discrimination statutes and has represented some workers in litigation. There are three ways the EEOC can help improve federal discrimination law.

(1) The EEOC should use its authority to challenge the fakers and floodgates argument.
(2) The EEOC should decide what kinds of employment actions constitute discrimination and retaliation.
(3) Given the disarray in the adjudication of traditional discrimination claims, the EEOC should provide leadership on the traditional core of intent-based discrimination claims.

1. Floodgates and Fakers. The EEOC should respond to the fakers/floodgates myth. When the EEOC is a party in a case, it can repudiate potential fakers and floodgates claims in several ways. First, the EEOC should challenge the courts' authority to prioritize court-created arguments about fakers and floodgates over Congress's intent to prohibit discrimination. Second, it should explicitly rebut the fakers and floodgates claim and should explicitly state that the sheer number of claims—a number that is in decline, no less—is not a proper basis to limit the reach of discrimination law.

2. Adverse Action Doctrine. The EEOC should issue guidance on what kinds of employment actions constitute discrimination and retaliation. For discrimination cases, the EEOC should provide a definition for the phrase "terms, conditions, or privileges" that adequately describes these broad words, relying on a wealth of decisions in other areas of law to support a broad meaning.

The EEOC should also explain how the second main provision in Title VII and the ADEA affects the adverse action and severe or pervasive doctrines. That provision prohibits employers from taking actions that "limit, segregate, or classify his employees or applicants for employment in any way which would deprive or tend to deprive any individual of employment opportunities or otherwise adversely affect his status as an employee" because of a protected trait.[13] To date, the courts have largely ignored this second provision of Title VII and the ADEA. The EEOC should remind courts of this second provision and show how it broadens the adverse action doctrine.

In retaliation cases, the EEOC should research what action would dissuade a reasonable person from complaining about discrimination so that the standard corresponds with how people actually think and act.

3. Focus on the Core. The EEOC often focuses its efforts on emerging or cutting-edge issues in discrimination. However, this book shows how leadership is still needed to bolster traditional discrimination claims. The EEOC is one of the few institutional actors with sufficient knowledge of the frameworks and doctrines and their history. There is a great need for the EEOC to provide leadership on the frameworks and rules for establishing more traditional discrimination claims because the current rules do not adequately protect workers against discrimination. The EEOC can attempt to accomplish these goals through administrative guidance and taking on litigation matters that bring up these issues.

4. COURTS

Judges created many of the problems with the current state of discrimination law. These same judges have the power to fix these problems. There are several areas where judges can focus their attention to make discrimination law fairer and more coherent.

(1) Judges should reconsider the court-created doctrines and determine whether they are supported by the text and purpose of the discrimination statutes and whether they are consistent with the procedural rules that govern litigation.

(2) Courts should focus special attention on the doctrines that determine whether an action is serious enough to constitute discrimination.

(3) Judges should recognize that funneling the facts of a case through the available frameworks and doctrines may not help them determine whether discrimination happened. In fact, the frameworks and rules might distract judges from the central question in discrimination cases.

(4) Courts should abandon the "fakers and floodgates" rhetoric because it is not supported by fact.

Dismantle the Doctrines. Judges should dismantle many of the doctrines they created to limit discrimination claims. Most of the doctrines are not supported by the text of the discrimination statutes or their purposes. Many of these doctrines also do not comport with the procedural rules that restrict judges' abilities to take cases away from juries. Moreover, many of these doctrines are not based on any actual evidence.

One of the most important changes the courts can make is to abolish most of the frameworks the courts use to evaluate discrimination claims. In their place, the courts should construct the method of proof using the actual statutory language. The core language of Title VII makes it unlawful for an employer to do the following:

(1) to fail or refuse to hire or to discharge any individual, or otherwise to discriminate against any individual with respect to his compensation, *terms, conditions, or privileges* of employment, because of such individual's race, color, religion, sex, or national origin; or

(2) *to limit*, segregate, or classify his employees or applicants for employment *in any way which would deprive or tend to deprive any individual of employment opportunities or otherwise adversely affect his status as an employee*, because of such individual's race, color, religion, sex, or national origin.[14]

The elements of a discrimination claim, based on Title VII's statutory language, would require the establishment of (1) a hiring, termination, compensation decision, or other action(s) that affects the terms or conditions of employment or that limit, segregate, or classify employees or applicants for employment in any way that would deprive or tend to deprive any individual of employment opportunities or otherwise adversely affect his status as an employee, (2) that is taken because of (3) a protected trait.[15]

Using the text of the statutes to evaluate discrimination claims may seem controversial to some people, especially those who advocate for an expansive view of the discrimination statutes. After all, some judges have attempted to use textual analyses to limit the reach of discrimination law. However, the language of the statutes provides broad protections for workers.

The current discrimination analysis does not always protect workers in the "terms, conditions or privileges" of employment because the courts have largely focused on creating doctrines like the adverse action doctrine that are not tied to this language. The phrase "terms, conditions or privileges" traditionally has a broad meaning in labor and employment law, and it should retain the same meaning in the employment discrimination context. The current discrimination analysis also focuses primarily on the first provision to evaluate traditional discrimination cases. However, we propose more consideration of both portions of the statute's language because it is illegal for the employer to take the actions described in both sections (1) and (2).

The proposed inquiry of three elements based on the text of Title VII is similar to the inquiry that courts undertake in many other legal contexts. For example, negligence cases are generally described through basic elements. Often the elements alone are enough to assist a court in resolving a case, but at times, supporting doctrines are used. Crafting general elements of a discrimination claim from the statutes' language has many benefits. The language's plain meaning is given primacy, rather than the court-created tests. In turn, it allows courts to use simpler inquiries to resolve many cases.

Using the suggested approach does not mean that discrimination law no longer requires definition by appellate courts. Important questions still remain to be answered, such as whether the "because of" language in the federal employment discrimination statutes would hold an employer liable for unconscious discrimination.[16] Focusing less on frameworks will allow the courts to concentrate on the important questions.

Underlying the appeal of the frameworks is the idea that they are necessary to help lower courts decide employment discrimination cases. However, the need for the frameworks has never been supported. There is nothing especially complex about employment discrimination law that suggests it should work differently than other cases such as negligence cases. In many cases, the Supreme Court has assumed that lower courts are confused about employment discrimination law and then mandated that lower courts think about discrimination problems through frameworks. The *McDonnell Douglas* burden-shifting test, the severe or pervasive test in harassment cases, and parts of the disparate impact structure were all created before there was a demonstrated need for them.

To impose so many frameworks is not only unusual among statutory regimes, but it also gives the mistaken impression that employment discrimination cases are somehow different or more difficult than other cases judges handle. The assumption that the frameworks are needed is also belied by the fact that at least some of the frameworks are abandoned at trial. When cases go to the jury, juries are not instructed on many of these frameworks.[17] If juries do not need to use many of the frameworks to decide whether discrimination happened, judges should not need them either.

Some judges have started to examine the utility of the frameworks, and these discussions should continue. For example, Seventh Circuit case law does not require a worker to process through the *McDonnell Douglas* test.[18] The Seventh Circuit recognizes that the *McDonnell Douglas* test is not always the proper or the sole way to analyze these cases. As discussed earlier, a few judges are openly questioning whether the frameworks work at all. Lower courts should also engage in this type of formal discussion of the problems with the frameworks and doctrines.

Harm Doctrine. Currently, federal judges rely on the court-created doctrines of "adverse action" and the "serious or pervasive" concept in harassment cases to determine whether an employer discriminated against a worker. Instead, federal judges should create a harm doctrine in discrimination cases based on the words of the federal statutes.

As discussed earlier, under the statutes, discrimination occurs if an action negatively affected the terms, conditions, or privileges of employment. Actions that deprive or tend to deprive an employee of employment opportunities are also prohibited. The current harm doctrine underenforces the statute.

The harm doctrine also causes judges to invade the province of the jury. The job of judges is to distinguish those cases that could never result in liability from those that might possibly result in liability. Instead of doing this, many federal judges have tried to determine what specific facts constitute discrimination. Some judges declare that one touching of a breast is not discrimination, but three might be. Two racial epithets do not show evidence of bias, but more than two might. When judges engage in such line-drawing, they inevitably take over the role of the jury.

Moreover, for retaliation cases, the Supreme Court has declared that retaliation happens when an action taken against a worker would dissuade a reasonable person from complaining about discrimination. As we have stated, because of the elite backgrounds of many federal judges, their own work and financial situations are very different from the situations of most American workers. As a result, those judges may not be able to accurately decide what would dissuade most people. The earlier described empirical study shows that reasonable people would be dissuaded by a wide variety of employer actions, including negative evaluations—some of which courts do not recognize as retaliation. We encourage further empirical work in this area.

Stop Going Through the Motions. The discrimination law is complex because of the frameworks and doctrines created by courts. It takes time and experience for a person who specializes in discrimination law to understand it. Accordingly, federal judges who have a docket that includes cases from a variety of legal subjects have a significant task to understand all of those subjects and also all of the frameworks and doctrines in discrimination law.

As already discussed, a few federal judges have started to publicly question the current state of discrimination law. We encourage judges to continue this discussion. They should consider whether the existing frameworks and doctrines comport with the text and purposes of the discrimination statutes. Moreover, they should examine whether the court-created doctrines like the same-actor inference and the honest-belief rule comport with the procedural rules that govern litigation. Additionally, as discussed in Chapter 6, Supreme Court precedent does not require judges to use the *McDonnell Douglas* test, and courts should feel free to examine whether the test helps them determine whether discrimination exists.[19] Even when judges feel compelled by the dictates of stare decisis and precedent to reach a decision, judges should openly question the current state of discrimination law in written decisions.

Cost and False Claims. As described in Chapter 8, when courts claim that a large number of false claims are flooding the courts, they do so with no empirical support. Nonetheless, these unsupported judicial assertions have played a role in shaping discrimination law. Courts should stop using this argument to make it harder for workers to establish discrimination claims. The argument prioritizes employer interests and the interest of courts in managing their dockets over the interest of the workers for whom Congress designed the discrimination laws.

5. NEW COALITIONS

It is also time to recognize a new politics of discrimination law. The old politics assume that anything that narrows discrimination law is good for employers, and anything that expands it is bad for those same employers. This way of thinking about discrimination law misses some important points. There is now support from many public companies for the core protections of discrimination law. The cliché that large employers always want to restrict discrimination law is no longer true. In fact, some employers have recently played key roles in opposing discrimination and tried to create more equal workplaces.

The problem is that once a case is before a judge, employers have incentives to encourage judges to narrow discrimination law. Litigation is a zero-sum game. One party will win on a claim, and the other party will not. Often, narrowing the substantive law is a good way to make sure the judge dismisses the case, which counts as a win for the employer. In these instances, it is not in the employers' interest to protect the traditional core of discrimination law. This is true even if the particular employer is otherwise trying to eliminate discrimination in its everyday business practices.

Employers who support protection against discrimination under the law should consider how their litigation tactics in particular discrimination cases impacts the overall discrimination law. A coalition of companies should consider ways to align their litigation strategy with their commitments to antidiscrimination principles outside the litigation context.

Employers may require some inducement to do this. Recently, people have been able to encourage companies to change corporate policies through social media. People could express disappointment and anger to employers who claim to adhere to antidiscrimination principles in public but then make legal arguments to narrow the reach of discrimination law. Social media makes it possible to hold employers accountable for making arguments during litigation that narrow discrimination law by allowing people to discuss and publicize these positions. Here, advocacy groups and scholars can play an important role. The compelling stories of real cases need to be shared with a broader audience. This book provides a jumping off point for that discussion.

6. CONCLUDING THOUGHTS

Courts use a host of evidentiary rules and inferences to evaluate discrimination claims. Together, these rules and inferences create a mental road map for judges to think through discrimination cases. Many of the court-created inferences are unique to discrimination law and are not supported by evidence. They prioritize the employer's explanations and judicial concerns over those of discrimination victims.

These frameworks and their supporting cast of rules define what counts as discrimination and what does not. They serve as gatekeepers that control the substantive discrimination narratives juries hear, and they structure the ways that judges and lawyers think about discrimination. Over the past thirty years, courts have defined many key concepts within discrimination law narrowly. Rather than define terms expansively to protect potential victims of discrimination, some courts interpret the statutes to serve other values, such as reducing the number of claims filed.

Workers have a right to a jury trial for intentional discrimination claims. However, courts now use various procedural and substantive devices to prevent the jury from hearing cases or to narrow the way that juries are allowed to frame discrimination questions. This is problematic because discrimination cases are highly fact specific, making them particularly suitable for a decision by a jury.

Over the past few decades, the courts have interpreted discrimination statutes narrowly to dismiss workers' claims. It is time for the courts to fully enforce the statutes Congress wrote.

CHAPTER 1

1. Lyndon B. Johnson, Remarks upon Signing the Civil Rights Bill (July 2, 1964), *available at* http://millercenter.org/president/speeches/speech-3525.

2. A few states had employment discrimination laws of their own before Congress enacted Title VII. *See, e.g.*, 43 PA. CONS. STAT. ANN. §§ 952, 955 (West 1991) (originally enacted prior to passage of Title VII in 1964 and the ADEA in 1967).

3. This fact pattern is based on a hypothetical created by the United States Court of Appeals for the District of Columbia. Douglas v. Donovan, 559 F.3d 549, 555 (D.C. Cir. 2009).

4. Saidu-Kamara v. Parkway Corp., 155 F. Supp. 2d 436, 439 (E.D. Pa. 2001).

5. Ash v. Tyson Foods, Inc., No. CIV.A. 96-RRA-3257-M, 2004 WL 5138005, at *1, 5 (N.D. Ala. Mar. 26, 2004), *aff'd in part, rev'd in part*, 129 F. App'x 529 (11th Cir. 2005), *vacated and remanded*, 546 U.S. 454 (2006).

6. *Ash v. Tyson Foods*, 2004 WL 5138005, at *6.

7. *Id.* at *5–6.

8. *Id.* at *7.

9. *Id.* at *6.

10. Ash v. Tyson Foods, Inc., 129 F. App'x 529, 531 (11th Cir. 2005), *vacated and remanded*, 546 U.S. 454 (2006).

11. *See generally infra* Chapter 3.

12. *See generally infra* Chapter 3; *see also* Mendoza v. Borden, Inc., 195 F.3d 1238, 1246 (11th Cir. 1999) (collecting cases).

13. The law has the capacity to be much broader, and we are not making any claims about the validity of affirmative action or the capacity of the law to cover unconscious discrimination or other similar claims.

14. William N. Eskridge, Jr. & John Ferejohn, *Super-Statutes*, 50 DUKE L.J. 1215 (2001).

15. *See, e.g.*, Griggs v. Duke Power Co., 401 U.S. 424, 427 (1971).

16. McMonigle v. Delta Air Lines, Inc., 556 F.2d 1261, 1263 (5th Cir. 1977).

17. Corning Glass Works v. Brennan, 417 U.S. 188, 191 n.2 (1974).

18. *See, e.g.*, Leticia M. Saucedo, *Addressing Segregation in the Brown Collar Workplace: Toward A Solution for the Inexorable 100%*, 41 U. MICH. J.L. REFORM 447, 452 (2008) (discussing "brown collar" jobs).

19. Devah Pager, *The Mark of a Criminal Record*, 108 Am. J. of Sociology 937, 955 (2003).

20. *Id.* at 955.

21. *Id.* at 957.

22. *Id.* at 955.

23. *Id.* at 957.

24. *Id.* at 958.

25. Devah Pager, *The Use of Field Experiments for Studies of Employment Discrimination: Contributions, Critiques, and Directions for the Future*, 609 Annals Am. Acad. Political and Soc. Sci. 104, 112 (2007).

26. *See, e.g.*, Bureau of Labor Statistics, Employment Status of the Civilian Population by Race, Sex, and Age, *available at* http://www.bls.gov/news.release/empsit.t02. htm (last modified Nov. 4, 2016).

27. Gregory Wallace, *Only 5 Black CEOs at 500 Biggest Companies*, CNN Money, Jan. 29, 2015, *available at* http://money.cnn.com/2015/01/29/news/economy/ mcdonalds-ceo-diversity/.

28. Claire Zillman, *Microsoft's New CEO: One Minority Exec in a Sea of White*, Fortune, Feb. 4, 2014, *available at* http://fortune.com/2014/02/04/microsofts-new-ceo-one-minority-exec-in-a-sea-of-white/.

29. Justin Wolfers, *Fewer Women Run Big Companies Than Men Named John*, N.Y. Times (Mar. 2, 2015), http://www.nytimes.com/2015/03/03/upshot/fewer-women-run-big-companies-than-men-named-john.html.

30. Farhad Manjoo, *Exposing Hidden Bias at Google*, N.Y. Times (Sept. 14, 2014), at B1, http://www.nytimes.com/2014/09/25/technology/exposing-hidden-biases-at-google-to-improve-diversity.html.

31. *Id.*

32. *Id.*

33. Catalyst, *2014 Catalyst Census: Women Board Directors* (2015), *available at* http:// www.catalyst.org/system/files/2014_catalyst_census_women_board_directors_ 0.pdf.

34. *Women and Minorities at Law Firms by Race and Ethnicity—New Findings for 2015*, NALP Bulletin (Jan. 2016), http://www.nalp.org/0116research.

35. American Bar Ass'n, Standing Committee on Judicial Independence, *National Database on Judicial Diversity in State Courts* (June 2010), *available at* http://apps. americanbar.org/abanet/jd/display/national.cfm.

36. American Bar Ass'n, Commission on Women in the Profession, *A Current Glance at Women in the Law* (July 2014), *available at* http://www.americanbar.org/content/ dam/aba/marketing/women/current_glance_statistics_july2014.authcheckdam.pdf.

37. *Id.*

38. *Id.*

39. *Id.*

40. *Id.*

41. U.S. Dep't of Labor, Bureau of Labor Statistics, Labor Force Statistics from the Current Population Survey, Median Weekly Earnings of Full-Time Wage and Salary Workers by Detailed Occupation and Sex, 2014 (2015), *available at* http:// www.bls.gov/cps/cpsaat39.htm (last modified Feb. 10, 2016).

42. Ariane Hegewisch, Emily Ellis & Heidi Hartmann, Ph.D., Institute for Women's Policy Research, *The Gender Wage Gap: 2014; Earnings Differences by Race and Ethnicity* (Mar. 2015), http://www.iwpr.org/publications/pubs/the-gender-wage-gap-2014-earnings-differences-by-race-and-ethnicity.

43. Paul Weiler, *The Wages of Sex: The Uses and Limits of Comparable Worth*, 99 HARV. L. REV. 1728, 1784 (1986) (placing the gap at 10 to 15 percent); Am. Ass'n of Univ. Women, *The Simple Truth About the Gender Pay Gap* (2015), *available at* http://www.aauw.org/files/2015/02/The-Simple-Truth_Spring-2015.pdf.

44. AM. ASS'N OF UNIV. WOMEN, THE CENTRAL TRUTH ABOUT THE GENDER PAY GAP (2015), *available at* http://www.aauw.org/files/2015/02/The-Simple-Truth_Spring-2015.pdf.

45. *Id.*

46. Michael Selmi, *Why Are Employment Discrimination Cases So Hard to Win?*, 61 LA. L. REV. 555, 563 (2001).

47. Manjoo, *supra* note 30 (Ch. 1); *see also* Richard Delgado, *On Telling Stories in School: A Reply to Farber and Sherry*, 46 VAND. L. REV. 665, 671 (1993) (noting the popular narrative that overt racism is sporadic and rare).

48. Laura Beth Nielsen & Robert L. Nelson, *Rights Realized? An Empirical Analysis of Employment Discrimination Litigation as a Claiming System*, 2005 WIS. L. REV. 663, 665 (2005) (summarizing narratives about discrimination cases).

49. Richard Thompson Ford, *Bias in the Air: Rethinking Employment Discrimination Law*, 66 STAN. L. REV. 1381, 1396 (2014).

50. Wendy Parker, *Lessons in Losing: Race Discrimination in Employment*, 81 NOTRE DAME L. REV. 889, 890 (2006) (noting that the system works well at identifying cases where an individual manager fires an employee after making negative comments about a protected trait).

51. Eskridge & Ferejohn, *supra* note 14 (Ch. 1), at 1240.

52. For discussions of structural discrimination and identity performance as a source of discrimination, see, e.g., Samuel R. Bagenstos, *The Structural Turn and the Limits of Antidiscrimination Law*, 94 CAL. L. REV. 1 (2006); Tristin K. Green, *Work Culture and Discrimination*, 93 CAL. L. REV. 623, 625 (2005); Devon W. Carbado & Mitu Gulati, *Working Identity*, 85 CORNELL L. REV. 1259, 1262 (2000) (discussing how work structure pressures employees to behave in certain ways to perform a work identity).

53. Tristin K. Green, *A Structural Approach as Antidiscrimination Mandate: Locating Employer Wrong*, 60 VAND. L. REV. 849, 850 (2007).

54. Amy L. Wax, *Discrimination as Accident*, 74 IND. L.J. 1129, 1130 (1999).

55. Manjoo, *supra* note 30 (Ch. 1). The following articles are helpful for understanding unconscious or implicit bias. Samuel R. Bagenstos, *Implicit Bias, "Science," and Antidiscrimination Law*, 1 HARV. L. AND POL'Y REV. 477 (2007); R. Richard Banks, Jennifer L. Eberhardt & Lee Ross, *Discrimination and Implicit Bias in a Racially Unequal Society*, 94. CAL. L. REV. 1169 (2006); Anthony G. Greenwald & Linda Hamilton Krieger, *Implicit Bias: Scientific Foundations*, 94 CAL. L. REV. 945 (2006); Olatunde C.A. Johnson, *Disparity Rules*, 107 COLUM. L. REV. 374 (2007); Christine Jolls & Cass R. Sunstein, *The Law of Implicit Bias*, 94. CAL. L. REV. 969 (2006); Jerry Kang, *Trojan Horses of Race*, 118 HARV. L. REV. 1489, 1510 (2005); Jerry Kang & Mahzarin R. Banaji,

Fair Measures: A Behavioral Realist Revision of "Affirmative Action," 94 CAL. L. REV. 1063 (2006); Linda Hamilton Krieger & Susan T. Fiske, *Behavioral Realism in Employment Discrimination Law: Implicit Bias and Disparate Treatment,* 94 CAL. L. REV. 997 (2006); Charles R. Lawrence III, *The Id, the Ego, and Equal Protection: Reckoning with Unconscious Racism,* 39 STAN. L. REV. 317 (1987).

56. *See generally* MAHZARIN R. BANAJI AND ANTHONY G. GREENWALD, BLINDSPOT: HIDDEN BIASES OF GOOD PEOPLE (2013).

57. Nicholas Kristof, *Our Biased Brains,* N.Y. TIMES, May 7, 2015, at A29, *available at* http://www.nytimes.com/2015/05/07/opinion/nicholas-kristof-our-biased-brains. html.

58. Elizabeth G. Olson, *How Corporate America Is Tackling Unconscious Bias,* FORTUNE (Jan. 15, 2015), *available at,* http://fortune.com/2015/01/15/how-corporate-america-is-tackling-unconscious-bias/.

59. Wax, *supra* note 54 (Ch. 1), at 1133; *but see* Melissa Hart, *Subjective Decisionmaking and Unconscious Discrimination,* 56 ALA. L. REV. 741, 743 (2005) (arguing that the legal system can address unconscious bias).

60. Wax, *supra* note 54 (Ch. 1), at 1133.

61. Addison v. Bd. of Educ., No. 4:12CV1601 HEA, 2012 WL 4058369, at *1 (E.D. Mo. Sept. 14, 2012).

62. 42 U.S.C. § 2000e-5(e)(1), (f)(1) (2015).

63. *Id.* The ADEA has a slightly different administrative procedure that does not require a worker to obtain a Right to Sue letter. Smithson v. Hamlin Pub, Inc., No. 15-CV-11978, 2016 WL 465564, at *5 (E.D. Mich. Feb. 8, 2016).

64. Griffin v. Pasqual, No. 5:14-CV-1030 MAD, 2015 WL 1967537, at *2, 9 (N.D.N.Y. Apr. 30, 2015) (noting California statute of limitations for personal injury claims is two years and for professional negligence is three years); *In re* Avandia Mktg., Sales Practices & Prods. Liab. Litig., No. 07-MD-1871, 2015 WL 1728127, at *2 (E.D. Pa. Apr. 10, 2015) (noting New York statute of limitations for certain products liability claims, including negligence, is three years).

65. *See, e.g.,* 735 ILL. COMP. STAT. 5/13–206 (providing a ten-year window to file suit on some claims, including claims brought under a written contract); Guzman v. Bridgepoint Educ., Inc., No. 11-CV-69-BAS WVG, 2015 WL 1396650, at *20 (S.D. Cal. Mar. 26, 2015) (noting consumer protection statute of limitations were as much as ten years).

66. Thomas v. City of E. St. Louis, No. CIV. 11-921-GPM, 2012 WL 1405719, at *2 (S.D. Ill. Apr. 21, 2012).

67. Starceski v. Westinghouse Elec. Corp., 54 F.3d 1089, 1104 (3d Cir. 1995). In many states, workers can also sue under state law. This book focuses on federal causes of action. Some states provide greater remedies for discrimination than federal law provides.

68. 42 U.S.C. § 1981a(b)(1) (2015).

69. 42 U.S.C. § 1981a(b)(3).

70. 42 U.S.C. § 1981a(b)(3)(D).

71. There is one exception to these limits. There is a separate federal statute that prohibits race discrimination. 42 U.S.C. § 1981. This statute does not require administrative exhaustion. It also does not contain damages caps.

72. 42 U.S.C. § 2000e(b); 29 U.S.C. § 630(b).

73. 42 U.S.C. § 2000e-2(a).

74. Broussard v. L.H. Bossier, Inc., 789 F.2d 1158, 1160 (5th Cir. 1986) (holding that independent contractors are not protected by Title VII); Smith v. Berks Cmty. Television, 657 F. Supp. 794, 795 (E.D. Pa. 1987) (same for volunteers).

75. 42 U.S.C. § 2000e-2(e) & (h).

CHAPTER 2

1. For a case with similar facts, see *Demmons v. Fulton County*, No. 1:09-CV-2312-TWT-WEJ, 2010 WL 3418325, at *7–8 (N.D. Ga. Aug. 2, 2010), *report and recommendation adopted*, No. 1:09-CV-2312-TWT, 2010 WL 3418328 (N.D. Ga. Aug. 25, 2010).

2. *See id.*

3. Stewart J. Schwab & Michael Heise, *Splitting Logs: An Empirical Perspective on Employment Discrimination Settlements*, 96 CORNELL L. REV. 931, 932–33 (2011); Minna J. Kotkin, *Outing Outcomes: An Empirical Study of Confidential Employment Discrimination Settlements*, 64 WASH. AND LEE L. REV. 111, 126 (2007).

4. Marc Galanter, *A World Without Trials?*, 2006 J. DISP. RESOL. 7, 8 (2006).

5. Federal Judicial Caseload Statistics, U.S. District Courts—Civil Cases Terminated, by Nature of Suit and Action Taken—During the 12-Month Period Ending Mar. 31, 2014 (2014), http://www.uscourts.gov/statistics/table/c-4/federal-judicial-caseload-statistics/2014/03/31.

6. Laura Beth Nielsen et al., *Uncertain Justice: Litigating Claims of Employment Discrimination in the Contemporary United States* 19 (Am. Bar Found., Research Paper No. 08-04, 2008), *available at* http://papers.ssrn.com/sol3/papers.cfm?abstract_id=1093313.

7. Katie R. Eyer, *That's Not Discrimination: American Beliefs and the Limits of Anti-Discrimination Law*, 96 MINN. L. REV. 1275, 1282–83 (2012) (internal citations omitted); *see also* Ruth Colker, *Winning and Losing Under the Americans with Disabilities Act*, 62 OHIO ST. L.J. 239, 252 (2001) (discussing ADA cases).

8. Kevin M. Clermont et al., *How Employment-Discrimination Plaintiffs Fare in the Federal Courts of Appeals*, 7 EMP. RTS. AND EMP. POL'Y J. 547, 547–48 (2003) (internal citation omitted).

9. Eyer, *supra* note 7 (Ch. 2), at 1284–85.

10. FED. R. CIV. P. 12(b)(6).

11. St. John v. Cach, LLC, No. 14-2760, 2016 WL 2909195, at *1 (7th Cir. May 19, 2016).

12. Bell Atlantic Corp. v. Twombly, 550 U.S. 544 (2007); Ashcroft v. Iqbal, 556 U.S. 662 (2009).

13. Conley v. Gibson, 355 U.S. 41, 45–46 (1957).

14. *Twombly*, 550 U.S. at 556; *Iqbal*, 556 U.S. at 663.

15. *Iqbal*, 556 U.S. at 679.

16. *See, e.g.*, Am. Bar Ass'n, Commission on Women in the Profession, A Current Glance at Women in the Law (July 2014), *available at* http://www.americanbar.org/content/dam/aba/marketing/women/current_glance_statistics_july2014.authcheckdam.pdf; Russell Wheeler, *The Changing Face of the Federal Judiciary* 1 (Governance Studies

at Brookings Aug. 2009), http://www.brookings.edu/~/media/research/files/papers/
2009/8/federal-judiciary-wheeler/08_federal_judiciary_wheeler.pdf.

17. *See, e.g.,* Savage v. Secure First Credit Union, 107 F. Supp. 3d 1212, 1216 (N.D. Ala.
2015); *see also* Alexander A. Reinert, *Measuring the Impact of Plausibility Pleading,*
101 Virg. L. Rev. 2117, 2124 (2015) (finding an increased dismissal of civil rights
cases under new standard); Brian S. Clarke, *Grossly Restricted Pleading:* Twombly/
Iqbal, Gross, *and Cannibalistic Facts in Compound Employment Discrimination
Claims,* 2010 Utah L. Rev. 1101, 1103 (2010); Scott Dodson, *A New Look: Dismissal
Rates of Federal Civil Claims,* 96 Judicature 127, 128 (2012); Victor D. Quintanilla,
Beyond Common Sense: A Social Psychological Study of Iqbal's *Effect on Claims of
Race Discrimination,* 17 Mich. J. Race and L. 1 (2011).

18. *See* Reinert, *supra* note 17 (Ch. 2), at 2124 (finding an increase in dismissals for civil
rights and employment cases).

19. Vasquez v. Empress Ambulance Serv., Inc., No. 14 CIV. 8387 NRB, 2015 WL
5037055, at *1 (S.D.N.Y. Aug. 26, 2015), *reversed by* 835 F. 3d 267 (2d Cir. 2016).

20. *Id.* at *1–2.

21. *Id.* at *2.

22. Fed. R. Civ. P. 56(a).

23. *Id; see also* Suja A. Thomas, *Summary Judgment and the Reasonable Jury
Standard: A Proxy for A Judge's Own View of the Sufficiency of the Evidence?,* 97
Judicature 222, 223 (2014) (discussing ambiguity in reasonable jury standard).

24. Gallagher v. Delaney, 139 F.3d 338, 342–43 (2d Cir. 1998); *see also* Ann C. McGinley,
Cognitive Illiberalism, Summary Judgment, and Title VII: An Examination of Ricci
v. DeStefano, 57 N.Y.L. Sch. L. Rev. 865 (2013); Dan M. Kahan et al., *Whose Eyes
Are You Going to Believe?* Scott v. Harris *and the Perils of Cognitive Illiberalism,* 122
Harv. L. Rev. 837 (2009).

25. Nat'l Women's Law Ctr., Women in the Federal Judiciary: Still a Long
Way to Go 2 n.2 (Feb. 2016).

26. Russell Wheeler, *The Changing Face of the Federal Judiciary* 1 (Governance Studies
at Brookings Aug. 2009), www.brookings.edu/~/media/research/files/papers/
2009/8/federal-judiciary-wheeler/08_federal_judiciary_wheeler.pdf.

27. *See* Suja A. Thomas, *The Fallacy of Dispositive Procedure,* 50 B.C. L. Rev. 759 (2009).

28. Arraleh v. Cnty. of Ramsey, 461 F.3d 967, 980 (8th Cir. 2006) (Heaney, J., dissenting).

29. *Id.* at 974.

30. *Id.* at 980.

31. *Id.* at 980.

32. Williamson v. Adventist Health Sys./Sunbelt, Inc., No. 608-CV-32-ORL-31GKJ, 2009
WL 1393471, at *5 (M.D. Fla. May 18, 2009), *aff'd,* 372 F. App'x 936 (11th Cir. 2010).

33. Danzer v. Norden Sys., Inc., 151 F.3d 50, 53 (2d Cir. 1998).

34. *Id.*

35. *Id.*

36. In this case, the trial court's grant of summary judgment in the employer's favor
was later reversed on appeal. *Id.*

37. It is possible for a worker who loses a pretrial motion to appeal that ruling to an
appellate court. However, one study found that appellate courts only reverse these

trial court rulings on pretrial motions about 10 percent of the time. Clermont et al., *supra* note 8 (Ch. 2), at 553.

38. Memorandum from Joe Cecil and George Cort of The Federal Judicial Center to Hon. Michael Baylson (June 15, 2007), *available at* http://www.fjc.gov/public/pdf. nsf/lookup/sujufy06.pdf/$file/sujufy06.pdf; Nielsen, *supra* note 6 (Ch. 2).

39. Amanda Farahany & Tanya McAdams, *Analysis of Employment Discrimination Claims for Cases in Which an Order Was Issued on Defendant's Motion for Summary Judgment in 2011 and 2012 in the U.S. District Court for the Northern District of Georgia* (Sept. 16, 2013), *available at* http://www.ssrn.com/abstract=2326697.

40. FED. R. CIV. P. 50(a) & (b).

41. FED. R. CIV. P. 50(a) & (b).

42. For an example of a case applying remittitur, see *Tanzini v. Marine Midland Bank*, 978 F. Supp. 70, 73 (N.D.N.Y. 1997).

43. Suja A. Thomas, *Re-examining the Constitutionality of Remittitur Under the Seventh Amendment*, 64 OHIO ST. L.J. 731, 735 (2003).

44. *Id.*

45. 42 U.S.C. § 1981a(c).

46. FED. R. CIV. P. 50(a) & (b), 56(a).

47. Ash v. Tyson Foods, Inc., 546 U.S. 454, 455 (2006).

48. *Id.*

49. *Id.* at 456.

50. *Id.*

51. Ash v. Tyson Foods, Inc., No. CIV.A. 96-RRA-3257-M, 2004 WL 5138005, at *1, 6 (N.D. Ala. Mar. 26, 2004), *aff'd in part, rev'd in part*, 129 F. App'x 529 (11th Cir. 2005), *vacated*, 546 U.S. 454 (2006).

52. Ash v. Tyson Foods, Inc., 546 U.S. 454, 456 (2006).

53. Ash v. Tyson Foods, Inc., No. CIV.A. 96-RRA-3257-M, 2004 WL 5138005, at *1, 7 (N.D. Ala. Mar. 26, 2004).

54. *Id.* at *6.

55. *Id.* at *1.

56. *See* 42 U.S.C. § 1981a(b)(1).

57. Ash v. Tyson Foods, Inc., No. CIV.A. 96-RRA-3257-M, 2004 WL 5138005, at *10 (N.D. Ala. Mar. 26, 2004).

58. Ash v. Tyson Foods, Inc., 129 F. App'x 529, 531 (11th Cir. 2005), *vacated and remanded*, 546 U.S. 454 (2006).

59. 129 F. App'x at 533.

60. *Id.* at 536.

61. Hithon v. Tyson Foods, Inc., No. CIV A 96-RRA-3257-M, 2008 WL 4921515, at *10 (N.D. Ala. Sept. 30, 2008), *rev'd sub nom.* Ash v. Tyson Foods, Inc., 392 F. App'x 817 (11th Cir. 2010), *vacated and aff'd*, 664 F.3d 883 (11th Cir. 2011).

62. *See, e.g.*, DeJarnette v. Corning Inc., 133 F.3d 293, 300 (4th Cir. 1998).

63. Clermont et al., *supra* note 8 (Ch. 2), at 552.

64. *Id.* at 554.

65. Kevin M. Clermont & Theodore Eisenberg, *Anti-Plaintiff Bias in the Federal Appellate Courts*, 84 JUDICATURE 128, 129 (2000).

66. Clermont et al., *supra* note 8 (Ch. 2), at 552.
67. Clermont & Eisenberg, *supra* note 65 (Ch. 2), at 129.
68. Clermont et al., *supra* note 8 (Ch. 2), at 555.
69. Reeves v. Sanderson Plumbing Prods., Inc., 530 U.S. 133, 137 (2000).
70. *Id.*
71. Reeves v. Sanderson Plumbing Prods., Inc., 197 F.3d 688, 691 (5th Cir. 1999), *rev'd*, 530 U.S. 133 (2000).
72. *Reeves*, 197 F.3d at 693.

CHAPTER 3

1. Barrow v. Ga. Pac. Corp., 144 F. App'x 54, 57 (11th Cir. 2005).
2. *Id.*
3. *Id.* In this case, the court dismissed the plaintiff's harassment claim on two grounds: (1) the plaintiff's allegations of harassment were not serious enough to be harassment, and (2) the worker had failed to complain about the harassment.
4. Saidu-Kamara v. Parkway Corp., 155 F. Supp. 2d 436, 439 (E.D. Pa. 2001).
5. *See* cases cited throughout this chapter; *see also* Guthrie v. Waffle House, Inc., 460 F. App'x 803, 805 (11th Cir. 2012); Mendoza v. Borden, Inc., 195 F.3d 1238, 1246 (11th Cir. 1999) (collecting cases); Lowe v. Cardinal Health Inc., 61 F. Supp. 3d 1228, 1236 (N.D. Ala. 2014); Matherne v. Ruba Mgmt., No. CIV.A. 12-2461, 2014 WL 2938100, at *6 (E.D. La. June 27, 2014), *aff'd*, 624 F. App'x 835 (5th Cir. 2015) (collecting cases); Redd v. N.Y. State Div. of Parole, No. 07-CV-120(NGG)(LB), 2010 WL 1177453, at *3 (E.D.N.Y. Mar. 24, 2010), *vacated in part sub nom.* Redd v. N.Y. Div. of Parole, 678 F.3d 166 (2d Cir. 2012); Smith v. Am. Online, Inc., 499 F. Supp. 2d 1251, 1261 (M.D. Fla. 2007) (collecting cases).
6. U.S. Equal Employment Opportunity Commission, Laws, Regulations, Guidance & MOUs, Harassment (undated), http://www.eeoc.gov/laws/types/harassment.cfm.
7. *Id.*
8. Mitchell v. Pope, 189 F. App'x 911, 913 n.3 (11th Cir. 2006).
9. *Id.* at 913.
10. *Id.*
11. Hill v. Guyoungtech USA, Inc., No. CIV A 07-0750-KD-M, 2008 WL 4073638, at *8 (S.D. Ala. Aug. 26, 2008).
12. 477 U.S. 57, 59 (1986).
13. *Id.* at 65.
14. *Id.* at 67.
15. *Id.* (internal citations omitted).
16. *Id.* at 60.
17. Harris v. Forklift Sys., Inc., 510 U.S. 17, 22 (1993).
18. *Id.* at 23.
19. *See, e.g.*, Hockman v. Westward Commc'ns, 407 F.3d 317, 328 (5th Cir. 2004).
20. Davis v. Baroco Elec. Constr. Co., No. 99-1055-S, 2000 WL 33156436, at *2 (S.D. Ala. Dec. 15, 2000).
21. *Id.*

22. *See* Matherne v. Ruba Mgmt., No. CIV.A. 12-2461, 2014 WL 2938100, at *6 (E.D. La. June 27, 2014) (characterizing the holding of *Landers v. CHLN, Inc.*, Civ. A. No. 07-75, 2009 WL 803777 (E.D. Ky. Mar. 25, 2009), which concluded that multiple comments about plaintiff's breasts, requests to lick whipped cream and wine off of her, inappropriate touching while hugging plaintiff, requests to go out, rubbing plaintiff's shoulders, arms, and rear end, and inappropriate text messages were not sufficiently severe or pervasive under Kentucky state law, using similar standard as federal law).

23. Baldwin v. Blue Cross/Blue Shield of Ala., 480 F.3d 1287, 1292, 1294, 1303 (11th Cir. 2007). In this case, the trial court held that the conduct was not severe or pervasive enough to constitute harassment. The appellate court affirmed the dismissal but based its reasoning on agency principles.

24. Bonora v. UGI Utils., Inc., No. CIV.A. 99-5539, 2000 WL 1539077, at *4 (E.D. Pa. Oct. 18, 2000) (characterizing the facts of *Weiss v. Coca-Cola Bottling Co. of Chicago*, 990 F.2d 333 (7th Cir. 1993)).

25. Brooks v. City of San Mateo, 229 F.3d 917, 921 (9th Cir. 2000).

26. Quinn v. Green Tree Credit Corp., 159 F.3d 759, 768 (2d Cir. 1998).

27. Barnett v. Boeing Co., 306 F. App'x 875, 879 (5th Cir. 2009) (worker had evidence that a coworker leered at her and "touched her in sexually inappropriate and unwelcome ways"); Adusumilli v. City of Chicago, 164 F.3d 353 (7th Cir. 1998) (affirming grant of summary judgment; incidents where worker presented evidence that coemployees teased plaintiff, made sexual jokes aimed at her, repeatedly stared at her chest, and made unwelcome contact with her arm, fingers, and buttocks were not sufficiently severe or pervasive to create a hostile work environment); *see also* *supra* note 5 (Ch. 3).

28. Freeman v. Dal-Tile Corp., 750 F.3d 413, 420–21 (4th Cir. 2014) (reversing the district court's grant of summary judgment on this set of facts).

29. Hill v. Guyoungtech USA, Inc., No. CIV A 07-0750-KD-M, 2008 WL 4073638, at *8 (S.D. Ala. Aug. 26, 2008).

30. *Id.* at *10.

31. *Id.* at *8 (internal citations omitted).

32. *Id.* at *9–10 (internal citations omitted).

33. Boyer-Liberto v. Fontainebleau Corp., No. CIV. JKB-12-212, 2013 WL 1413031, at *3 (D. Md. Apr. 4, 2013), *aff'd*, 752 F.3d 350 (4th Cir. 2014), *vacated on reh'g*, 786 F.3d 264 (4th Cir. 2015) (en banc). The supervisor denied making the comments.

34. *Id.*

35. Boyer-Liberto v. Fontainebleau Corp., 752 F.3d 350, 357 (4th Cir. 2014), *vacated on reh'g*, 786 F.3d 264 (4th Cir. 2015) (en banc).

36. Boyer-Liberto v. Fontainebleau Corp., 786 F.3d 264 (4th Cir. 2015) (en banc).

37. Curry v. SBC Commc'ns, Inc., 669 F. Supp. 2d 805, 835 (E.D. Mich. 2009) (noting the use of the epithet alone would not create a hostile environment, but it could be added to other factors to allow claim to proceed); Cargo v. Kan. City S. Ry. Co., No. CIV.A. 05-2010, 2012 WL 4596757, at *7 (W.D. La. Oct. 1, 2012) (holding that isolated use of racial slurs does not constitute racial harassment).

38. Redd v. N.Y. Div. of Parole, 678 F.3d 166, 179 (2d Cir. 2012); Stathatos v. Gala Res., LLC, No. 06 CIV. 13138 RLC, 2010 WL 2024967, at *5 (S.D.N.Y. May 21, 2010) (noting

that allegation that person "intentionally groped [worker's] buttocks can alone defeat defendants' motion for summary judgment."); *see also* Thomas v. Willie G's Post Oak, Inc., No. H-04-4479, 2006 WL 1117959 (S.D. Tex. Apr. 25, 2006) (denying summary judgment where plaintiff's manager had touched plaintiff's buttocks twice and had touched his arm muscles or rubbed his shoulders four or five times).

39. Harvill v. Westward Commc'ns, L.L.C., 433 F.3d 428, 438 (5th Cir. 2005); Hockman v. Westward Commc'ns, 407 F.3d 317, 328 (5th Cir. 2004).

40. Faragher v. City of Boca Raton, 524 U.S. 775, 806–07 (1998); Burlington Indus., Inc. v. Ellerth, 524 U.S. 742, 773 (1998).

41. *See, e.g.*, Black v. Zaring Homes, Inc., 104 F.3d 822, 823–24 (6th Cir. 1997) (reversing jury verdict and finding conduct over four-month period was "sex-based" but insufficiently severe or pervasive to constitute actionable claim, where alleged conduct included repeated sexual jokes; one occasion of looking plaintiff up and down, smiling, and stating, there's "nothing I like more in the morning than sticky buns"; suggesting land area be named "Titsville" or "Twin Peaks"; asking plaintiff, "Say, weren't you there [at a biker bar] Saturday night dancing on the tables?"; stating, "Just get the broad to sign it"; telling plaintiff she was "paid great money for a woman"; laughing when plaintiff mentioned the name of Dr. Paul Busam, apparently pronounced as "bosom"); *see also* Mendoza v. Borden, Inc., 195 F.3d 1238, 1247 (11th Cir. 1999).

42. Throughout this book we alter the names of the workers and companies involved in these cases because the names are not relevant to the general concepts that we discuss. Sally's story is based on the case *Baskerville v. Culligan International Co.*, 50 F.3d 428, 430 (7th Cir. 1995).

43. *Id.*

44. *Id.* at 431.

45. Douglas v. Donovan, 559 F.3d 549, 555 (D.C. Cir. 2009).

46. *Id.* at 556 (Tatel, C.J., dissenting).

47. *See, e.g.*, Sotomayor v. City of New York, 862 F. Supp. 2d 226, 254 (E.D.N.Y. 2012), *aff'd*, 713 F.3d 163 (2d Cir. 2013); Taylor v. N.Y.C. Dep't of Educ., 11-CV-3582, 2012 WL 5989874, at *7 (E.D.N.Y. Nov. 30, 2012) (being rated as having unsatisfactory performance not sufficient to constitute an adverse action); Siddiqi v. N.Y.C. Health & Hosps. Corp., 572 F. Supp. 2d 353, 367 (S.D.N.Y. 2008).

48. Alvarado v. Tex. Rangers, 492 F.3d 605, 612 (5th Cir. 2007); Santana v. U.S. Tsubaki, Inc., 632 F. Supp. 2d 720, 721 (N.D. Ohio 2009).

49. *See, e.g.*, Lara v. Unified Sch. Dist. # 501, 350 F. App'x 280, 284 (10th Cir. 2009) (threatened transfer not enough to constitute an unlawful employment practice); Sanchez v. Denver Pub. Sch., 164 F.3d 527, 532 (10th Cir. 1998) (job transfer that increased teacher's commute from a few minutes to between thirty and forty minutes not sufficient); Harlston v. McDonnell Douglas Corp., 37 F.3d 379, 382 (8th Cir. 1994) (being given more stressful job duties not sufficient); Williams v. Bristol-Myers Squibb Co., 85 F.3d 270, 274 (7th Cir. 1996); Craven v. Tex. Dep't of Criminal Justice, 151 F. Supp. 2d 757, 766 (N.D. Tex. 2001); *but see* Collins v. Illinois, 830 F.2d 692, 703 (7th Cir. 1987) (finding an adverse action occurred when employer moved employee's office to undesirable location); Czekalski

v. Peters, 475 F.3d 360, 364 (D.C. Cir. 2007) (noting that some lateral transfers do constitute adverse actions).

50. Chukwuka v. City of New York, 795 F. Supp. 2d 256, 262 (S.D.N.Y. 2011), *aff'd*, 513 F. App'x 34 (2d Cir. 2013).

51. *Id.*

52. Myers v. Maryland Auto. Ins. Fund, No. CIV. CCB-09-3391, 2010 WL 3120070, at *5 (D. Md. Aug. 9, 2010).

53. Han v. Whole Foods Mkt. Grp., Inc., 44 F. Supp. 3d 769, 789 (N.D. Ill. 2014).

54. White v. Hall, 389 F. App'x 956, 960 (11th Cir. 2010).

55. *See, e.g.*, EEOC v. Audrain Health Care, Inc., 756 F.3d 1083, 1085 (8th Cir. 2014).

56. EEOC v. v. Audrain Health Care, Inc., No. 2:11-CV-57 NAB, 2013 WL 317311, at *1 (E.D. Mo. Jan. 28, 2013), *aff'd* , 756 F.3d 1083 (8th Cir. 2014).

57. Sotomayor v. City of New York, 862 F. Supp. 2d 226, 252, 254 (E.D.N.Y. 2012), *aff'd*, 713 F.3d 163 (2d Cir. 2013) (no adverse action when employee alleged employer subjected her to frequent performance evaluations, negative evaluations, denial of her preferred teaching assignment, and assigned her a heavier teaching load than other teachers).

58. Tepperwien v. Entergy Nuclear Operations, Inc., 663 F.3d 556, 572 (2d Cir. 2011); Dixon v. Office Depot, Inc., Civ. No. 05-cv-01197-MSK-MJW, 2006 WL 3328124, at *3 (D. Colo. Nov. 15, 2006).

59. 42 U.S.C. § 2000e-2(a)(1)-(2) (emphasis added). The ADEA uses similar language to define prohibited conduct. 29 U.S.C. § 623(a)(1)-(2). The ADA's first operative provisions also contain similar prohibitions, but the wording and construction of the ADA is slightly different. 42 U.S.C. § 12112(a) ("No covered entity shall discriminate against a qualified individual on the basis of disability in regard to job application procedures, the hiring, advancement, or discharge of employees, employee compensation, job training, and other terms, conditions, and privileges of employment."). The ADA contains a second provision that further defines what it means to discriminate. *Id.* at § 12112(b). Given the ADA's accommodation requirement, the ADA provides a longer list of harms than found in Title VII and the ADEA.

60. *See, e.g.*, Martinez v. Coatings Inc. & Co., 251 F. Supp. 2d 1058, 1068 (D. P.R. 2003) (demotion constitutes an adverse action).

61. Ford Motor Co. (Chicago Stamping Plant) v. NLRB, 571 F.2d 993, 997 (7th Cir. 1978).

62. *Id.* at 1000 (providing examples of other subjects that qualify).

63. NLRB v. Gulf Power Co., 384 F.2d 822, 825 (5th Cir. 1967).

64. S.S. Kresge Co. v. NLRB, 416 F.2d 1225, 1229–1230 (6th Cir. 1969).

65. NLRB v. Washington Aluminum Co., 370 U.S. 9, 16 (1962).

66. Blue Circle Cement Co., Inc. v. NLRB, 107 F.3d 880 (10th Cir. 1997).

67. S. Cal. Edison Co. v. NLRB, 852 F.2d 572 (9th Cir. 1988).

68. *See, e.g.*, Hook v. UBS Fin. Servs., Inc., No. 3:10CV950 JBA, 2011 WL 1741997, at *4 (D. Conn. May 4, 2011) (noting that in the arbitration context, such language relates to all disputes involving employment); Raw v. Bank of N.Y. Mellon Corp., No. CIV.A. 09-4341 DRH, 2010 WL 4236941, at *3 (E.D.N.Y. Oct. 21, 2010), *aff'd*, 447 F. App'x 268 (2d Cir. 2012). Unlike in discrimination law, the law of at-will

employment also broadly defines these words "terms or conditions" of employment. At-will employment describes the rules that generally govern employment in the United States. At-will employment exists unless a contract or a specific law protects an employee. Under the at-will doctrine, an employer has the power to make employment decisions for a good reason, a bad reason, or no reason at all. For example, an employer could give an employee an office in the basement because she likes the music of Michael Bolton or because she wears mismatched socks. These reasons have very little to do with an employee's work performance, but most of American employment law does not require an employer to make decisions based on merit or for good reasons. So long as a contract or an existing law does not limit the employer's options, employers have discretion to make employment decisions. *See, e.g.*, Franklin v. Pinnacle Entm't, Inc., 1 F. Supp. 3d 979, 989 (E.D. Mo. 2014) (at-will employment includes decisions about whether to transfer employees); Salazar v. Monaco Enters., Inc., No. CV-12-0186-LRS, 2014 WL 1976601, at *4 (E.D. Wash. May 15, 2014) (handbook noting that at-will employment includes employer's right to transfer or discipline employees).

69. *See supra* notes 47–54 (Ch. 3).
70. 42 U.S.C. § 2000e-3(a) (Title VII); 29 U.S.C. § 623(d) (ADEA); 42 U.S.C. § 12203(a), (b) (ADA).
71. Univ. of Tex. Sw. Med. Sch. v. Nassar, 570 U.S. ___, 133 S. Ct. 2517, 2525 (2013); Crawford v. Metro. Gov't of Nashville & Davidson Cnty., Tenn., 555 U.S. 271, 274 (2009) (discussing opposition and participation conduct).
72. Faragher v. City of Boca Raton, 524 U.S. 775, 806–07 (1998); Burlington Indus., Inc. v. Ellerth, 524 U.S. 742, 773 (1998).
73. *See, e.g.*, 42 U.S.C. § 2000e-5(e)(1) & (f)(1).
74. *See, e.g.*, Hellman v. Weisberg, 360 F. App'x 776, 779 (9th Cir. 2009); Brown v. SDH Educ. E. LLC, No. 312-cv-2961-TLW, 2014 WL 468974, at *7 (D.S.C. Feb. 4, 2014); Gutierrez v. GEO Grp., No. 11-cv-02648-PAB-KLM, 2012 WL 2030024, at *3 (D. Colo. June 6, 2012); Jantz v. Emblem Health, No. 10 Civ. 6076 (PKC), 2012 WL 370297, at *14 (S.D.N.Y. Feb. 6, 2012); Pugni v. Reader's Digest Ass'n, No. 05 Civ. 8026 (CM), 2007 WL 1087183, at *23 (S.D.N.Y. Apr. 9, 2007).
75. *See, e.g.*, Gomez-Perez v. Potter, 452 F. App'x 3, 8 (1st Cir. 2011); Sconfienza v. Verizon Pa. Inc., 307 F. App'x 619, 622, 624 (3d Cir. 2008); Sesay-Harrell v. N.Y.C. Dep't of Homeless Servs., No. 12 Civ. 925(KPF), 2013 WL 6244158, at *19 (S.D.N.Y. Dec. 2, 2013); Augustus v. Napolitano, No. 11-120-JJB, 2013 WL 530586, at *5 (M.D. La. Feb. 11, 2013); Wilson-Robinson v. Our Lady of the Lake Reg'l Med. Ctr., Inc., No. 10-584, 2012 WL 5940912, at *5–7 (M.D. La. Nov. 27, 2012); Palmer-Williams v. Yale New Haven Hosp., Civ. No. 3:08cv1526 (JBA), 2011 WL 1226022, at *10 (D. Conn. Mar. 27, 2011); Carmellino v. Dist. 20 of N.Y.C. Dep't of Educ., No. 03 Civ. 5942 PKC, 2006 WL 2583019, at *32 (S.D.N.Y. Sept. 6, 2006).
76. *See, e.g.*, Littleton v. Pilot Travel Ctrs., LLC, 568 F.3d 641, 644 (8th Cir. 2009); Ballard v. Donahoe, No. 2:11-cv-2576 JAM AC PS, 2014 WL 1286193, at *13 (E.D. Cal. Mar. 27, 2014); Baloch v. Kempthorne, 550 F.3d 1191, 1199 (D.C. Cir. 2008); *see also* Chang v. Safe Horizons, 254 F. App'x 838, 839 (2d Cir. 2007) (holding that oral reprimands were not sufficient).

77. Bridgeforth v. Jewell, 721 F.3d 661, 662 (D.C. Cir. 2013).

78. *See, e.g.*, McKneely v. Zachary Police Dep't, No. 12-354-SDD-RLB, 2013 WL 4585160, at *10–11 (M.D. La. Aug. 28, 2013); Muse v. Jazz Casino Co., No. 09-0066, 2010 WL 2545278, at *3 (E.D. La. June 16, 2010).

79. *See, e.g.*, Lushute v. La. Dep't. of Soc. Servs., 479 F. App'x 553, 555 (5th Cir. 2012) (analyzing an action arising from the Family and Medical Leave Act (FMLA) using a Title VII standard); *McKneely*, 2013 WL 4585160, at *10.

80. *See, e.g.*, Rodriguez-Monguio v. Ohio State Univ., 499 F. App'x 455, 464 (6th Cir. 2012).

81. *See, e.g., Littleton*, 568 F.3d at 644.

82. Bridgeforth v. Salazar, 831 F. Supp. 2d 132, 144 (D.D.C. 2011).

83. *See, e.g.*, Barefield v. Bd. of Trustees of Cal. State Univ., Bakersfield, 500 F. Supp. 2d 1244, 1272 (E.D. Cal. 2007) (finding that a negative evaluation was an adverse action for purposes of retaliation law because it could affect the worker's future job prospects and her exclusion from a ball held by her school could also be an adverse action).

84. Burlington N. & Santa Fe Ry. v. White, 548 U.S. 53, 57 (2006).

85. Further information about the survey can be found at Sandra F. Sperino, *Retaliation and the Reasonable Person*, 67 FLA. L. REV. 2031 (2015).

86. As with many of the doctrines discussed in this book, courts do not approach the retaliation standard in a uniform way. Some courts will allow cases to proceed if an employer threatens to fire a worker or gives her a negative evaluation. Bixby v. JP Morgan Chase Bank, N.A., No. 10 C 405, 2012 WL 832889, at *13 (N.D. Ill. Mar. 8, 2012); Eldredge v. City of St. Paul, 809 F. Supp. 2d 1011, 1036 (D. Minn. 2011); EEOC v. Collegeville/Imagineering, No. CV-05-3033-PHX-DGC, 2007 WL 2051448, at *8 (D. Ariz. July 16, 2007). Courts have held that a written warning or letter of counseling may rise to the level of an adverse employment action "if it affects the likelihood that the plaintiff will be terminated, undermines the plaintiff's current position, or affects the plaintiff's future employment opportunities." Medina v. Income Support Div., 413 F.3d 1131, 1137 (10th Cir. 2005); *see also* Roberts v. Roadway Express, 149 F.3d 1098, 1104 (10th Cir. 1998) (holding that the plaintiff's written warnings constituted adverse employment actions, where "the record indicate[d] that the more warnings an employee received, the more likely he or she was to be terminated for a further infraction").

87. *See, e.g.*, Taylor v. Cardiovascular Specialists, P.C., 4 F. Supp. 3d 1374, 1378 (N.D. Ga. 2014). This requirement only applies to conduct that the courts call opposition conduct, such as complaining to an employer about discrimination. When a worker engages in participation conduct (such as filing a Charge of Discrimination with the EEOC or an administrative agency), courts will not impose a reasonable belief requirement. *See, e.g.*, Ray v. Ropes & Gray LLP, 799 F.3d 99, 110 (1st Cir. 2015).

88. Deborah L. Brake, *Retaliation in an EEO World*, 89 IND. L.J. 115, 136 (2014).

89. *Id.* at 139.

90. 536 F.3d 1209 (11th Cir. 2008).

91. *Id.* at 1210.

92. *Id.* at 1212.
93. *Id.* at 1213.
94. Boyer-Liberto v. Fontainebleau Corp., No. 13-1473, 786 F.3d 264 (4th Cir. 2015).
95. *Id.* at 283.
96. Little v. United Tech., Carrier Transicold Div., 103 F.3d 956, 958 (11th Cir. 1997).
97. Van Portfliet v. H & R Block Mortg. Corp., 290 F. App'x 301, 302 (11th Cir. 2008).
98. Hill v. Guyoungtech USA, Inc., Civ. No. 07-0750-KD-M, 2008 WL 4073638, at *9 (S.D. Ala. Aug. 26, 2008).
99. Brake, *supra* note 88 (Ch. 3), at 238.
100. SOCIETY FOR HUMAN RESOURCE MANAGEMENT, ABOUT THE SOCIETY FOR HUMAN RESOURCE MANAGEMENT, http://www.shrm.org/about/pages/default.aspx.
101. SOCIETY FOR HUMAN RESOURCE MANAGEMENT, SAMPLE EMPLOYEE HANDBOOK, *available at* http://www.shrm.org/TemplatesTools/Samples/Documents/Sample%20 Handbook_FINAL.doc (last visited Oct. 8, 2015).
102. *Id.*
103. *Id.*
104. *Id.* In some states, these facts might create a breach of contract claim. However, many employers include language in their handbooks stating that the handbook is not a contract; and many courts have refused to enforce handbooks as contracts.
105. King v. Piggly Wiggly Ala. Distrib. Co., 929 F. Supp. 2d 1215, 1228 (N.D. Ala. 2013) (internal citation omitted).
106. Brake, *supra* note 88 (Ch. 3), at 132–33.
107. Univ. of Tex. Sw. Med. Ctr. v. Nassar, 570 U.S. ___, 133 S. Ct. 2517, 2537 (2013) (internal citation omitted); Burlington N. & Santa Fe Ry. v. White, 548 U.S. 53, 67 (2006).
108. Burlington Indus., Inc. v. Ellerth, 524 U.S. 742, 764 (1998).
109. *Id.*
110. Kolstad v. Am. Dental Ass'n, 527 U.S. 526 (1999).
111. *See* Brake, *supra* note 88 (Ch. 3), at 130.
112. *See* cases cited throughout this chapter; *but see* Schatzman v. Martin Newark Dealership, Inc., 158 F. Supp. 2d 392, 403 (D. Del. 2001) (allowing retaliation claim to proceed based on the reporting of one comment).
113. Anderson v. United Parcel Serv., Inc., 248 F. App'x 97, 100 (11th Cir. 2007); Morgan v. Vilsack, 715 F. Supp. 2d 168, 175 (D.D.C. 2010).
114. *See, e.g.*, Valtchev v. City of New York, 400 F. App'x 586, 589 (2d Cir. 2010); Dimitracopoulos v. City of New York, 26 F. Supp. 3d 200, 212 (E.D.N.Y. 2014); Bostic v. AT&T of Virgin Islands, 166 F. Supp. 2d 350, 358 (D.V.I. 2001). For harassment cases, the courts created the idea of a continuing violation. A supervisor might make a discriminatory comment one day, but days, weeks, or even months might go by before he engages in other discriminatory conduct. Because a single comment is usually not enough to establish a harassment claim, the worker can wait until the entire course of events is considered serious enough to be called harassment. As long as a worker goes to the EEOC within the appropriate 180 or 300 days of one harassing act, she can use the entire course of conduct

to support her harassment claim. Taylor v. Brandywine Sch. Dist., 202 F. App'x 570, 574 (3d Cir. 2006).

115. Mveng-Whitted v. Va. State Univ., No. 3:11-CV-00842-JAG, 2012 WL 3686285, at *5 (E.D. Va. Aug. 24, 2012).

116. Miller v. New Hampshire Dep't of Corr., 296 F.3d 18, 22 (1st Cir. 2002).

CHAPTER 4

1. For a case with similar facts, see *Behnia v. Shapiro*, No. 96 C 7646, 1998 WL 381041, at *3 (N.D. Ill. July 1, 1998). There, the court allowed one of plaintiff's claims to proceed, but it is not clear from the opinion whether the court credited any of the remarks as part of the evidence in support of the worker's case.

2. *Id.*

3. For a case with similar facts, see *Auguster v. Vermilion Parish School Board*, 249 F.3d 400, 401 (5th Cir. 2001).

4. *Id.* at 401.

5. *Id.*

6. *Id.*

7. *Id.* at 404–05.

8. Chappell v. The Bilco Co., No. 3:09CV00016 JLH, 2011 WL 9037, at *9 (E.D. Ark. Jan. 3, 2011), *aff'd*, 675 F.3d 1110 (8th Cir. 2012) (affirming summary judgment).

9. O'Connor v. Consol. Coin Caterers Corp., 56 F.3d 542, 551 (4th Cir. 1995) (Butzner, J., dissenting), *rev'd*, 517 U.S. 308 (1996).

10. For more discussion of the stray remarks doctrine, see Kerri Lynn Stone, *Taking in Strays: A Critique of the Stray Comment Doctrine in Employment Discrimination Law*, 77 Mo. L. Rev. 149 (2012).

11. Mosberger v. CPG Nutrients, Civ. No. 01-100, 2002 WL 31477292, at *7, 8 (W.D. Pa. Sept. 6, 2002) ("Discriminatory stray remarks are generally considered in one of three categories—those made (1) by a non-decisionmaker; (2) by a decisionmaker but unrelated to the decision process; or (3) by a decisionmaker but temporally remote from the adverse employment decision.") (internal quotations and citations omitted); *see also generally* Stone, *supra* note 10 (Ch. 4).

12. 490 U.S. 228 (1989).

13. *Id.* at 235.

14. *Id.*

15. *Id.*

16. *Id.* at 277 (O'Connor, J., concurring) (internal citation omitted).

17. Stone, *supra* note 10 (Ch. 4), at 170.

18. Ferrand v. Credit Lyonnais, No. 02 CIV.5191(VM), 2003 WL 22251313, at *1 (S.D.N.Y. Sept. 30, 2003), *aff'd*, 110 F. App'x 160 (2d Cir. 2004).

19. Price v. Marathon Cheese Corp., 119 F.3d 330, 337 (5th Cir. 1997).

20. Pronin v. Raffi Custom Photo Lab., Inc., 383 F. Supp. 2d 628, 638 (S.D.N.Y. 2005).

21. Engstrand v. Pioneer Hi-Bred Int'l, Inc., 946 F. Supp. 1390, 1399 (S.D. Iowa 1996), *aff'd*, 112 F.3d 513 (8th Cir. 1997).

22. Nesbit v. Pepsico, Inc., 994 F.2d 703, 705 (9th Cir. 1993).

23. Harrison v. Formosa Plastics Corp. Tex., 776 F. Supp. 2d 433, 442 (S.D. Tex. 2011).

24. Sweezer v. Mich. Dep't of Corr., 229 F.3d 1154 (6th Cir. 2000).

25. Suja A. Thomas, *Summary Judgment and the Reasonable Jury Standard: A Proxy for a Judge's Own View of the Sufficiency of the Evidence?*, 97 Judicature 222 (2014).

26. Bagwe v. Sedgwick Claims Mgmt. Servs., Inc., No. 11 CV 2450, 2014 WL 4413768, at *13 (N.D. Ill. Sept. 5, 2014).

27. For a case with similar facts, see *Bagwe, id.*, 2014 WL 4413768 at *13.

28. *Id.*

29. *Id.; see also* Overly v. Keybank Nat'l Ass'n, 662 F.3d 856, 865 (7th Cir. 2011) (finding that supervisor calling plaintiff a "bitch" after she resigned was insufficient "to be regarded by a reasonable jury as a confession that any previous, adverse conduct was taken for a discriminatory purpose").

30. *Overly*, 662 F.3d at 862.

31. *Id.* at 865.

32. Diaz v. Jiten Hotel Mgmt., Inc., 762 F. Supp. 2d 319, 335 (D. Mass. 2011).

33. *Id.* at 337.

34. *See, e.g.*, Ash v. Tyson Foods, Inc., 129 F. App'x 529, 531 (11th Cir. 2005), *vacated and remanded*, 546 U.S. 454 (2006).

35. Michael J. Zimmer, *Slicing & Dicing of Individual Disparate Treatment Law*, 61 La. L. Rev. 577 (2001).

36. Holmes v. Marriott Corp., 831 F. Supp. 691, 704 (S.D. Iowa 1993).

37. Sweezer v. Mich. Dep't of Corr., 229 F.3d 1154 (6th Cir. 2000); Ferrand v. Credit Lyonnais, No. 02 CIV. 5191(VM), 2003 WL 22251313, at *10 (S.D.N.Y. Sept. 30, 2003), *aff'd*, 110 F. App'x 160 (2d Cir. 2004).

38. Boyer-Liberto v. Fontainebleau Corp., No. 13-1473, 2015 WL 2116849, at *1 (4th Cir. May 7, 2015) (referring to black employee as a "porch monkey" was evidence of discrimination); Crisonino v. N.Y.C. Hous. Auth., 985 F. Supp. 385, 389 (S.D.N.Y. 1997) (using the term "dumb bitch" to refer to a female employee is not a stray remark).

39. *See, e.g.*, Armendariz v. Pinkerton Tobacco Co., 58 F.3d 144, 153 (5th Cir. 1995); Lassetter v. Strategic Materials, Inc., 192 F. Supp. 2d 698, 704 (N.D. Tex. 2002), *aff'd*, 72 F. App'x 106 (5th Cir. 2003) (trial court granted employer's motion for judgment as a matter of law even though worker presented evidence of age-related comments); Palasota v. Haggar Clothing Co., No. CIV.A. 3:00CV1925G, 2002 WL 1398556, at *4 (N.D. Tex. June 26, 2002), *rev'd*, 342 F.3d 569 (5th Cir. 2003).

40. Alvarado-Santos v. Dep't of Health of P.R., 619 F.3d 126, 128 (1st Cir. 2010).

41. *Id.*

42. *Id.* at 127.

43. *Id.*

44. *Id.* at 133.

45. Ash v. Tyson Foods, Inc., 546 U.S. 454, 455–56 (2006).

46. Ash v. Tyson Foods, Inc., No. CIV.A. 96-RRA-3257-M, 2004 WL 5138005, at *1, 6 (N.D. Ala. Mar. 26, 2004), *aff'd in part, rev'd in part*, 129 F. App'x 529 (11th Cir. 2005), *vacated*, 546 U.S. 454 (2006).

47. *Ash*, 2004 WL 5138005, at *6.

48. Ash v. Tyson Foods, Inc., 129 F. App'x 529, 533 (11th Cir. 2005), *vacated*, 546 U.S. 454 (2006).

49. 546 U.S. at 456.

50. Ash v. Tyson Foods, Inc., 190 F. App'x 924, 926 (11th Cir. 2006).

51. *Id.* at 927.

52. Ash v. Tyson Foods, Inc., 392 F. App'x 817, 833 (11th Cir. 2010) *opinion vacated on reconsideration*, 664 F.3d 883 (11th Cir. 2011).

53. *Id.* at 833 (Dowd, J., dissenting).

54. Ash v. Tyson Foods, Inc., 664 F.3d 883, 897 (11th Cir. 2011).

55. *Id.* at 887.

56. Reeves v. Sanderson Plumbing Prods., Inc., 530 U.S. 133, 137 (2000).

57. *Id.*

58. Reeves v. Sanderson Plumbing Prods., Inc., 197 F.3d 688, 691 (5th Cir. 1999), *rev'd*, 530 U.S. 133 (2000).

59. *Reeves*, 197 F.3d at 693.

60. 530 U.S. at 151.

61. 82 F.3d 651, 658 (5th Cir. 1996).

62. *Id.* at 658.

63. *Id.* at 656.

64. *Id.*

65. *Id.*

66. *Id.*

67. *Id.*

68. Brown v. CSC Logic, Inc., 82 F.3d 651, 658 (5th Cir. 1996) (internal citations omitted). There is a long line of cases applying the same protected class inference. *See, e.g.*, Elrod v. Sears, Roebuck and Co., 939 F.2d 1466, 1471 (11th Cir. 1991); Cartee v. Wilbur Smith Assocs., Inc., No. C/A 3:08-4132, 2010 WL 5059643, at *5 (D.S.C. Oct. 6, 2010); Demesme v. Montgomery Cnty. Gov't, 63 F. Supp. 2d 678, 683 (D. Md. 1999). However, courts also reject the same protected class inference. Kadas v. MCI Systemhouse Corp., 255 F.3d 359, 361 (7th Cir. 2001).

69. *Brown*, 82 F.3d at 658 (internal citations omitted); *see also* DeJarnette v. Corning Inc., 133 F.3d 293, 298 (4th Cir. 1998) (internal citations omitted).

70. Amirmokri v. Balt. Gas & Elec. Co., 60 F.3d 1126, 1128 (4th Cir. 1995).

71. *Id.* at 1130.

72. *Id.* at 1131.

73. Proud v. Stone, 945 F.2d 796, 796–97 (4th Cir. 1991).

74. Natasha T. Martin, *Immunity for Hire: How the Same-Actor Doctrine Sustains Discrimination in the Contemporary Workplace*, 40 Conn. L. Rev. 1117, 1135 (2008).

75. Carlton v. Mystic Transp., Inc., 202 F.3d 129, 132 (2d Cir. 2000).

76. Martin, *supra* note 74 (Ch. 4), at 1128.

77. Stone, *supra* note 10 (Ch. 4), at 183–84.

78. Perez v. Thorntons, Inc., 731 F.3d 699, 710 (7th Cir. 2013).

79. There is not one uniform understanding of the honest belief rule. Different appellate courts describe the test in different ways.

80.	Ralph Richard Banks & Richard Thompson Ford, *(How) Does Unconscious Bias Matter?: Law, Politics, and Racial Inequality*, 58 EMORY L.J. 1053, 1088 (2009).
81.	*See, e.g.*, Obike v. Applied EPI, Inc., No. CIV.02-1653 (JRT/FLN), 2004 WL 741657, at *5 (D. Minn. Mar. 24, 2004) (discussing reluctance of some courts to use doctrine).
82.	Dailey v. Accubuilt, Inc., 944 F. Supp. 2d 571, 580 (N.D. Ohio 2013).
83.	Hamilton v. Boise Cascade Exp., 280 F. App'x 729, 729 (10th Cir. 2008).
84.	*Id.* at 732.
85.	*Id.* at 737 (Ebel, J., dissenting).
86.	*Id.* at 729, 734.
87.	For a case with similar facts, see *Hale v. Mercy Health Partners*, No. 14-3522, 2015 WL 1637896, at *10 (6th Cir. Apr. 14, 2015) (White, J., concurring in part and dissenting in part).
88.	Wilson v. Cleveland Clinic Found., 579 F. App'x 392, 408 (6th Cir. 2014) (Cole, C.J., dissenting in part).
89.	*Id.* at 407.
90.	Seeger v. Cincinnati Bell Tel. Co., 681 F.3d 274, 290 (6th Cir. 2012) (Tarnow, J., dissenting) (discussing honest-belief doctrine in context of the Family and Medical Leave Act, which is a similar analysis to that used in discrimination cases); *see also* Kariotis v. Navistar Int'l Transp. Corp., 131 F.3d 672, 677 (7th Cir. 1997) (describing employer investigation as "careless").
91.	Clack v. Rock-Tenn Co., 304 F. App'x 399, 403 n.2 (6th Cir. 2008).
92.	*Id.*
93.	*Id.*
94.	*Id.*
95.	*Id.* at 405.
96.	*See, e.g.*, Loyd v. Saint Joseph Mercy Oakland, 766 F.3d 580, 597 (6th Cir. 2014) (Clay, J., dissenting).
97.	Walton v. McDonnell Douglas Corp., 167 F.3d 423, 426 (8th Cir. 1999).
98.	*Id.*
99.	*Id.*
100.	Smith v. Chrysler Corp., 155 F.3d 799, 806 (6th Cir. 1998).
101.	Bhama v. Mercy Mem'l Hosp. Corp., 416 F. App'x 542, 557 (6th Cir. 2011) (White, J., dissenting).
102.	*Id.*
103.	*See, e.g.*, Kurincic v. Stein Inc., 30 F. App'x 420, 430 (6th Cir. 2002) (Gibson, J., dissenting) (arguing that other judges had substituted a different reason for the employer's action); Hamilton v. Boise Cascade Exp., 280 F. App'x 729, 737–38 (10th Cir. 2008) (Ebel, J., dissenting).
104.	St. Mary's Honor Ctr. v. Hicks, 509 U.S. 502, 511 (1993).
105.	*See, e.g.*, Clack v. Rock-Tenn Co., 304 F. App'x 399, 403, 408 (6th Cir. 2008); Seeger v. Cincinnati Bell Tel. Co., 681 F.3d 274, 287–290 (6th Cir. 2012) (discussing honest-belief doctrine in FMLA context).
106.	Ernest F. Lidge III, *The Courts' Misuse of the Similarly Situated Concept in Employment Discrimination Law*, 67 MO. L. REV. 831, 877 (2002).

107. Charles A. Sullivan, *Circling Back to the Obvious: The Convergence of Traditional and Reverse Discrimination in Title VII Proof*, 46 WM. AND MARY L. REV. 1031, 1115–16 (2004).

108. McDonnell Douglas v. Green, 411 U.S. 792, 797 (1973).

109. DeJarnette v. Corning Inc., 133 F.3d 293, 299 (4th Cir. 1998).

110. *Id.*

111. *Id.* (considering employer's motion for judgment as a matter of law).

112. Wolf v. Buss (Am.) Inc., 77 F.3d 914, 918 (7th Cir. 1996).

113. *Id.* at 923 (granting employer's motion for summary judgment).

114. *See, e.g.*, DeJarnette v. Corning Inc., 133 F.3d 293, 299 (4th Cir. 1998); Jones v. Polk Ctr., No. CIV.A. 07-204, 2009 WL 700686, at *6 (W.D. Pa. Mar. 11, 2009).

115. *See, e.g., DeJarnette*, 133 F.3d at 299; Ramos v. Molina Healthcare, Inc., 963 F. Supp. 2d 511, 523 (E.D. Va. 2013), *aff'd*, No. 13-2117, 2015 WL 1137091 (4th Cir. Mar. 16, 2015) (evidence from plaintiff and coworker calling into question claim that plaintiff was belligerent during a meeting was not tethered to other evidence of age discrimination); Jones v. Polk Ctr., No. CIV.A. 07-204, 2009 WL 700686, at *6 (W.D. Pa. Mar. 11, 2009).

116. *See, e.g.*, DeJarnette v. Corning Inc., 133 F.3d 293, 299 (4th Cir. 1998); Jones v. Polk Ctr., No. CIV.A. 07-204, 2009 WL 700686, at *6 (W.D. Pa. Mar. 11, 2009).

117. McDonnell Douglas v. Green, 411 U.S. 792, 797 (1973); Reeves v. Sanderson Plumbing Prods., Inc., 530 U.S. 133, 143 (2000).

118. *See, e.g.*, Ash v. Tyson Foods, Inc., No. CIV.A. 96-RRA-3257-M, 2004 WL 5138005, at *1, 6 (N.D. Ala. Mar. 26, 2004), *aff'd in part, rev'd in part*, 129 F. App'x 529 (11th Cir. 2005), *vacated*, 546 U.S. 454 (2006).

119. *Reeves*, 530 U.S. at 147.

120. *See, e.g.*, Ash v. Tyson Foods, Inc., No. CIV.A. 96-RRA-3257-M, 2004 WL 5138005, at *1, 6 (N.D. Ala. Mar. 26, 2004), *aff'd in part, rev'd in part*, 129 F. App'x 529 (11th Cir. 2005), *vacated*, 546 U.S. 454 (2006).

121. *See, e.g.*, Ham v. Washington Suburban Sanitary Comm'n, 158 F. App'x 457, 466 (4th Cir. 2005).

122. Keaton v. Cobb Cnty., 545 F. Supp. 2d 1275, 1280 (N.D. Ga. 2008).

123. *Id.* at 1292.

124. *Id.* at 1301.

125. Bryant v. Dougherty Cnty. Sch. Sys., No. 1:05-CV-142WLS, 2009 WL 3161678, at *13 (M.D. Ga. Sept. 28, 2009), *aff'd*, 382 F. App'x 914 (11th Cir. 2010) (internal citations omitted).

126. Ash v. Tyson Foods, Inc., 546 U.S. 454, 457 (2006).

127. *Id.* at 458. Despite the *Ash* decision, lower courts continue to reject evidence that a worker was better qualified. While courts should not use the "slap you in the face" standard that the Supreme Court rejected, some courts seem to continue to use a similarly high standard for viewing a worker's evidence. Bryant v. Dougherty Cnty. Sch. Sys., No. 1:05-CV-142WLS, 2009 WL 3161678, at *13 (M.D. Ga. Sept. 28, 2009), *aff'd*, 382 F. App'x 914 (11th Cir. 2010) (internal citations omitted). Recently, a court stated that evidence that a worker was better qualified than the chosen applicant constitutes evidence of discrimination only if

the differences between candidates "are so favorable to the plaintiff that there can be no dispute among reasonable persons of impartial judgment that the plaintiff was clearly better qualified for the position at issue." Carlson v. CSX Transp., Inc., No. 3:12-CV-00195-RLY-WGH, 2015 WL 400633, at *6 (S.D. Ind. Jan. 28, 2015); *see also* Mlynczak v. Bodman, 442 F.3d 1050, 1059–60 (7th Cir. 2006).

128. See cases cited *supra* note 127 (Ch. 4).

129. Hasham v. Cal. State Bd. of Equalization, 200 F.3d 1035, 1046 (7th Cir. 2000).

130. Ransdell v. Russ Berrie & Co., Chicago, No. 87 C 4628, 1991 WL 101658, at *2 (N.D. Ill. June 6, 1991).

131. Ramos v. Molina Healthcare, Inc., 963 F. Supp. 2d 511, 526 (E.D. Va. 2013), *aff'd*, No. 13-2117, 2015 WL 1137091 (4th Cir. Mar. 16, 2015).

132. Millbrook v. IBP, Inc., 280 F.3d 1169, 1181 (7th Cir. 2002); *see also* Bryant v. Honeywell Int'l, No. 3:11 CV 495, 2014 WL 1316949, at *7 (N.D. Ind. Mar. 28, 2014) (internal citations omitted).

133. Wexler v. White's Fine Furniture, Inc., 246 F.3d 856, 859-60, 863 (6th Cir. 2001), *reh'g en banc granted, judgment vacated* (July 12, 2001), *opinion superseded on reh'g*, 317 F.3d 564 (6th Cir. 2003).

134. 246 F.3d at 861.

135. *Id.* at 864 (affirming summary judgment for the employer).

136. *Id.* at 874 (Gilman, J., dissenting).

137. *See* Suzanne B. Goldberg, *Discrimination by Comparison*, 120 Yale L.J. 728 (2011); Stone, *supra* note 10 (Ch. 4); Martin, *supra* note 74 (Ch. 4).

138. Rojas v. Florida, 285 F.3d 1339, 1341 (11th Cir. 2002).

139. *Id.* at 1343.

140. *Id.* at 1341.

141. *Id.* at 1343.

142. *Id.* at 1342.

143. *Id.* at 1342 n.3.

144. *Id.* at 1341, 1344 n.4.

145. *Id.* at 1342.

146. *Id.* at 1343. The court also excluded the comment from Nancy's coworker, finding that it was inadmissible hearsay

147. *Id.*

148. Brief for Appellee at *5, Rojas v. Florida, 285 F.3d 1339 (11th Cir. 2002) (No. 01-11070-JJ), 2001 WL 34089992, at *5.

CHAPTER 5

1. This fact pattern is very loosely based on the case of *Boyd v. State Farm Insurance Cos.*, 158 F.3d 326, 327 (5th Cir. 1998). There, the worker alleged that the company failed to promote him and later fired him. The worker also alleged a violation of the Family and Medical Leave Act. The fact pattern does not discuss the termination claim. The employer asserted that the employee was fired for missing work without proper medical documentation.

2. *Id.* at 329.

3. *Id.*

4. *Id.* at 329–30.
5. *Id.* at 329.
6. Montgomery v. John Deere & Co., 169 F.3d 556, 559–60 (8th Cir. 1999).
7. *Id.*
8. Ferrand v. Credit Lyonnais, No. 02 CIV.5191(VM), 2003 WL 22251313, at *10 (S.D.N.Y. Sept. 30, 2003), *aff'd*, 110 F. App'x 160 (2d Cir. 2004).
9. *See, e.g.,* Arraleh v. Cnty. of Ramsey, 461 F.3d 967, 975 (8th Cir. 2006).
10. Tristin K. Green, *Work Culture and Discrimination*, 93 CAL. L. REV. 623, 640 (2005).
11. Price Waterhouse v. Hopkins, 490 U.S. 228, 231–32 (1989).
12. *Id.* at 232–33.
13. *Id.* at 233.
14. *Id.* at 235.
15. *Id.*
16. *Id.*
17. *Id.* at 234–35.
18. Farmer v. Camden City Bd. of Educ., No. CIV. 03-685JBS, 2005 WL 1683745, at *1 (D.N.J. July 19, 2005).
19. *Id.* at *5.
20. Cerutti v. BASF Corp., 349 F.3d 1055, 1062 (7th Cir. 2003).
21. *Id.*
22. *Id.* at 1063.
23. Cole v. Mgmt. & Training Corp., No. 4:11CV-118-JHM, 2014 WL 2612561, at *4 (W.D. Ky. June 11, 2014).
24. For a case with similar facts, see *Ferrand v. Credit Lyonnais*, No. 02 CIV.5191(VM), 2003 WL 22251313, at *1, *10 (S.D.N.Y. Sept. 30, 2003), *aff'd*, 110 F. App'x 160 (2d Cir. 2004).
25. For similar reasoning, see *Ferrand*, 2003 WL 22251313, at *9.
26. Cook v. IPC Int'l Corp., 673 F.3d 625, 628 (7th Cir. 2012).
27. Staub v. Proctor Hosp., 562 U.S. 411, 422 (2011) (footnote omitted). Although the Supreme Court decided the *Staub* case under a different statute—that protected discrimination on the basis of military status as opposed to discrimination under Title VII and other general discrimination statutes—the *Staub* decision frequently referenced those other discrimination laws, and courts use the *Staub* standard in general discrimination cases.
28. *See, e.g.,* Anderson v. Northland Rest. Grp., LLC, No. CIV 14-5005, 2016 WL 1258748, at *2 (D.S.D. Mar. 28, 2016) (holding that the worker did not present evidence that the decision maker relied on the opinion of the jilted lover); Baron v. Maxam N. Am., Inc., No. 3:11-CV-198 JCH, 2012 WL 1247257, at *7 (D. Conn. Apr. 13, 2012).
29. Thomas v. Berry Plastics Corp., 803 F.3d 510, 513 (10th Cir. 2015).
30. *Id.* at 516–17.
31. Hill v. Lockheed Martin Logistics Mgmt., Inc., 354 F.3d 277, 282 (4th Cir. 2004); *see also* Hebert v. JPMorgan Chase Bank, N.A., No. 13 C 4358, 2016 WL 245570, at *5 (N.D. Ill. Jan. 21, 2016).
32. *Hill*, 354 F.3d at 283.
33. *Id.*

34. Vasquez v. Empress Ambulance Serv., Inc., No. 14 CIV. 8387 NRB, 2015 WL 5037055, at *1 (S.D.N.Y. Aug. 26, 2015), *vacated by* 835 F. 3d 267 (2d Cir. 2016).

35. *Id.* at 2.

36. Vasquez v. Cnty. of Los Angeles, 349 F.3d 634, 647 (9th Cir. 2004) (internal citations omitted); *see also* Burlington v. News Corp., 55 F. Supp. 3d 723, 740 (E.D. Pa. 2014).

37. This hypothetical is similar to one provided in RESTATEMENT (SECOND) OF TORTS § 432, illus. 1 (1965).

38. Gross v. FBL Fin. Servs., 557 U.S. 167 (2009).

39. Univ. of Tex. Sw. Med. Ctr. v. Nassar, 570 U.S. __, 133 S. Ct. 2517 (2013).

40. Savage v. Secure First Credit Union, No. 2:14-cv-02468-WMA, 2015 U.S. Dist. LEXIS 60507, at *6 (N.D. Ala. May 8, 2015); *see also* Culver v. Birmingham Bd. of Educ., 646 F. Supp. 2d 1270, 1272 (N.D. Ala. 2009); Barnes v. McHugh, No. CIV.A. 12-2491, 2013 WL 3561679, at *12 (E.D. La. July 11, 2013) (stating that worker must choose between age and other reasons for employment actions to proceed on age discrimination claim); Woldetadik v. 7-Eleven, Inc., 881 F. Supp. 2d 738, 742 (N.D. Tex. 2012) (allowing claims of age and national origin discrimination to proceed past the pleading stage, but noting that worker may not be "able to recover on both his age discrimination claim and national origin claim" at trial). Even when courts recognize that two motives can be at issue, they may not allow a worker to proceed with a claim. *See, e.g.,* Kelmendi v. Detroit Bd. of Educ., No. 12-CV-14949, 2015 WL 4394134, at *9 (E.D. Mich. July 16, 2015) (allowing worker's national origin claim to proceed, but not allowing age discrimination claim to proceed even though there was evidence that a committee who hired a worker commented on the chosen worker's youth).

41. Leal v. McHugh, 731 F.3d 405, 415 (5th Cir. 2013).

42. Price Waterhouse v. Hopkins, 490 U.S. 228, 231–32 (1989).

43. *Id.* at 236–37.

44. *Id.* at 237. At the time of *Price Waterhouse,* Title VII did not provide for a jury trial, so cases were bench tried. This means that the trial court judge sat as the fact-finder in the case.

45. *Id.* at 240.

46. *Id.* at 240–41; 262 (O'Connor, J., concurring) (Justice O'Connor thought that the two-step process ultimately resulted in a but for cause inquiry; however, she noted that the worker should not be required to carry the entire causation burden).

47. *Id.* at 240 (plurality opinion).

48. *Id.* at 241.

49. *Id.* at 241–48. Congress later amended Title VII to change this portion of the *Price Waterhouse* decision. If an employer makes the required showing, it can limit its damages, but it does not escape liability. 42 U.S.C. §§ 2000e-2(m) & 2000e-5(g)(2) (B).

50. 490 U.S. at 266 (O'Connor, J., concurring).

51. *Id.*

52. Gross v. FBL Fin. Servs., Inc., 557 U.S. 167, 170 (2009).

53. *Id.* at 171.

54. *Id.*
55. *Id.*
56. The *Gross* case raised the question of whether a worker must present direct evidence of discrimination to obtain a "mixed-motive" instruction in an ADEA case. 557 U.S. at 172. In *Price Waterhouse v. Hopkins*, there was a plurality opinion, two concurring opinions, and a dissent. 490 U.S. 228 (1989). The plurality opinion garnered the votes of four Justices, which is not a majority of the Court. Although six of the Justices agreed about the causation test, they could not agree on the reasons for the test. In instances where there is not a majority opinion, courts will often determine the holding of a case by looking for agreement among the plurality opinion and concurring opinions. In *Price Waterhouse*, Justice O'Connor stated that a worker was entitled to proceed under the motivating factor test if she presented direct evidence of discrimination. 490 U.S. at 276. Direct evidence is evidence that establishes discrimination without any need for speculation or inference. For example, if a supervisor states, "I did not hire Suzy because she is a woman," this statement would be direct evidence of discrimination. Direct evidence is contrasted with circumstantial evidence. If a supervisor said he did not like women and then did not hire Suzy, this would be circumstantial evidence. After *Price Waterhouse*, lower courts struggled with the question of whether workers had to present direct evidence of discrimination to proceed under the motivating factor framework.
57. Interestingly, *Gross* did not come before the Court as a causation case. When a litigant wants to have a case heard by the Supreme Court he presents certain questions for the Court to consider. The question the Court accepted was whether a worker must present direct evidence of age discrimination to claim the benefit of a motivating factor analysis under the ADEA. 557 U.S. at 172. The Court did not answer this question. Rather, the Court answered the very different question of whether the ADEA allowed a motivating factor analysis at all.
58. When Congress created the ADEA, it adopted the original operative language of Title VII. Thus, both statutes prohibit an employer from making employment decisions "because of" an employee's protected trait. 42 U.S.C. § 2000e-2(a)(1)-(2) (Title VII); 29 U.S.C. § 623(a)(1)-(2) (ADEA). In 1991, Congress amended Title VII. It added a new provision to Title VII that expressly codified the motivating factor standard enunciated in *Price Waterhouse*. 42 U.S.C. §§ 2000e-2(m) & 2000e-5(g)(2)(B). Congress also made the statute more worker-friendly. Under *Price Waterhouse*, if the employer considered an impermissible trait but proved the same outcome would happen without consideration of the protected trait, the employer would win the case. However, Congress thought the worker should win once the worker proved the impermissible factor was a motivating factor. Congress chose to allow the employer to escape liability for certain kinds of damages if it could show it would have made the same decision absent consideration of the impermissible trait. *Id.* Congress did not make similar amendments to the ADEA or the retaliation provision in Title VII. In *Gross*, the Court characterized Congress's failure to amend the main provisions of the ADEA as proof that the causation analysis should proceed differently under the two statutes. 557 U.S. at 174–75.

59. Univ. of Tex. Sw. Med. Ctr. v. Nassar, 570 U.S. __, 133 S. Ct. 2517 (2013).

60. *Workplace Fairness: Has the Supreme Court Been Misinterpreting Laws Designed to Protect American Workers from Discrimination? Hearing Before the S. Comm. on the Judicary*, 111th Cong. 4–5 (2009) (statement of Jack Gross), *available at* http://www.judiciary.senate.gov/imo/media/doc/10-07-09%20Gross%20testimony.pdf.

61. Gross v. FBL Fin. Grp., Inc., 489 F. App'x 971, 972–73 (8th Cir. 2012).

62. *Workplace Fairness: Has the Supreme Court Been Misinterpreting Laws Designed to Protect American Workers from Discrimination? Hearing Before the S. Comm. on the Judiciary*, 111th Cong. 2 (2009) (statement of Sen. Patrick Leahy, Chairman, S. Comm. on the Judiciary), *available at* http://www.judiciary.senate.gov/imo/media/doc/leahy_statement_10_07_09a.pdf.

63. *Id.*

64. 908 F. Supp. 2d 686, 693 (D. Md. 2012), *aff'd in part, rev'd in part on reconsideration*, No. CIV. TJS-10-1933, 2013 WL 5487813 (D. Md. Sept. 27, 2013).

65. *Id.*

66. *Id.*

67. *Id.*

68. *Id.* at 694–95.

69. *Id.* at 695.

70. *Id.* at 696.

71. *Id.* at 708.

72. Foster v. Univ. of Md. E. Shore, No. CIV. TJS-10-1933, 2013 WL 5487813, at *7 (D. Md. Sept. 27, 2013), *reversed on other grounds*, 787 F.3d 243 (4th Cir. 2015) (trial court dismissing case on summary judgment). Interestingly, the appellate court applied a different causation analysis to the retaliation claim.

73. Meyers v. Medco Health Solutions, Inc., No. 09 CIV. 09216 (RKE), 2015 WL 1500217, at *4 (S.D.N.Y. Mar. 31, 2015) (internal citation omitted).

74. Sass v. MTA Bus Co., 6 F. Supp. 3d 229, 235 (E.D.N.Y. 2014).

75. Courts are split about which standard should apply to disability discrimination claims. Francis v. Wyckoff Heights Med. Ctr., No. 13-cv-2813(DLI)(MDG), 2016 WL 1273235, at *8 n.7 (E.D.N.Y. Mar. 30, 2016) (noting disagreement); Savage v. Secure First Credit Union, 107 F. Supp. 3d 1212, 1217 (N.D. Ala. 2015) (applying but for cause to ADA claim); Vale v. Great Neck Water Pollution Control Dist., 80 F. Supp. 3d 426, 437 (E.D.N.Y. 2015).

76. Mathews v. Massage Green LLC, No. 14-CV-13040, 2016 WL 1242354, at *18 (E.D. Mich. Mar. 30, 2016) (internal citation omitted); Hendon v. Kamtek, Inc., 117 F. Supp. 3d 1325, 1334 (N.D. Ala. 2015) (noting that a worker cannot prove retaliation "if her firing was prompted by both legitimate and illegitimate factors") *see also* Vickers v. Hyundai Motor Mfg. of Alabama, LLC, No. 2:14-CV-126-WKW (WO), 2015 WL 5736909, at *8 (M.D. Ala. Sept. 30, 2015).

CHAPTER 6

1. Harris v. Forklift Sys., Inc., 510 U.S. 17 (1993); Meritor Sav. Bank, FSB v. Vinson, 477 U.S. 57 (1986).

2. Sandoval v. Am. Bldg. Maint. Indus., Inc., 578 F.3d 787, 801 (8th Cir. 2009).

3. *Harris*, 510 U.S. at 22.

4. *Id.* at 23.

5. Faragher v. City of Boca Raton, 524 U.S. 775 (1998); Burlington Indus. v. Ellerth, 524 U.S. 742 (1998).

6. *See, e.g.*, Stone v. Autoliv ASP, Inc., 210 F.3d 1132, 1137 (10th Cir. 2000) (indicating that a company policy could be kind of evidence to qualify as direct evidence of discrimination). While the definition of "direct evidence" appears to vary slightly by circuit, direct evidence of discrimination can be described as "evidence, that, if believed, proves the existence of a fact in issue without inference or presumption ... [and] is composed of only the most blatant remarks, whose intent could be nothing other than to discriminate on the basis of some impermissible factor." Rojas v. Fla., 285 F.3d 1339, 1342 n.2 (11th Cir. 2002) (internal quotation marks and citation omitted). One court has described direct evidence as that which "essentially requires an admission by the employer" and explained that "such evidence is rare." Argyropoulos v. City of Alton, 539 F.3d 724, 733 (7th Cir. 2008) (internal citations omitted). "A statement that can plausibly be interpreted two different ways—one discriminatory and the other benign—does not directly reflect illegal animus, and, thus, does not constitute direct evidence." Vaughn v. Epworth Villa, 537 F.3d 1147, 1154–55 (10th Cir. 2008).

7. The Eleventh Circuit uses a slightly different formulation. It allows litigants to proceed under a direct evidence framework if they can establish a "convincing mosaic of circumstantial evidence." *See, e.g.*, King v. Ferguson Enters., Inc., 568 F. App'x 686, 689 (11th Cir. 2014).

8. 411 U.S. 792 (1973).

9. *Id.* at 802 (describing the shifting burdens of a prima facie case for a failure to rehire case).

10. *Id.*

11. *Id.* at 804.

12. *Id.* at 802 n.13.

13. Tex. Dep't of Cmty. Affairs v. Burdine, 450 U.S. 248 (1981); St. Mary's Honor Ctr. v. Hicks, 509 U.S. 502 (1993); O'Connor v. Consol. Coin Caterers Corp., 517 U.S. 308 (1996); Reeves v. Sanderson Plumbing, 530 U.S. 133 (2000); *see also* Gross v. FBL Fin. Servs., Inc., 557 U.S. 167, 175 n.2 (2009) (noting that the Supreme Court has never decided whether the test applies to ADEA cases); Pingle v. Richmond Heights Local Sch. Dist. Bd. of Educ., No. 1:12-CV-2892, 2015 WL 6501449, at *10 (N.D. Ohio Oct. 27, 2015) (describing a widespread circuit split in how to apply test to reverse discrimination cases).

14. *McDonnell Douglas*, 411 U.S. at 802 & n.13.

15. 42 U.S.C. §§ 2000e-2(m) & 2000e-5(g)(2)(B).

16. *Id.*

17. *See, e.g.*, Earnest v. Clarksdale Mun. Sch. Dist., No. 4:14-CV-094-JMV, 2015 WL 5712242, at *8 (N.D. Miss. Sept. 29, 2015).

18. Quigg v. Thomas Cty. Sch. Dist., 814 F.3d 1227, 1238–39 (11th Cir. 2016) (discussing the mixed-motive issue). The Supreme Court has provided lower courts

no guidance on how the higher causation standard affects the *McDonnell Douglas* test. Many courts continue to use the *McDonnell Douglas* test in age discrimination cases.

19. Univ. of Tex. Sw. Med. Ctr. v. Nassar, 570 U.S. __, 133 S. Ct. 2517 (2013); Gross v. FBL Fin. Servs., Inc., 557 U.S. 167 (2009). The Supreme Court has not decided that the *McDonnell Douglas* test applies to age cases. *Gross*, 557 U.S. at 175 n.2.

20. *Nassar*, 133 S. Ct. at 2523; Aguiar v. Morgan Corp., 27 F. App'x 110, 112 (3d Cir. 2002). Some circuits incorporate the retaliation inquiry into the *McDonnell Douglas* test. *See, e.g.*, Wimes v. Health, 157 F. App'x 327, 327 (2d Cir. 2005).

21. Tex. Dep't of Cmty. Affairs v. Burdine, 450 U.S. 248 (1981); St. Mary's Honor Ctr. v. Hicks, 509 U.S. 502 (1993); O'Connor v. Consol. Coin Caterers Corp., 517 U.S. 308 (1996); Reeves v. Sanderson Plumbing, 530 U.S. 133 (2000).

22. Weimer v. Honda of Am. Mfg., Inc., 356 Fed. App'x 812, 817–18 (6th Cir. 2009) (noting that "it is generally inappropriate to instruct a jury on the *McDonnell Douglas* analysis as such"); Whittington v. Nordam Grp. Inc., 429 F.3d 986, 998 (10th Cir. 2005); Sanders v. N.Y.C. Human Res. Admin., 361 F.3d 749, 758 (2d Cir. 2004); Kanida v. Gulf Coast Med. Pers. LP, 363 F.3d 568, 576 (5th Cir. 2004); Sanghvi v. City of Claremont, 328 F.3d 532, 539–40 (9th Cir. 2003); Watson v. Se. Pa. Transp. Auth., 207 F.3d 207, 221–22 (3d Cir. 2000) (indicating that it is proper "to instruct the jury that it may consider whether the factual predicates necessary to establish the prima facie case have been shown," but noting that it is error to instruct as to the *McDonnell Douglas* burden-shifting scheme); Dudley v. Wal-Mart Stores, Inc., 166 F.3d 1317, 1322 (11th Cir. 1999). *But see* Rodriguez-Torres v. Caribbean Forms Mfr., Inc., 399 F.3d 52, 58 (1st Cir. 2005) (finding that the district court instructed the jury to evaluate the evidence by applying the *McDonnell Douglas* burden-shifting framework); Kozlowski v. Hampton Sch. Bd., 77 Fed. App'x 133, 141 (4th Cir. 2003) (discussing use of *McDonnell Douglas* framework in jury instructions); Brown v. Packaging Corp. of Am., 338 F.3d 586, 595 (6th Cir. 2003) (Clay, J., concurring) (approving the use of *McDonnell Douglas* in jury instructions).

23. EEOC v. Abercrombie & Fitch Stores, Inc., 135 S. Ct. 2028 (2015).

24. *Id.* at 2031.

25. *Id.*

26. EEOC v. Abercrombie & Fitch Stores, Inc., 731 F.3d 1106, 1123 (10th Cir. 2013), *cert. granted*, 135 S. Ct. 44 (2014), *rev'd*, 135 S. Ct. 2028 (2015).

27. 135 S. Ct. 2028 (2015).

28. 517 U.S. 308 (1996).

29. O'Connor v. Consol. Coin Caterers Corp., 829 F. Supp. 155, 158 (W.D.N.C. 1993).

30. *Id.* at 158.

31. *O'Connor*, 517 U.S. at 312–13.

32. Harmon v. Earthgrains Baking Cos., No. 08-5227, 2009 WL 332705, at *1 (6th Cir. Feb. 11, 2009).

33. *Id.*

34. *Id.*

35. *Id.*

36. *Id.* at *4.

37. *Id.* at *2.
38. *Id.*
39. *Id.* at *1, 2, 7.
40. *Id.* at *3.
41. *Id.* at *5, 7.
42. *See* Noah D. Zatz, *Managing the Macaw: Third-Party Harassers, Accommodation, and the Disaggregation of Discriminatory Intent*, 109 Colum. L. Rev. 1357, 1368 (2009) (noting that "[f]ew propositions are less controversial or more embedded in the structure of Title VII analysis than that the statute recognizes only 'disparate treatment' and 'disparate impact' theories of employment discrimination.").
43. Coleman v. Donahoe, 667 F.3d 835, 863 (7th Cir. 2012) (Wood, C.J., concurring).
44. *Id.*
45. *Id.*
46. Timothy M. Tymkovich, *The Problem with Pretext*, 85 Denv. U. L. Rev. 503, 521–22 (2008); *see also* Griffith v. City of Des Moines, 387 F.3d 733, 740 (8th Cir. 2004) (criticizing the *McDonnell Douglas* test).

CHAPTER 7

1. *See, e.g.,* Americans with Disabilities Amendments Act of 2008, Pub. L. No. 110-325, 122 Stat. 353 (2008) (superseding several Supreme Court decisions narrowing the definition of disability); CBOCS W., Inc. v. Humphries, 553 U.S. 442 (2008) (discussing how the Civil Rights Act of 1991 superseded *Patterson v. McLean Credit Union*, 491 U.S. 164 (1989)); Wards Cove Packing Co. v. Atonio, 490 U.S. 642 (1989), *superseded by statute*, Civil Rights Act of 1991 § 105, Pub. L. No. 102-166, 105 Stat. 1071; Price Waterhouse v. Hopkins, 490 U.S. 228 (1989) (mixed motives), *superseded by statute*, Civil Rights Act of 1991 § 107(a), Pub. L. No. 102-166, 105 Stat. 1075.
2. *See, e.g.,* Univ. of Tex. Sw. Med. Ctr. v. Nassar, 570 U.S. ___, 133 S. Ct. 2517 (2013); Wal-Mart Stores, Inc. v. Dukes, 564 U.S. 338 (2011); Gross v. FBL Fin. Servs., Inc., 557 U.S. 167 (2009); Ricci v. DeStefano, 557 U.S. 557 (2009).
3. Problems with the political bias account also show up in causation doctrine. Many Supreme Court judges appointed by Republican Presidents voted in favor of the motivating factor standard in *Price Waterhouse v. Hopkins*, 490 U.S. 228 (1989).
4. *See supra* note 2 (Ch. 7); Lilly Ledbetter Fair Pay Act, 42 U.S.C. § 2000e-5(e)(3) (A) (amending the Civil Rights Act of 1964; signed into law by President Obama in January 2009); Newport News Shipbuilding & Dry Dock Co. v. EEOC, 462 U.S. 669, 676 (1983) (noting how the Pregnancy Discrimination Act superseded a Supreme Court decision); *see also* W. Va. Univ. Hosps., Inc. v. Casey, 499 U.S. 83, 113 (1991) (Stevens, J., dissenting) (discussing how Supreme Court has frequently interpreted discrimination statutes in a way contrary to congressional intent).
5. Civil Rights Act of 1991, Pub. L. No. 102-166, 105 Stat 1071.
6. ADA Amendments Act of 2008, Pub. L. No. 110-325, 122 Stat 3553 (2008).
7. Michael Selmi, *The Supreme Court's Surprising and Strategic Response to the Civil Rights Act of 1991*, 46 Wake Forest L. Rev. 281, 293–94 (2011). Professor Selmi excluded cases brought under the ADA from his sample. *Id.* at 292.

8. *Id.* at 293–94.

9. Margaret H. Lemos, *The Consequences of Congress's Choice of Delegate: Judicial and Agency Interpretations of Title VII*, 63 VAND. L. REV. 363, 390 (2010).

10. *Id.* at 366.

11. Courts have created doctrines to describe when and how they will defer to administrative agencies. Chevron U.S.A. Inc. v. Natural Res. Def. Council, Inc., 467 U.S. 837 (1984); Skidmore v. Swift & Co., 323 U.S. 134 (1944). The level of deference due to the EEOC varies depending on the statute at issue and whether the EEOC issued regulations to describe the law. Nancy M. Modesitt, *The Hundred-Years War: The Ongoing Battle Between Courts and Agencies Over the Right to Interpret Federal Law*, 74 MO. L. REV. 949, 976–77 (2009) (discussing how Congress did not provide rule-making authority to the EEOC under Title VII); ADA Amendments Act of 2008, Pub. L. No. 110-325, 122 Stat. 3553, § 6 (granting EEOC authority to issue regulations).

12. *Id.* at 388–89.

13. *Id.* at 390.

14. *Id.*

15. Selmi, *supra* note 7 (Ch. 7), at 295.

16. Ash v. Tyson Foods, Inc., 129 F. App'x 529, 533 (11th Cir. 2005), *vacated*, 546 U.S. 454 (2006).

17. *Id.*

18. 135 S. Ct. 2028 (2015).

19. *Id.* at 2031.

20. EEOC v. Abercrombie & Fitch Stores, Inc., 798 F. Supp. 2d 1272, 1287 (N.D. Okla. 2011), *rev'd*, 731 F.3d 1106 (10th Cir. 2013), *cert. granted*, 135 S. Ct. 44 (2014), *rev'd*, 135 S. Ct. 2028 (2015).

21. 135 S. Ct. at 2031.

22. EEOC v. Abercrombie & Fitch Stores, Inc., 731 F.3d 1106, 1123 (10th Cir. 2013) *cert. granted*, 135 S. Ct. 44 (2014), *rev'd*, 135 S. Ct. 2028 (2015).

23. 135 S. Ct. at 2034.

24. Selmi, *supra* note 7 (Ch. 7), at 298.

25. *See, e.g.,* Crawford v. Metro. Gov't of Nashville & Davidson Cnty., 555 U.S. 271 (2009); Burlington N. & Santa Fe Ry. Co. v. White, 548 U.S. 53 (2006).

26. *See, e.g.,* St. Mary's Honor Ctr. v. Hicks, 509 U.S. 502 (1993).

27. Harris v. Forklift Sys., Inc., 510 U.S. 17 (1993); Meritor Sav. Bank, FSB v. Vinson, 477 U.S. 57 (1986).

28. Burlington Northern & Santa Fe Ry. v. White, 548 U.S. 53, 57 (2006).

29. *See, e.g.,* Pauline T. Kim, *Deliberation and Strategy on the United States Courts of Appeals: An Empirical Exploration of Panel Effects*, 157 U. PA. L. REV. 1319, 1327 (2009); Cass R. Sunstein et al., *Ideological Voting on Federal Courts of Appeals: A Preliminary Investigation*, 90 VA. L. REV. 301 (2004); Michael J. Songer, *Decline of Title VII Disparate Impact: The Role of the 1991 Civil Rights Act and the Ideologies of Federal Judges*, 11 MICH. J. RACE AND L. 247, 248, 254 (2005); Jennifer L. Peresi, *Female Judges Matter: Gender and Collegial Decisionmaking in the Federal Appellate Court*, 114 YALE L.J. 1759 (2005).

30. Sunstein, *supra* note 29 (Ch. 7), at 319.

31. *Id.* at 324.

32. Songer, *supra* note 29 (Ch. 7), at 258–59.

33. *Id.* at 262–63.

34. FEDERAL JUDICIAL CENTER, HOW THE FEDERAL COURTS ARE ORGANIZED, http://
www.fjc.gov/federal/courts.nsf/autoframe?openagent&nav=menu1&page=/fed-
eral/courts.nsf/page/183. There are also 515 full- or part-time federal magistrate
judges.

35. Kim, *supra* note 29 (Ch. 7), at 1321–22.

36. Sunstein, *supra* note 29 (Ch. 7), at 304.

37. *See, e.g.*, Pat K. Chew, *Judges' Gender and Employment Discrimination Cases:
Emerging Evidence-Based Empirical Conclusions*, 14 J. GENDER RACE AND JUST.
359, 371 (2011) (collecting studies); Sue Davis et al., *Voting Behavior and Gender on
the U.S. Court of Appeals*, 77 JUDICATURE 129, 131 (1993).

38. Chew, supra note 37 (Ch. 7), at 366 (collecting studies).

39. Jennifer L. Peresie, Note, *Female Judges Matter: Gender and Collegial Decisionmaking
in the Federal Appellate Courts*, 114 YALE L.J. 1759, 1769, 1776 (2005).

40. Kim, *supra* note 29 (Ch. 7), at 1368.

41. Civil Rights Act of 1991, Pub. L. No. 102-166, 105 Stat 1071.

42. Americans With Disabilities Amendments Act of 2008, Pub. L. No. 110-325, 122
Stat. 353 (2008).

43. 411 U.S. 792 (1973).

44. Griggs v. Duke Power Co., 401 U.S. 424 (1971).

45. *Id.* at 430.

46. *See, e.g.*, Univ. of Tex. Sw. Med. Ctr. v. Nassar, 133 S. Ct. 2517 (2013); Wal-Mart
Stores, Inc. v. Dukes, 564 U.S. 338 (2011); Gross v. FBL Fin. Servs., Inc., 557 U.S. 167
(2009); Ricci v. DeStefano, 557 U.S. 557 (2009).

47. *See, e.g.*, EEOC v. Abercrombie & Fitch Stores, Inc., 135 S. Ct. 2028 (2015); Crawford
v. Metro. Gov't of Nashville & Davidson Cnty., 555 U.S. 271 (2009); Burlington
N. & Santa Fe Ry. Co. v. White, 548 U.S. 53 (2006).

48. Brief for Exxon Mobil as Amicus Curiae Supporting Neither Party, Grutter
v. Bollinger, 539 U.S. 306 (2003) (Nos. 02-241, 02-516, 2003 WL 554411, at *2).

49. Brief for BP America Inc. as Amicus Curiae Supporting Neither Party, Grutter
v. Bollinger, 539 U.S. 306 (2003) (Nos. 02-241, 02-516, 2003 WL 1339512, at *2).

50. *Id.*

CHAPTER 8

1. Kirsten Downey Grimsley, *Worker Bias Cases Are Rising Steadily*, L.A. TIMES
(May 12, 1997), http://articles.latimes.com/1997-05-12/business/fi-58080_1_dis-
crimi nation-lawsuits.

2. Tschappat v. Reich, 957 F. Supp. 297, 299 (D.D.C. 1997).

3. Kristoferson v. Otis Spunkmeyer, Inc., 965 F. Supp. 545, 548 (S.D.N.Y. 1997); *see
also* Vasquez v. Cty. of Los Angeles, 307 F.3d 884, 898 (9th Cir. 2002), *opinion with-
drawn*, 341 F.3d 869 (9th Cir. 2003), *superseded* by 349 F.3d 634 (9th Cir. 2003),
amended Jan. 2, 2004; Griswold v. Fresenius USA, Inc., 978 F. Supp. 718, 729 (N.D.

Ohio 1997) (noting that another court was concerned about floodgates of litigation); Does 1, 2, 3, 4 v. Covington Cty. Sch. Bd., 969 F. Supp. 1264, 1279 (M.D. Ala. 1997); Guice-Mills v. Brown, 882 F. Supp. 1427, 1430 (S.D.N.Y. 1995) (noting court was inundated); EEOC v. MCI Int'l, Inc., 829 F. Supp. 1438, 1456 (D.N.J. 1993).

4. Scott v. Sulzer Carbomedics, Inc., 141 F. Supp. 2d 154, 160–61 (D. Mass. 2001), *amended* June 21, 2001.

5. Univ. of Tex. Sw. Med. Ctr. v. Nassar, 570 U.S. __, 133 S. Ct. 2517, 2532 (2013).

6. Nancy Gertner, *Losers' Rules*, 122 YALE L.J. ONLINE 109, 117 (2012), *available at* http://yalelawjournal.org/forum/losers-rules.

7. *Nassar*, 133 S.Ct. at 2523.

8. *Id.*

9. Nassar v. Univ. of Tex. Sw. Med. Ctr., 674 F.3d 448, 450 (5th Cir. 2012), *vacated*, 570 U.S. __, 133 S. Ct. 2517 (2013).

10. *Nassar*, 133 S. Ct. at 2523.

11. *Id.* at 2524.

12. *Id.*

13. *Id.*

14. 674 F.3d at 451.

15. *Id.* at 452.

16. *Id.* at 454 (internal citation omitted). Despite the jury verdict, the appellate court decided that there was insufficient evidence to support the plaintiff's claim of discrimination).

17. 42 U.S.C. § 2000e-3(a).

18. 133 S. Ct. at 2531–32.

19. *Id.* at 2532. In the past, other lower court judges had expressed similar fears about discrimination and retaliation claims. Capo v. Pittsburgh Bd. of Pub. Educ., No. 2:04CV1473, 2007 WL 760513, at *8 (W.D. Pa. Mar. 8, 2007); Munford v. James T. Barnes & Co., 441 F. Supp. 459, 464 (E.D. Mich. 1977).

20. *Id.* at 2547 (Ginsburg, J., dissenting).

21. Mathis v. City of St. Augustine Beach, No. 3:13-CV-1015-J-34JRK, 2015 WL 1470762, at *22 (M.D. Fla. Mar. 31, 2015); Taylor v. Donahoe, No. 13-2216-STA-DKV, 2014 WL 5798549, at *8 (W.D. Tenn. Nov. 7, 2014); Conner v. Ass'n of Flight Attendants-CWA, No. CIV.A. 13-2464, 2014 WL 6973298, at *6 (E.D. Pa. Dec. 10, 2014); Childs-Bey v. Mayor of Baltimore, No. TJS-10-2835, 2013 WL 5718747, at *2 (D. Md. Oct. 17, 2013); Foster v. Univ. of Md. E. Shore, No. TJS-10-1933, 2013 WL 5487813, at *2 (D. Md. Sept. 27, 2013); *see also* Chase v. U.S. Postal Serv., No. 12-11182-DPW, 2013 WL 5948373, at *11 (D. Mass. Nov. 4, 2013) (citing concerns in FMLA context).

22. *See* U.S. DEP'T OF JUSTICE, BUREAU OF JUSTICE STATISTICS SPECIAL REPORT, NCJ 173427, CIVIL RIGHTS COMPLAINTS IN U.S. DISTRICT COURTS, 1990–98, at 4 tbl.3 (Jan. 2000, *rev'd* 2/22/00), *available at* http://www.bjs.gov/content/pub/pdf/crcusdc.pdf.

23. U.S. COURTS, STATISTICS AND REPORTS, TBLC-2, CIVIL CASES COMMENCED, BY BASIS OF JURISDICTION AND NATURE OF SUIT, DURING THE 12-MONTH PERIOD ENDING MAR. 31, 2003, *available at* http://www.uscourts.gov/uscourts/Statistics/FederalJudicialCaseloadStatistics/2003/tables/C02Mar03.pdf.

24. U.S. COURTS, STATISTICS AND REPORTS, TBLC-1, CIVIL CASES FILED, BY JURISDICTION AND NATURE OF SUIT, DURING THE 12-MONTH PERIODS ENDING DEC. 31, 2012 AND 2013, *available at* http://www.uscourts.gov/statistics/table/c-2/statistical-tables-federal-judiciary/2013/12/31 (also noting 1,883 ADA employment cases). *See generally* U.S. COURTS, FEDERAL JUDICIAL CASELOAD STATISTICS, *available at* http://www.uscourts.gov/statistics-reports/analysis-reports/federal-judicial-caseload-statistics; *see also* U.S. COURTS, STATISTICS AND REPORTS, TBLC-2A, CIVIL CASES FILED, BY NATURE OF SUIT, DURING THE 12-MONTH PERIODS ENDING SEPT. 30, 2008 THROUGH 2012 (Sept. 30, 2012), *available at* http://www.uscourts.gov/uscourts/Statistics/JudicialBusiness/2012/appendices/C02ASep12.pdf (showing caseloads for civil rights employment cases in the 13,000–15,000 range from 2008 through 2012); U.S. COURTS, STATISTICS AND REPORTS, TBLC-2A, CIVIL CASES FILED, BY NATURE OF SUIT, DURING THE 12-MONTH PERIODS ENDING SEPT. 30, 1999 THROUGH 2003, *available at* http://www.uscourts.gov/uscourts/Statistics/JudicialBusiness/2003/appendices/c2a.pdf (showing caseloads for civil rights employment cases in the 20,000–22,000 range). Commentators have noted this sharp drop in employment discrimination claims since 1999. Kevin M. Clermont & Stewart J. Schwab, *Employment Discrimination Plaintiffs in Federal Court: From Bad to Worse?*, 3 HARV. L. AND POL'Y REV. 103, 117–18 (2009).

25. U.S. COURTS, STATISTICS AND REPORTS, TBLC-2, CIVIL CASES FILED, BY JURISDICTION AND NATURE OF SUIT, DURING THE 12-MONTH PERIODS ENDING MAR. 31, 2002 AND 2003, *available at* http://www.uscourts.gov/uscourts/Statistics/FederalJudicialCaseloadStatistics/2003/tables/C02Mar03.pdf.

26. U.S. COURTS, STATISTICS AND REPORTS, TBLC-2, CIVIL CASES FILED, BY JURISDICTION AND NATURE OF SUIT, DURING THE 12-MONTH PERIODS ENDING DEC. 31, 2012 AND 2013, *available at* http://www.uscourts.gov/statistics/table/c-2/statistical-tables-federal-judiciary/2013/12/31.

27. *Id.*

28. U.S. Dep't of Labor, Bureau of Labor Statistics, Employment Status of the Civilian Noninstitutional Population, 1944 to Date (2014), *available at* http://www.bls.gov/cps/cpsaat01.pdf.

29. Some of those workers are not eligible to file claims, however. For example, their employer may be too small to be covered by the discrimination law, or they may not be considered employees.

30. Univ. of Tex. Sw. Med. Ctr. v. Nassar, 570 U.S. __, 133 S. Ct. 2517, 2524 (2013).

31. Deborah L. Brake & Joanna L. Grossman, *The Failure of Title VII as a Rights-Claiming System*, 86 N.C. L. REV. 859, 882–83, 900–05 (2008).

32. *Id.* at 897–900 (summarizing social science literature).

33. Smith v. Tower Auto. Operations USA I, L.L.C., No. 4:12-CV-93-CWR-FKB, 2013 WL 6240247, at *7 (S.D. Miss. Dec. 3, 2013).

34. *See, e.g.*, Robinson v. Alameda Cnty., No. 12-CV-00730-JCS, 2013 WL 4494655, at *21 (N.D. Cal. Aug. 19, 2013); Brooks v. Capistrano Unified Sch. Dist., 1 F. Supp. 3d 1029, 1037 (C.D. Cal. 2014); *see also* cases cited *supra* note 21 (Ch. 8).

35. *See generally* Suja A. Thomas, *Frivolous Cases*, 59 DEPAUL L. REV. 633 (2010).

36. FED. R. CIV. P. 11(b), (c).

37. 28 U.S.C. § 1927 (2015).
38. Fed. R. Civ. P. 26(g)(1) & (3); Fed. R. Civ. P. 37.
39. Shepherd v. Am. Broad. Cos., 62 F.3d 1469, 1472 (D.C. Cir. 1995) ("As old as the judiciary itself, the inherent power enables courts to protect their institutional integrity and to guard against abuses of the judicial process with contempt citations, fines, awards of attorneys' fees, and such other orders and sanctions as they find necessary, including even dismissals and default judgments.").
40. 42 U.S.C. § 2000e-5(k).
41. 42 U.S.C. § 1981a(b)(1), (3) (2015). Starceski v. Westinghouse Elec. Corp., 54 F.3d 1089, 1104 (3d Cir. 1995). In many states, workers can also sue under state law, and state laws, too, can limit damages.
42. Luciano v. Olsten Corp., 110 F.3d 210, 221 (2d Cir. 1997).
43. 42 U.S.C. § 2000e-5(b).
44. 509 U.S. 502, 508 (1993).
45. *Id.* at 521.
46. *Id.* at 521–22.
47. *Id.* at 520–21.
48. *Id.*
49. *Id.*
50. Russell v. Principi, 257 F.3d 815, 818–19 (D.C. Cir. 2001); *see also* Casey v. Mabus, 878 F. Supp. 2d 175, 183 (D.D.C. 2012).
51. Siddiqi v. N.Y.C. Health & Hosps. Corp., 572 F. Supp. 2d 353, 367 (S.D.N.Y. 2008).
52. Nelson v. Univ. of Me. Sys., 923 F. Supp. 275, 283 (D. Me. 1996).
53. For a case with similar facts, see *Demmons v. Fulton Cnty.*, No. 1:09-CV-2312-TWT-WEJ, 2010 WL 3418325, at *7–8 (N.D. Ga. Aug. 2, 2010), *report and recommendation adopted*, No. 1:09-CV-2312-TWT, 2010 WL 3418328 (N.D. Ga. Aug. 25, 2010). The employer denied that the supervisor engaged in this activity. *Id.*
54. *Id.* at *12.
55. *Id.*

CHAPTER 9

1. Michael J. Zimmer, *Slicing & Dicing of Individual Disparate Treatment Law*, 61 La. L. Rev. 577 (2001).
2. Stern v. Trustees of Columbia Univ. in City of N.Y., 131 F.3d 305, 314 (2d Cir. 1997). At times, the jury does not get to consider the entire case because the judge has sliced and diced the case before it goes to trial by dismissing some claims or by making evidentiary rulings that exclude relevant evidence.
3. Clack v. Rock-Tenn Co., No. 1:06-CV-119, 2007 WL 1983802, at *2 (E.D. Tenn. July 3, 2007), *aff'd*, 304 F. App'x 399 (6th Cir. 2008).
4. *Id.* at *2.
5. *Id.*
6. *Id.* at *3
7. *Id.*
8. *Id.*
9. *Id.* at *4.

10. *Id.*
11. *Id.* at *6.
12. *Id.* at *6.
13. *Id.* at *7.
14. *Id.*
15. *Id.*
16. *Id.*
17. *Id.*
18. *Id.* at *19.
19. *Id.* at *18.
20. *Id.* at *19 (internal citations omitted).
21. *Id.* at *22.
22. *Id.* at *21.
23. *Id.* at *22.
24. *Id.* at *22.
25. Clack v. Rock-Tenn Co., 304 F. App'x 399, 400 (6th Cir. 2008).
26. Professor Thomas has argued that this standard is unconstitutional under the Seventh Amendment. Suja A. Thomas, *Why Summary Judgment Is Unconstitutional*, 93 VA. L. REV. 139 (2007). She argues for the "consensus requirement." When one judge believes that a reasonable jury could find for the plaintiff employee, a court should not order summary judgment or judgment as a matter of law for the defendant employer. SUJA A. THOMAS, THE MISSING AMERICAN JURY: RESTORING THE FUNDAMENTAL CONSTITUTIONAL ROLE OF THE CRIMINAL, CIVIL, AND GRAND JURIES 237 (2016).
27. Aka v. Wash. Hosp. Ctr., 116 F.3d 876, 880 (D.C. Cir. 1997), *vacated on reh'g en banc*, 124 F.3d 1302 (D.C. Cir.), *opinion reinstated in part on reh'g*, 156 F.3d 1284 (D.C. Cir. 1998).
28. Delville v. Firmenich Inc., 920 F. Supp. 2d 446, 458 (S.D.N.Y. 2013) (internal citations omitted).
29. White v. Baxter Healthcare Corp., 533 F.3d 381, 402 (6th Cir. 2008) (internal citations omitted).
30. Barbour v. Browner, 181 F.3d 1342, 1354 (D.C. Cir. 1999).
31. *Id.* at 1355.
32. Nancy Gertner, *Losers' Rules*, 122 YALE L.J. ONLINE 109, 117 (2012), *available at* http://yalelawjournal.org/forum/losers-rules.

CHAPTER 10

1. Boyer-Liberto v. Fontainebleau Corp., No. CIV. JKB-12-212, 2013 WL 1413031, at *3 (D. Md. Apr. 4, 2013), *aff'd*, 752 F.3d 350 (4th Cir. 2014), *vacated on reh'g en banc*, No. 13-1473, 2015 WL 2116849 (4th Cir. May 7, 2015). There was conflicting evidence about whether the worker who made the comments was a supervisor or a coworker, and the courts differed on how they characterized this worker.
2. Boyer-Liberto v. Fontainebleau Corp., 752 F.3d 350, 357 (4th Cir. 2014), *vacated on reh'g en banc*, No. 13-1473, 2015 WL 2116849 (4th Cir. May 7, 2015).
3. Boyer-Liberto v. Fontainebleau Corp., No. 13-1473, 2015 WL 2116849, at *13 (4th Cir. May 7, 2015).

4. Rodgers v. W.-S. Life Ins. Co., 12 F.3d 668, 675 (7th Cir. 1993); *see also* Bailey v. Binyon, 583 F. Supp. 923, 927 (N.D. Ill. 1984) ("The use of the word 'n*****' automatically separates the person addressed from every non-black person; this is discrimination *per se*.").

5. H.R. 3721, 111th Cong. §2(a)-(b) (2009).

6. ADA Amendments Act of 2008, Pub. L. No. 110-325, 122 Stat. 3553 (2008).

7. *Id.*

8. *Id.*

9. Price Waterhouse v. Hopkins, 490 U.S. 228 (1989).

10. *Id.* at 238.

11. 42 U.S.C. § 2000e-2(m).

12. 29 U.S.C. § 623. The Court chose to interpret the fact that Congress did not amend the ADEA as proof that Congress intended for the ADEA to have a higher causal standard. Gross v. FBL Fin. Servs., Inc., 557 U.S. 167, 174 (2009). However, equally plausible explanations are that Congress forgot to amend the ADEA or that Congress intended *Price Waterhouse* to apply to ADEA cases. The least plausible explanation is that Congress's expansion of Title VII signaled its intention to limit age discrimination cases.

13. 42 U.S.C. § 2000e-2(a)(1)–(2).

14. 42 U.S.C. § 2000e-2(a)(1)–(2) (emphasis added). The ADEA uses similar language to define prohibited conduct. 29 U.S.C. § 623(a)(1) & (2). The ADA's first operative provisions also contain similar prohibitions, but the wording and construction of the ADA is slightly different. 42 U.S.C. § 12112(a), (b). Given the ADA's accommodation requirement, the ADA provides a longer list of harms than that found in Title VII and the ADEA.

15. Retaliation and accommodation cases may require a separate set of elements when they derive from different statutory provisions than pure discrimination claims.

16. *See generally* Mary Ellen Maatman, *Choosing Words and Creating Worlds: The Supreme Court's Rhetoric and Its Constitutive Effects on Employment Discrimination Law*, 60 U. Pitt. L. Rev. 1 (1998) (discussing the Supreme Court's various approaches to causation analysis in Title VII cases).

17. *See, e.g.*, Messin v. Kroblin Transp. Sys., Inc., 903 F.2d 1306, 1308 (10th Cir. 1990) (indicating *McDonnell Douglas* framework is too complex for jury instructions).

18. *See* Hooper v. Proctor Health Care Inc., 804 F.3d 846 (2015); Simpson v. Beaver Dam Cmty. Hosps., Inc., 780 F.3d 784 (2015); Coleman v. Donahoe, 667 F.3d 835 (2012).

19. McDonnell Douglas Corp. v. Green, 411 U.S. 792, 802 n.13 (1973).